Christ and Horrors

Who would the Savior have to be to rescue human beings from the meaning-destroying experiences of their lives? This book offers a systematic Christology that is at once biblical and philosophical. Starting with human radical vulnerability to horrors such as permanent pain, sadistic abuse, or genocide, it develops what must be true about Christ if He is the horror-defeater who ultimately resolves all the problems affecting the human condition and Divine–human relations. Distinctive elements of Marilyn McCord Adams' study are her defense of the two-natures theory and of Christ as Inner Teacher and a functional partner in human flourishing, and her arguments in favor of literal bodily resurrection (Christ's and ours) and of a strong doctrine of corporeal eucharistic presence. The book concludes that Christ is the One in Whom not only Christian doctrine, but also cosmos, church, and the human psyche hold together.

MARILYN MCCORD ADAMS is Regius Professor of Divinity, University of Oxford, and Canon of Christ Church Cathedral, Oxford. She has published extensively in academic philosophy and theology.

CURRENT ISSUES IN THEOLOGY

General Editor:
Iain Torrance
*Professor in Patristics and Christian Ethics, Master of Christ's College,
and Dean of the Faculty of Arts & Divinity, University of Aberdeen*

Editorial Advisory Board:

David Ford   *University of Cambridge*
Bryan Spinks   *Yale University*
Kathryn Tanner   *University of Chicago*
John Webster   *University of Aberdeen*

There is a need among upper-undergraduate and graduate students of
theology, as well as among Christian teachers and church professionals, for a
series of short, focussed studies of particular key topics in theology written by
prominent theologians. *Current Issues in Theology* meets this need.

The books in the series are designed to provide a "state-of-the-art"
statement on the topic in question, engaging with contemporary thinking as
well as providing original insights. The aim is to publish books which stand
between the static monograph genre and the more immediate statement of a
journal article, by authors who are questioning existing paradigms or
rethinking perspectives.

Other titles in the series:

Holy Scripture   John Webster
The Just War Revisited   Oliver O'Donovan
Bodies and Souls, or Spirited Bodies?   Nancey Murphy

MARILYN McCORD ADAMS

Christ and Horrors

The Coherence of Christology

CAMBRIDGE
UNIVERSITY PRESS

CAMBRIDGE UNIVERSITY PRESS
Cambridge, New York, Melbourne, Madrid, Cape Town,
Singapore, São Paulo, Delhi, Mexico City

Cambridge University Press
The Edinburgh Building, Cambridge CB2 8RU, UK

Published in the United States of America by Cambridge University Press, New York

www.cambridge.org
Information on this title: www.cambridge.org/9780521686006

First published 2006
Reprinted 2008

A catalogue record for this publication is available from the British Library

ISBN 978-0-521-86682-8 Hardback
ISBN 978-0-521-68600-6 Paperback

For

John Hick and Allan B. Wolter,
excellent mentors

Contents

Preface

In my earlier book, *Horrendous Evils and the Goodness of God*, I registered my discontent with standard "big-picture" and "free-will" theodicies. Not only do *they* not do justice to the very worst evils – the ones I identified as "horrendous." I argued that, where horrors are concerned, *no* solution within the confines of a religion-neutral value-theory is possible. By contrast, a range of options opens up if one turns to the wider resources of Christian theology. One methodological moral of my story was that, in explaining how Christian faith can be coherent, Christian philosophers should not act as if Christian beliefs sum to "restricted-standard theism" – the claim that there exists an omniscient, omnipotent, and perfectly good God. Instead, Christian philosophers should bring the richer and more nuanced doctrines of the Trinity, Incarnation, and atonement into play.

My own wrestlings with evil convinced me that, while sin and horrors are both problems, horrors are the more fundamental problem. My opening question in this book is: what does Christology look like, if rescuing the world from horrendous evils is the Savior's principal job? Where *Horrendous Evils and the Goodness of God* urged philosophers to be more theological, *Christ and Horrors: The Coherence of Christology* invites theologians to define the soteriological problem in a philosophical way. I myself am committed to this approach and its consequences. Naturally, I hope my arguments will convince many readers. Others will know in advance, however, that their commitment to centering soteriology around solving the sin-problem is too deep to budge. I make bold to suggest that even these should not stop reading, but instead regard themselves as invited into a thought experiment in systematic theology. Studying Riemannian geometry to see what happens when Euclid's parallel postulate is taken away helps one understand Euclidean geometry better. Besides, even those who start with sin will have to account for horrors. What follows may furnish them with some transplantable ideas! A Christology that is philosophical as well as biblical owes an account of the metaphysics of the Incarnation (which I offer in chapter 5). I have structured the book in such a way that readers less interested in metaphysics can pass over chapter 5 without losing the thread of the argument of the other chapters.

That Christology would be the place for me to start in doing systematic theology was probably already determined by the Jesus-centered faith of my bible-belt upbringing. It was reinforced by my Anglo-Catholic mentors and the Incarnational vision of the great turn-of-the-twentieth-century Anglicans surveyed in Archbishop Michael Ramsey's wonderful little book *An Era in Anglican Theology, from Gore to Temple: Anglican Theology between Lux Mundi and the Second World War 1889–1939*.[1] It was fed by the medieval theologians I have spent most of my adult life studying, great thinkers who have their own marvelous Christological visions and who also made philosophy the backbone of their extensive theological reflections.

The materials in this book took some years in developing. Parts were presented in Gifford lectures (the University of St. Andrew's, November 1999), DuBose lectures (Sewanee, the University of the South School of Theology, October 2003), and Warfield lectures (Princeton Theological Seminary, April 2005). I am grateful to these schools for inviting me and to the individuals who attended for many probing and provocative questions. I am happy to thank Yale University for sabbatical leave and the Luce Foundation for a Henry Luce III Fellowship in Theology (2002–2003) that supported my work.

---

[1] Arthur Michael Ramsey, *An Era in Anglican Theology, from Gore to Temple: Anglican Theology between* Lux Mundi *and the Second World War 1889–1939* (New York: Scribner, 1960).

Special thanks go to the Rockefeller Foundation Study Center at Bellagio, Italy, whose extravagant hospitality provided the spiritual leisure to finish this project.

During my ten Yale years, I enjoyed many stimulating class sessions and conversations with excellent students, who are now moving into their own careers. Among them, I mention Michael Barnwell, Wendy Boring, Alice Chapman, Andrew Chignell, Shannon Craigo-Snell, Andrew Dole, Stephen Edmondson, Christine Helmer, Cynthia Hess, Ruthanna Hooke, Maurice Lee, Todd Ohara, Edwin van Driel, and Edward Waggoner (who also did a spectacular job as my research assistant). For me, working with them was the academy at its best! Kathryn Tanner offered useful and insightful feedback in her role as Luce Conference commentator. Rowan Greer was an invaluable guide to turn-of-the-twentieth-century Anglican authors. Robert Merrihew Adams has facilitated this project with scholarly critique and moral support that did not stint at transatlantic relocation! He also joined Oxford colleagues Jane Shaw and Sarah Ogilvie in brainstorming a new title. I am indebted to all of these persons in many and various ways.

This book is a sequel to *Horrendous Evils and the Goodness of God*. The conception of horrendous evils and their anthropological consequences, which I worked out in the earlier book, has been appropriated and reasserted here. Some other ideas in this book have been previewed or overviewed in the following published articles:

"Biting and Chomping Our Salvation! Eucharistic Presence, Radically Understood," in *Redemptive Transformation in Practical Theology*, ed. Dana Wright and John D. Kuentzel (Grand Rapids, MI: Eerdmans, 2004), 69–94.

"The Coherence of Christology: God Enmattered and Enmattering," *Princeton Seminary Bulletin*, vol. 26, no. 2, new series (2005), 157–179.

"*Cur Deus Homo?* Priorities Among the Reasons," *Faith and Philosophy* 21:2 (April 2004), 1–18.

"Three Great Theological Ideas from the Middle Ages" (The Dubose
Lectures), *Sewanee Theological Review* 47:2 (Easter 2004), 129–180:
"The Metaphysical Size Gap," 129–144;
"Courtesy, Divine and Human," 145–163;
"The Primacy of Christ," 164–180.
"Trinitarian Friendship: Same Gender Models of Godly Love in
Richard of St. Victor and Aelred of Rievaulx," in *Theology and
Sexuality: Ancient and Contemporary Readings*, ed. Eugene F.
Rogers, Jr. (Oxford: Blackwell, 2001), 322–339.

I am grateful to these journals and anthologies for permission to
incorporate some of these materials into the present work.

When my attention was absorbed by the details of medieval metaphysics, two people in different ways reminded me that Christology
centers my driving questions: John Hick and Allan B. Wolter OFM,
both of them intellectual adventurers who follow questions where
they lead and seek truth where it may be found. This book is dedicated
to them with thanks for their inspiring examples.

1 | Christology as natural theology: methodological issues

1. Introduction

My topic is Christology; my thesis, the coherence of Christology; my theme, Christ as the One in Whom all things hold together. Metaphysically, Christ is the center both of Godhead and cosmos. Existentially, Christ is the integrator of individual positive personal meaning; psychologically, our inner teacher; body-politically, the organizer of Godward community. Christ saves us by virtue of being real and really present: Emmanuel, God with us, sharing our human condition; ascended to His most glorious throne in heaven at God's right hand; in the most blessed sacrament of the altar; and in the hearts of all His faithful people. Switching from object- to metalanguage, from the order of reality to the order of theory, turn-of-the-twentieth-century Anglicans declare that Christology is the centerpiece of systematic theology, that which integrates the creed, that from which we reason up to the Trinity, down to creation, out through the Church to the world. My own conviction is that they got this substantially right. Thus, in arguing for the coherence of Christology, I will take the coherence of theism for granted. But I will not treat Christology as an optional supplement to generic – what philosophers of religion often call "restricted-standard" – theism. My contention is that, because of its explanatory power, Christology has an integrating force of its own.

In the order of discovery, my argument begins with soteriology: with the fact that the human condition generally and Divine–human relations in particular are non-optimal. Christ becomes an explanatory posit, which shows how these non-optimality problems

1

can be solved. More particularly, my argument will be that a Christology that is *metaphysically high* – interpreting Chalcedon, one that posits that in Christ the Divine Word assumes a complete human nature, so that there is one person or supposit and two natures – and *materially low* – following nineteenth- and twentieth-century tendencies to see Christ's human being as much more like ours than patristic or medieval western scholastic theology would ever allow – solves the problem of horrendous evils. Chapter 2 will present the soteriological explananda. Chapter 3 will examine what Christ's human nature would have to be like for Him to carry out those soteriological jobs. Chapters 4 and 5 will turn to attempts to make sense of a God-man in terms of the conceptualities of psychology and metaphysics. Among other things, I hope to show that the turn away from medieval metaphysics – sometimes towards other philosophical outlooks but more often resolutely away from philosophy to other disciplines – has left contemporary Anglo-American Christology in shambles, where it has not altogether washed it away. My remedy is a return to philosophical theology and to metaphysics in Christology, where medieval metaphysics is my favorite (although not the only) option!

Theoretical coherence is exhibited in part by showing how a single explanatory posit can do many explanatory jobs. My analysis of human non-optimality problems and their solution so integrates God's creative purposes with Christ's saving work as to usher Christ into a variety of theoretical roles. Chapter 6 focusses on Christ as Inner Teacher; Chapter 7 as cosmic center; Chapter 8 as the first-born in resurrection and harbinger of cosmic renewal; Chapter 9 as priest and victim in cosmic sacrifice; and Chapter 10 as really present in the sacrament of the altar.

1.1. The scandal of Christology

To many, these agenda will seem not only unpromising but perverse. This book began as Gifford lectures, which are supposed to be on *natural* religion, a syllabus designation that presupposes a divide between *natural* theology (which is understood to cover whatever could be proved *sola ratione* to all reasonable human beings) and *revealed* theology (which is epistemologically dependent upon revelation). The idea that some religious tenets could be proved to every rational person has an ancient and honorable tradition, reaching back through thirteenth- and fourteenth-century philosophical theology all the way to Aristotle's *Posterior Analytics* Euclidian model of science. It persisted into the modern period through Descartes, Leibniz, Samuel Clarke, and Christian Wolf. It flourishes in the present, not least among neo-scholastics and neo-Thomists. Depending on the optimism of the period and particular thinkers, the existence of God, some or all of His perfection-making attributes (knowledge, wisdom, power, goodness; sometimes simplicity, immutability, incorruptibility, eternity), and some generic features of His providential design have occupied the turf of natural theology. But Trinity, Christology (Incarnation and Atonement), and the sacraments have been paradigms of revealed theology.

So far from a likely meeting ground for all reasonable persons, Christology is arguably the *root* of Christian revealed theology and so is fundamentally divisive. Religiously, Christ is a point of contention among Jewish, Christian, and Muslim adherents of biblical religion, not to mention among theists generally, *a fortiori* between Christianity and South and East Asian religions. Sociopolitically, Christ is held guilty by association with Roman, "Holy Roman," and British imperialism. For centuries, the charge of "Christ-killer" fueled anti-Jewish pogroms, the pejorative "infidel" sponsored the disastrous Crusades, suspected insincerity in the profession of Christ justified the Inquisition, etc. Even in the present, many missionary efforts continue to manifest cultural arrogance.

Most obviously, Christology seems bound to be divisive because it rocks and reels on epistemologically quaking ground. Trends in biblical criticism – which first surfaced in the Enlightenment (with Spinoza and Lessing) and gained momentum at the end of the

3

nineteenth century, avalanching into the twentieth – took the step of counting the Bible generally and the New Testament in particular among historical documents rightly subjected to the analysis of historical methods, and then (over several decades) proceeded to undermine confidence in their historical reliability. Many circles have abandoned the search for *Jesus ipse* or for *ipsissima verba*, conceding that we are left with (at best) second- and third-generation polemical documents that (via the methods of social history) tell us more about the communities from which they emerged and their struggles than about Jesus himself and what he said and did. Even the evidentially more optimistic Schweitzer and succeeding generations of "questers" offer cold comfort, introducing to us a series of culturally conditioned "historical" Jesuses, each in his own way theologically unpalatable to many.

Moreover, there was (and is) a mounting (not to say idolatrous) fascination with "the scientific worldview": with the triumphal claim of scientific method to be the one really "objective" source of knowledge, the one whose deliverances are and ought to be convincing to every rational person; with the accomplishments of science engendering the belief, fostering the hope, propounding the dogma, that science – biology, maybe just physics and chemistry – will be able to explain everything without remainder; with a picture of the universe as a closed system that, however probabilistic, admits of no miracles. Yet, for Christians, Christ not only performed miracles – exorcisms, cures, walking on water, multiplying loaves and fishes, changing water into wine – Christ was and *is* the biggest miracle, the Divine Word become flesh, surely a phenomenon well outside the explanatory scope and capacities of the natural sciences!

As St. Paul declared long ago, Christology is a scandal both to Jews and Greeks. How can we blame Christian theologians who find traditional Christology an embarrassment to be somehow de-emphasized, marginalized, reduced, or relativized? The demands of contemporary rationality and civility alike seem to require it.

1.2. Evasive maneuvers

At a very high level of generality, we can distinguish two types of reaction to these developments, by those who enter into them deeply and feel their power.

1.2.1. "Least-common-denominator"?

One response upholds the ancient and medieval ideal of a rationality common to all human beings. On this approach, least-common-denominator becomes *an epistemic norm*, dictating what can be counted as ground-level real. Least-common-denominator is also advanced as *a pragmatic counsel and moral norm*. How often do social scientists and political commentators in effect urge us to follow the Cliffordian deontological principle not to accept or embrace anything as true on insufficient evidence, in order to stifle irrational forces in our society, to bring an end to religious warfare and ethnic cleansing, because Clifford's principle will leave us unentitled to believe those things that divide. "*Eliminative*" versions require our many and varied cultural disagreements to be shaved away, skimmed off, and boiled down to a common core that everyone can accept. The trouble is that eliminative least-common-denominator outlooks are symbolically too impoverished to organize and orient human life. Liberal democracy advocates that the state restrict itself to a least-common-denominator ideology, but this is in order to leave room for different individuals and groups to embrace a variety of alternative and richer schemes. The original intention was not that the shared ground of civil religion should do the whole job.

"*Reductive*" least-common-denominator approaches continue to use God- or Christ-language as symbols, but subject them to reductive analyses in terms of states or aspects of what least-common-denominator identifies as fundamentally real. Thus, Gordon Kaufmann, in his book *In the Face of Mystery: Constructive Theology*, lets "God" stand for the serendipitous creativity that has evolved humankind and that moves creation forward in an ever more humane direction;[1] "Christ," not narrowly for the man Jesus, but for the whole new order of relationships which reveal the direction in which ultimate reality is moving – of self-sacrificing love and all-inclusive community – and so focus the norm and goal.[2] The idea is to borrow the motivational aura that still surrounds the old religious symbols, the better to focus a picture of the universe that will inspire and reinforce moral and humane behavior and projects. (Kaufmann does allow that other religions could offer the same sorts of reductive analyses. Insofar as they were well executed, religions would be on a par so far as their metaphysical grounding was concerned and superiority claims would have no justification. But not just any symbols would function to reveal the direction in which ultimate reality is moving and/or inspire human beings to live up to radical moral norms.) Yet, when all is said and done, reductionists like Kaufmann appear to "thin out" the significance of the old symbols so much that, while their approach does enable the present generation to keep up some ties (of *verbal* continuity) with their forebears by deploying the "same" symbols, it does not assign the symbols the kind of content that would keep the motivational aura from fading, and so does not endow the symbols with enough power to deter the younger generation from shedding religious labels as merely vestigial and adopt the framework of secular ethics instead.

1.2.2. Pluralisms

Pluralism begins from the other end of the spectrum. If least-common-denominator approaches arguably impoverish all competitors by deleting differences or explaining them away, pluralists pledge to preserve each of the world's great religions in all of their

---

[1] Gordon Kaufmann, *In the Face of Mystery: Constructive Theology* (Cambridge, MA, and London: Harvard University Press, 1993), e.g., ch. 23, 348–357, ch. 25, 375.
[2] Kaufmann, *In the Face of Mystery*, ch. 25, 382–391.

symbolic richness, and to appreciate how each is undergirded and textured by centuries of individual and collective religious experience. Yet, insofar as differences are retained, these systems can neither be held (at the theoretical level) all to be literally true at once (in the sense of corresponding with Reality with a capital "R",) nor (at the practical level) can they all be practiced at once.

Philosophically, members of the Rush-Rees Wittgensteinian school, represented most notably by D. Z. Phillips,[3] meet this difficulty by reaching for a form of *anti-realism.* They maintain that none of the religious language games or the belief-systems that go with them is true by correspondence with Reality with a capital "R," because there is no such thing as Reality with a capital "R." Rather, the criteria for what counts as real are *internal* to each language game. According to them, the notion of transcendent criteria of reality that operate outside any and every language game is philosophically incoherent, and turns the *external* question of which language game is really true into philosophical nonsense.

By contrast, in his *An Interpretation of Religion*, John Hick is a metaphysical realist in the sense that he believes in Reality with a capital "R" that transcends, is what it is, prior to and independently of any human conceptualities of it. Human "interaction" with Reality with a capital "R" evokes a variety of conceptual schemes and religious practices, such as are represented in the world's great religions. The problem is that Reality with a capital "R" is so disproportioned to our cognitive faculties that any ways of thinking or acting that we come up with are too distant from It to be *literally* true of (cannot nearly enough correspond to) It. Consequently, having begun his career defending the eschatological verifiability of religious language against second-quarter-of-the-twentieth-century logical positivism, Hick in effect concludes that religious outlooks and systems of thought do not have cognitive content but are at best

[3] D. Z. Phillips, *The Concept of Prayer* (New York: Schocken Books, 1966), esp. ch. 1, 1–29.

mythologically or *metaphorically true* by virtue of their capacity to advance the growth of their practitioners from a self-centered to an other-centered to a Reality-centered manner of life.[4] He thus agrees with Phillips that the rationale for choosing to embrace a given religion (to play a religious language game) is *pragmatic* or *moral* in nature.[5]

1.2.3. Christology, reduced anyway?

Since Christianity numbers among the world's great religions, one would expect Christ to be allowed to retain a central place in its worship and practice; insofar as theological reflection is permitted by pluralists (as it is by Hick but arguably isn't by Rush-Rees Wittgensteinians), one would expect Christology to remain key in Christian thought. It would seem consistent with pluralist approaches to leave the *content* of traditional "high" Christologies – e.g., the claim that Jesus is God, the Incarnate Divine Word – in place while altering the understanding of their truth conditions (denying literal correspondence with Reality with a capital "R").

In fact, this is not what happens. Even earlier pluralists, who – like Schleiermacher and Tillich – wanted to insist on some superiority for Christianity, felt it necessary to reconstruct traditional (patristic and scholastic) Christology in terms of their alternative soteriological requirements and philosophical commitments. More recently, pluralists – such as Hick[6] and Don Cupitt[7] – insist that belief in the superiority of Christianity has inspired Christians to do

---

[4] John Hick, *An Interpretation of Religion* (London: Macmillan Press, 1989), Part Four, ch. 19, 343–361.

[5] Phillips, *The Concept of Prayer*, ch. 2, 37, ch. 8, 149–160.

[6] John Hick, "An Inspiration Christology for a Religiously Plural World," in *Encountering Jesus: A Debate on Christology*, ed. Stephen T. Davis (Atlanta: John Knox Press, 1988), ch. 1, 5–22, 32–38, esp. 13–17. See also his *Interpretation of Religion*, Part Four, ch. 20, 371–372.

[7] Don Cupitt, "The Christ of Christendom," in *The Myth of God Incarnate*, ed. John Hick (Philadelphia: Westminster, 1977), ch. 7, 133–147, 205, esp. 137, 140–141.

many terrible things (to tolerate or promote anti-Semitic pogroms, to implement imperialist policies, etc.). Tracing the problem to the root of high Christology – the belief that Jesus is God and hence that *God* is the founder of Christianity – they conclude that high Christology fails their pragmatic test, and so must be supplanted by a low one, in which Christ is one remarkable religious leader among others, possessed of a high degree of God-consciousness and founder of an (until recently) highly successful religious movement. Belief systems of other religions might likewise need weeding by the pragmatic criteria. But Hick begins as a Christian, and for Hick repentance begins at home. Thus, while Hick has given considerable attention to Christology, it is largely by way of opposing traditional (patristic and medieval western) Christology as pernicious, and reinstating a Christ turn-of-the-twentieth-century "left-wing" liberal Protestantism would be happy with: Christ as one remarkable religious leader among others. Increasingly, in his later works, Hick's "soul-making" soteriology seeks ground common to the world's great religions – as Hick's description of the goal of spiritual development shifts from "Christ-centeredness" to "God-centeredness" to "other-centeredness" or "Reality-centeredness."

Hick's many books about religious pluralism are rich in provocative insights. All the same, his sociological objections to traditional (patristic and medieval western) Christology would be difficult to substantiate. It is not enough to point to *concomitance*: one must show that religion is a *salient* cause of the deplored effects. In fact, Christians do not seem *more* disposed to ethnic strife than others. Religion can be badge and banner, but it would be hard to show that the conflicts wouldn't have found some other equally handy pretext or "us-versus-them" marker. To target traditional (patristic and medieval western) Christology, one would have to show not simply that it was invoked, but that, apart from these doctrinal claims, the nefarious policies would not have been implemented, the horrendous action not undertaken. Hick's and Cupitt's thesis – that Chalcedonian Christology was invented because it was needed to support Constantinian political ideology – is historically belied by the fact that Arianism nearly triumphed in the early years of Christianity's being made an official religion in the Roman empire. Chalcedonian Christology cannot have figured as a motivator for many, insofar as it is not clear how widely the theological issue was understood.

2. Sceptical realism: the project, reconceived

By contrast, in matters philosophical and theological, I am *a sceptical realist*. I count myself *a realist* about philosophical and theological theories in that I believe (contrary to Rudolf Carnap[8]) that there is some fact of the matter, prior to and independently of what we think, believe, or conceive of in our theories – some Reality with a capital "R" to which our theories may or may not correspond. I am a *sceptic*, however, because I believe that the defense of any well-formulated philosophical/theological position of any interest will eventually involve premisses which are fundamentally controversial and so unable to command the assent of all reasonable persons. Moreover, sceptical realism (as I understand it) breaks the link between cognitive content and truth on the one hand, and epistemic decidability on the other. Thus, philosophical and theological claims – "Mental events are token-reducible to physical events," "A tree is a collection of ideas in the mind," "Mind and body are distinct substances," "The divine essence is supposited by three persons," "There is one person and two natures in Christ" – may be counted literally meaningful and asserted as true, even if human disagreements about them are naturally undecidable in this life. (An omnipotent God could, of course,

---

[8] Rudolf Carnap, "Empiricism, Semantics, and Ontology," in *Philosophy of Mathematics: Selected Readings*, ed. Paul Benacerraf and Hilary Putnam (Englewood Cliffs, NJ: Prentice-Hall, 1964), 233–248.

supernaturally produce consensus. My claim is that, even if God did, truth would not consist in the possibility or actuality of that consensus but would be prior to it in the order of explanation.)

Thus, I embrace *coherence*, not as a theory of *what truth consists in* (as a realist, I believe truth to be constituted by correspondence, once again, with Reality with a capital "R"), but as *a method of pursuing truth*. My assumption is that human reason's best chance at truth is won through the effort of integrating our data with our many and diverse intuitions into a coherent picture with the theoretical virtues of clarity, consistency, explanatory power, and fruitfulness. The process is difficult because our materials are so complex and pull in many different directions. It is dynamic because the twin desiderata of consistency and richness force many trial adjustments and alterations before a satisfactory organization, mastering complexity with simplicity, is achieved. The assignment is also fluid, because data and intuitions that strike us as bedrock at one time may become less entrenched later, and vice versa, forcing "Copernican revolutions" in our outlook.

Having abandoned the possibility of universal *sola ratione* convincement, the sceptical realist expects a plurality of positions to take the field and to commend themselves on the basis of their internal clarity, consistency, and coherence; on the basis of their explanatory power and fruitfulness. Most theories will exhibit costs and benefits, handle some problems and issues better than others: e.g. obviously and crudely, idealism does better with mind than with body; materialism the other way around; supralapsarian double predestination is strong on Divine sovereignty but weak on human freedom and responsibility in relation to God; eastern Trinitarian theology is firm on "three" but scrambles for "one," while Augustinian approaches easily accommodate "one" while somersaulting for "three." The goal of philosophizing and theologizing becomes to develop one's own outlook in such a way as to make it a credible competitor, overall getting roughly as good a rating for explaining, handling problems and difficulties, as the others. Happily, dispatch of this task is incompatible with arrogance toward and/or cultivated ignorance of alternative positions. On the contrary, it requires the intellectual flexibility to enter into the other theories, to appreciate their benefits as well as to assess their costs, to learn what, why, and how they handle issues well or badly. This exercise sparks ingenuity and inventiveness, which sees how to refine one's own approach to strengthen its vulnerable points, and win new advantages for itself.

Sceptical realism can count it rational – or at least, not irrational – to endorse one of the plurality of well-developed positions. From a sceptical realist point of view, a theory is not made discreditable, belief in it is not shown to be irrational, by the mere observation that there is some theoretical or practical alternative. One would have to establish that it is decidedly inferior to its competitors in ways that cannot be repaired. The obvious consequence is that there will be a variety of positions, each of which it could be rational to hold.

Thus, *pace* Hick, sceptical realism is able to win the advantages of pluralism without giving up on the *literal* truth-value of theological claims, much less accepting the disadvantages of Phillips' anti-realism. The theoretical market place opened by sceptical realism does not – like least-common-denominator approaches – wash out detail and texture, but drives the development of a plurality of richly nuanced positions. Moreover, sceptical realism is able to eat its realist cake while gulping down its epistemological "humble" pie, because the fact that the competing theories are on an epistemic par inhibits each and all from strutting their realist truth claims in an obnoxiously confident way. Thus, Christianity could present itself as *true* – not merely mythically and metaphorically on the grounds of its spiritually and morally formative effects, but in the sense of corresponding to Reality with a capital "R" – and still pay other religions the respect of willingness to learn from them something it might have de-emphasized or missed.

Within this sceptical realist frame, I wish to commend Christology. My apologetic goal is modest: viz., to re-present robust Christology as a viable competitor in the market place of religious and theological worldviews. I am thus not out to prove that Christianity is superior to other religions. My principal aim is not to persuade, much less demonstrate my position to, unbelievers, but rather to argue that it is not unreasonable for Christians to hold it. More urgently, I do hope to convince at least some of my fellow Christians that – even in these modern or postmodern times – there is no need to rush to eliminate or reductively reconstruct Christology into a shadow of its former self. My own conviction is that these moves will not be theoretically competitive, because Christ is the center of Christianity, the One without Whom the whole system falls to pieces.[9]

3. The dynamics of theory construction: reflective equilibrium

3.1. Terminological clarification

In talking about "theory"-construction, I have been using the term "theory" broadly. One might object that, unlike geometry, the world's great religions are complex cultural phenomena involving wide-ranging and diverse practices, institutions, scriptures, and traditions – which makes it more appropriate to speak with the Wittgensteinians of *forms of life* and *language games*. Even where the belief elements are concerned, they are apt to have narrative, even mythological, expression. Certainly, even where theology is regarded

---

[9] See William Temple, *Christus Veritas: An Essay* (London: Macmillan & Co, 1925), Preface, ix, where he makes the stronger claim that "belief in a specific revelation is only justified when it has been shown that the Theology in which it is articulated supplies a conception of reality which is *more* satisfactory as a philosophy than any other." I will be happy with a Christology that is *on a par* with other competitive philosophical positions.

as a "science," it straddles the Aristotelian theoretical/practical divide (between those that do and do not have to do with human choice and behavior). All of this might make it seem better to speak not of theories, but of *worldviews*.

I concede these points, but find the issue mainly verbal. All Aristotelian sciences – whether theoretical or practical – were to be modeled on Euclidean geometry. Thus, even if Christology and soteriology straddle the Aristotelian theoretical/practical divide, they would count as "sciences." Nowadays, we reserve "science" for the fields of physics, chemistry, astronomy, biology, etc., as distinct from the humanities. Within philosophy, we use "theory" to indicate a certain kind of systematic structuring of ideas, no matter whether those ideas are about the nature of matter or the norms of human behavior, and so count not only metaphysics and philosophy of mind but also certain kinds of ethical developments as theory. The main points of comparison that concern us here are the dynamics of constructing an explanatory system of ideas, and the resultant epistemic status of those ideas vis à vis competitors. Before going further, we need to scrutinize those dynamics in more detail.

3.2. Oversimple model

At a high level of abstraction, the task of theory-building seems straightforward. Begin with the data. Apply the explanatory model, which specifies what sorts of things need which types of explanations. Sort through the givens to identify the *explananda* (what needs to be explained), to see whether some of the givens explain others. If not, posit theoretical entities to do the job. Finally, read off a preliminary characterization of the *explanans* (the explainer) from the role-requirements. For example, Aquinas' explanatory model assumes that being and goodness require an explanation; that sufficient explanations are required; that things whose being and goodness are not self-explanatory cannot be *sufficient* explanations; and that things whose being and goodness are actually or possibly impermanent are things whose being and goodness are not self-explanatory. In the *Summa Theologica*, Aquinas applies this model in the First Way to things whose being is changeable, to infer the existence of an unmoved mover, and further – with the help of physical and metaphysical assumptions – that the first cause of motion is immutable, incorporeal, and not a subject of accidents.

3.3. *Interactive adjustments*

In fact, matters are messier. Sometimes – as above – one begins with a clear grip on the *explanandum* and explanatory model, and infers that and what the *explanans* must be. Sometimes this strategy is repeated with respect to a variety of *explananda*, for which the drive to simplicity demands a single *explanans*. Thus, to continue with Aquinas in the *Summa Theologica*, the explanatory model is applied not just to motion or change, but to beings whose existence is temporary or whose non-existence is possible, and to beings whose goodness and ordering to an end are not self-explanatory. Aquinas assumes that these explanatory roles are legitimately mapped on top of one another, that one and the same entity (the One "everyone calls 'God'") fills them all. He then uses their composite role description, along with other philosophical premises, to elaborate a further characterization of the explanatory posit Who fills these roles.

At other times, one identifies the *explanans* and allows actual features of the *explanans* to modify one's conception of the *explanandum* and/or the explanatory requirements. Again, multiple conceptualities are applied to the "same" data, to generate a variety of different diagnoses. The dual drives towards coherence and simplicity allow these to be mapped on top of one another in such a manner as to modify one another in various ways. Thus, much third-quarter-of-the-twentieth-century New Testament scholarship liked to tell how Christianity began within a sector of Judaism where the human condition generally and Divine–human relations in particular were judged non-optimal, and where both the problem and its remedy were mapped by a variety of competing conceptualities and plot lines, variously predicting the invasion of history by the apocalyptic Son of Man, the return of "home rule" under the ideal temporal ruler and Davidic Messiah, and/or worldwide redemption through the offices of God's Chosen Suffering Servant. Readers can watch how Gospel authors begin with the conviction that Jesus was and is God's agent of worldwide salvation, and address the scandal of the crucifixion that seemingly definitively disqualifies Him from this role, by making His actual career normative, so that Jesus defines what it is to be Messiah, Son of Man, Suffering Servant of God, and the latter conceptualities are adjusted against one another to fit Him.

Likewise, given the identification of Jesus as God's chosen agent, New Testament writers apply *a variety of conceptualities* to characterize the problem and the solution: *cultic* conceptuality portrays Jesus as high priest and pure sacrifice offered on our behalf; *legal* frameworks cast Jesus as the ransom paid to buy us out from under the powers of sin and death; *apocalyptic* theology as the warrior Who vanquishes the powers of hell; Hellenistic Judaism offers the category of preexistent Wisdom, the Divine Word through Whom all things were made; Pharisaic Judaism suggests the role of authoritative rabbi – by word and example – instructing the ignorant; the tradition of *prophecy* invites identification as the righteous prophet warning the resistant of the way of the Lord; Luke–Acts represents His cruciform–resurrection career as paradigm for disciples. Experience and simplicity demand that Jesus fits them all; coherence requires coloring and adjustments of these role definitions to fit Him and to mesh with one another.

The same exercise is repeated in medieval theology with an array of differently conceptualized roles: Christ is at once the One Who makes satisfaction for us, Who takes our punishment, Who pays the ransom; Christ is the paradigm of human nature, looking back to Eden, reaching forward to heaven, His Gospel career at once making gestures to win our love and exemplifying the virtues that we need to negotiate this passing life; Christ is high priest and perfect sacrifice; Christ is the head of the Church, the fontal source of all grace to His members.

3.4. Overlapping roles, consistent and complementary?

If cultic, legal, moral, and ecclesiastical conceptualities can conceive non-optimality problems from different angles, their conceptions of the agent–rescuer typically carry a variety of overlapping requirements. If all of these jobs are to be done by a single agent, coherence demands that the various job requirements be compatible with one another. It may happen that some jobs call for weaker, others stronger qualifications. But this creates no difficulty so long as the more qualified agent can still perform the other jobs. For example, in scholastic Christology, a sinless agent is required to make satisfaction, take our penalty, pay the ransom, be the pure sacrifice. But impeccability (incapacity for sin) is needed to anticipate our heavenly state. Maximal and perfect virtue would be demanded in a paradigm, but not for a strong example to chart our way. Likewise, spiritual wisdom would be required to instruct us in the way of the Lord, but not the beatific vision that will characterize our post-mortem careers, much less maximal knowledge that would go with paradigm humanity. In scholastic Christology, Christ takes the more demanding qualifications with him into the other roles.

3.5. Entrenched data

Where coherence demands harmonizing adjustments, sometimes entrenched data force alterations and modifications in roles and theories. For example, in New Testament Christology, not only are Messianic and apocalyptic roles tweaked by the scandal of the crucifixion, the delay of utopia forces Synoptic complications of traditional soteriological plots (first hidden arrival, then manifest eschatological fulfillment). Likewise, Israel's resistance to conversion, combined with Gentile influx into the Church, stimulates St. Paul to transform Isaiah's universalist plot – all Israel first, then Gentiles streaming to Zion – into one full of irony – first Jewish rejection making way for Gentile acceptance; then Jewish jealousy of Gentile participation in Kingdom rewards prompting Israel's repentance and return, and universal restoration.

3.6. Controlling roles, dominant and trumping

In striking the balance, sometimes one role dominates over others, whether because it is the first in the order of explanation, or the most important that the individual is held to fill. For example, where for Abelard pedagogy and making love's appeal predominate, Bonaventure and Aquinas give satisfaction center-stage and make love's appeal a secondary side effect.

I want to say that, in Christology, the problem – the non-optimality of the human condition generally and Divine–human relations in particular – and the key part of the solution – Jesus – are taken as givens. The effort is to find a coherent framework or frameworks to explain how – in view of His actual human career (as set forth in New Testament documents) – this can be so.

4. The data of Christology

4.1. Degrees of givenness

Any theory works with givens that it tries to organize into a coherent explanatory whole. By now – after two millennia – the data for Christology are vast and varied, and differ not only in kind, but also in *degree of givenness*. *Posterior Analytics*-style foundationalism takes as "givens" indubitable experiences and self-evident propositions (medieval *per se notae*), and tries to proceed from these by evident inferences to sure conclusions. To such deliverances of reason and experience, medieval theology added other infallible authorities: the Bible, the creeds, and select ecclesiastical pronouncements. Medieval school theologians also recognized *auctoritates* of lesser degree – in theology, the works of Augustine and other patristic authors; in philosophy, the writings of Aristotle, Seneca, and Boethius – works that – like the canon of any academic field – had to be seriously weighed and considered, that could not be lightly disregarded or overturned.

Neither for Anselm nor for thirteenth- and fourteenth-century school theology did "authority" or even infallible "givenness" mean "unquestionable." On the contrary, *auctoritates* were precisely those claims that one pitted against one another *pro et contra*, to formulate a problem; they constituted exactly those texts whose implications one questioned and disputed until a resolving integration was won.

My *method of coherence* recognizes that givenness comes in degrees by speaking of "*degrees of entrenchment.*" In a complex data set, it will usually not be straightforward how all of the pieces fit together. Some get marginalized and – whether by elimination or reduction – explained away: e.g., secondary qualities in Cartesian or corpuscularian accounts of matter; mental qualities by materialisms; biblical ascriptions of emotions to God by classical theories of Divine impassibility. Some data are virtually unbudgeable, items before which others must bend and bow. Still others fall somewhere in between.

Like the thinking of the great medieval theologians, my own theologizing is shaped by confessional and philosophical commitments. As an Anglo-Catholic Christian, I regard the Bible, the historic (Apostles' and Nicene) creeds, and the determinations of the ecumenical councils as having authoritative weight, and so a high level of entrenchment. As a historian of Christian doctrine, I pay patristic and medieval figures the respect of serious consideration. As an

Anglican, I also am formed and informed by the vision of turn-of-the-twentieth-century British theologians who front-and-centered the doctrine of the Incarnation and the sacramental universe. As a member of the worshiping community that seeks to grow in the knowledge and love of God and to be ever more conformed to Christ, I give serious consideration to Christian experience over the centuries, from the beginning until now.

Yet, as a sceptical realist, I regard only God as infallible. What God says to us is infallibly true, but human reception of revelation has to be filtered through our fallible cognitive faculties. Because this is true not only of our experiences but also of the written documents that give expression to what we hear God saying, I join many twentieth-century theologians in denying that the Bible, creeds, or conciliar documents are *infallibly* true. On my understanding, to take the Bible, creeds, and conciliar documents as *authoritative* is not to count them infallibly true, but rather to regard them as primary tools of spiritual formation, which shape Christian worship, devotional life, and wider praxis, as well as theological theory-making. To be a Christian is, among other things and in the words of that great Anglican divine Charles Gore, to put oneself to school to them on a daily basis, not only to those parts one finds congenial, but especially to those aspects that repel.[10] At the intellectual level, to be a Christian is to commit oneself to question and dispute these documents above all. Thus, Christian theology is tradition-based creativity, formed and informed by what we question and dispute all the days of our lives.

In a tradition so rich and diverse, I would not expect all of the data to be mutually consistent. This is true both within and across sources. To pretend otherwise sacrifices content, threatens to lose touch with what the human authors really meant and mean, with what they

---

[10] Charles Gore, "The Holy Spirit and Inspiration," in *Lux Mundi: A Series of Studies in the Religion of the Incarnation*, ed. Gore (London: John Murray, Albemarle Street, 1890), ch. 8, 315–362, esp. 349.

thought they heard God saying and how they struggled to conceptualize it, and so forfeits the opportunity to learn from the differences. Willy-nilly, Christian theology always involves some selection, and not just for emphasis. Thus, despite my great admiration for medieval theology, I do not believe that God is immutable and impassible.[11] My love for Holy Scripture notwithstanding, I believe that the human authors of Judges and I Samuel believed in a God who commanded the scorch-and-burn "holocaust" of holy war, *and* it is a consequence of my deepest theological convictions that they were wrong!

4.2. Scripture and historicity

Certainly, patristic/scholastic theologians were alert to the problems of integrating an embarrassingly rich database. Most recognized difficulties in maintaining every line of the Bible to be infallibly true and hence compatible with every other line of Scripture. They handled them by developing a flexible hermeneutic, which allowed what seemed otherwise obvious (e.g., from experience and extra-biblical learning) to influence the meaning assigned to the text of Scripture (e.g., Augustine's treatment of the six-day creation; non-univocal interpretations of statements about Divine emotions and changes of mind). They all recognized many layers of meaning in Scripture, not only literal but "spiritual" – allegorical, typological, moral, and mystagogical. For many, the infallibility of Scripture depended on the truth of the spiritual meanings, because literal construals were sometimes so obviously untrue.[12]

Within my own communion, turn-of-the-twentieth-century Anglicans were gripped by the idea that the New Testament is a *historical* document, indeed a largely reliable record of *historical* facts.

---

[11] See my *Horrendous Evils and the Goodness of God* (Ithaca, NY, and London: Cornell University Press, 1999), ch. 8, 168–174.

[12] See J. N. D. Kelly, *Early Christian Doctrines* (London: Adam and Charles Black, 1958), ch. 3, 69–75.

As we shall explore in more detail later (in my third chapter), they thought it was time for theology to drop its "*a priori*" approach and insisted that Christology should proceed "*a posteriori*" by making sure to square its portraits of Jesus with the "*historical facts.*"

Without pretending to enter higher critical debates about the historical Jesus in earnest, I want nevertheless to register my general methodological stance: *that the New Testament generally and the Gospels in particular are – among other things – second- and third-generation polemical documents intended to interpret the meaning of Jesus' career from the (individual or communal) author's point of view to particular contexts of controversy. Their focus is not primarily on what that career meant for Jesus, but on its significance for Israel, for His followers, indeed, for "the ends of the earth."* More particularly, many of these documents (especially the Gospels and Paul's letters) struggle with the distinctive problem (alluded to above) of how to relate Jesus' actual career to the theological expectations of Second Temple Judaism as to the character and role of the Divine agent who was to remedy the non-optimal condition of Israel and restore its relationship with God. Seizing the offensive and selecting irony as their weapon, many New Testament books argue that those very features of Jesus' career that most misfit the leading theological proposals – shameful death by crucifixion was no part of the scenarios associated with the Davidic Messiah or apocalyptic Son of Man – are the ones most essential to accomplishing His saving work (see I Corinthians 1:18ff.). Since New Testament documents thus reflect *an attempt to resystematize*, to offer complementary and overlapping theological interpretations of, Jesus' human career, the presentation of underlying historical data is *ipso facto* shaped by these systematic aims.[13]

---

[13] Note that the fact that these interpretations are given in *narrative* form is no proof against their *systematic* character. Roles also have definitions, in terms of qualifications and expectations. One would expect a systematic interpretation of the *saving work* of Christ to be given in terms of role definitions and job descriptions.

As a philosopher, I find "Third Quest" attempts to sort out "what Jesus was really like" from "what the Church projected upon Him" methodologically vexed. It is not that I agree with Wrede and Bultmann that the New Testament affords us no access to the historical Jesus, or that (as a theologian) I reject the general outlines of some "Third Quest" portraits. Rather, it seems to me that after the methodological "song and dance" is over, the historiographical criteria are uncritically applied. For example, how readily does John Maier cite the fact that some feature is mentioned in all four Gospels, or even the Gospels and the letters, as meeting the test of multiple attestation, without observing that historical probability considers not only the number of documents but also their (in this case, polemical) genre? Put otherwise, I see the quest for the historical Jesus as frustrated by a lack of documents. Not only are the witnesses few, but our fullest documents are of the wrong kind.

Happily, I have found a way to have my methodological cake and eat the contents, too: viz., by treating the New Testament documents as offering – among other things – *a variety of loosely integrated systematic proposals* which – insofar as Scripture is authoritative – demand the Christologian's serious consideration. This approach allows us to take New Testament conceptions to heart without risking exaggerated claims for their historical reliability. Turn-of-the-twentieth-century Anglicans such as Gore and Weston appealed to the "I AM" statements and the discourses of John's Gospel as *sufficient historical evidence* of Jesus' moral perfection and eventual consciousness of Divine Sonship. *Myth-of-God-Incarnate* authors, embracing further higher critical conclusions, find these arguments easy prey. It is another matter altogether to turn to John's Gospel for systematic proposals to be given authoritative weight and yet tested by systematic criteria: viz., how much they contribute to the consistency, coherence, explanatory power, and fruitfulness of the resultant theoretical whole. To defend these as systematic proposals one doesn't have to assert the historicity of each pericope or event. It is enough to say that this is what the New Testament authors – individual or communal – made of it. It may also be what Christ taught them to make of it. But we do not have to claim to *know* this on *historical* grounds in order to assess the systematic merits of the proposal.

4.3. Philosophical givens?

Metaphysical *realist* that I am, I join the great medieval theologians – Anselm, Bonaventure, Aquinas, Scotus, and Ockham – in affirming that Truth is one. That means that *truths* of physics and chemistry, geology and biology, philosophy and theology, cannot contradict but must be logically consistent with one another. *Metaphysical* realist that I am, I am a *philosophical* theologian, which means that I follow my medieval predecessors in thinking that the conceptuality of philosophy is appropriately marshaled to formulate Christian doctrines. For me as for them, the data to be harmonized and integrated into a theological theory thus include philosophical beliefs and commitments of various degrees of entrenchment.

Yet, in this century, the use of philosophy in theology has become highly controversial across the theological spectrum. Coming mostly from the right, some Barthians and Yale-school "narrative" theologians maintain that theology should restrict itself to the language of Scriptures and work within "the biblical worldview." Coming from the left, *The-Myth-of-God-Incarnate* authors object against the authority of Chalcedon, that we should not conceive of Jesus in terms other than those found in the New Testament or that go beyond the self-understandings attributed to Jesus there. Thus, Hick declares, the Bible does not assert, nor did Christ understand Himself to be God or teach others to believe He was. How dare theologians claim to know something so important about Jesus, when Jesus Himself appears to have been ignorant of it?[14]

---

[14] John Hick, *The Metaphor of God Incarnate: Christology in a Pluralistic Age* (Louisville, KY: Westminster/John Knox Press, 1993), ch. 3, 27–33, 39.

My reply to rightward-leaning Barthians and Yale schoolmen has many layers. First, to be philosophically nit-picking about it, there is no such thing as *the* (i.e., one and only one) biblical worldview. If the historical critical method has taught us anything, it is to recognize textual traces of many different worldviews over the roughly eighteen centuries covered, most of them radically different from our own. If one focusses instead on what the Church through the centuries has read out of or into the Bible, the history of exegesis once again will deliver a large variety of cosmic portraits.

Second, any reader of the Bible makes tacit philosophical assumptions, insofar as hermeneutics belongs to the subject matter of philosophy. The implicit philosophical commitments of most theologians go much further. My own contention is that the intellectual quality of theology would improve if theologians made these philosophical assumptions explicit, the better to expose them to discussion and critique, and so if theologians once again took responsibility for the *philosophical* adequacy of their proposals.

Third, in particular, the attempt to "seal off" theological discourse from the influence of other disciplines flirts with anti-realism. Once again, on metaphysical realist assumptions, Truth is one; the genuine truths of one science cannot be inconsistent with, but ought somehow to be integrable with, and possibly shed light on, those of others. To withdraw theology from the arena is to imply that either it, or the others, or both, should receive an anti-realist construal. On this point, D. Z. Phillips is refreshingly straightforward. He bites the anti-realist bullet, recognizes religions among the many language games that are played, and insists that they not be confused or conflated with ordinary language games about human persons and the material world. Asked how many can go together, reasonably be played by the same person at once, Phillips can say that pragmatic compatibility is all that matters, since he denies that there is any Reality with a capital "R" to which all alike should correspond. Phillips himself embraces the later Wittgensteinian rejection of metaphysics as a philosopher's confusion. Naturally, as a metaphysical realist, this is a position against which I stand firmly and fundamentally opposed.

Of course, I *do* agree – *pace* Clement of Alexandria, who thought the Bible read just like Plato – that Holy Scripture is not a library of philosophy. Notwithstanding the fact that its later human authors sometimes helped themselves to (often semi-popular versions of) then-current philosophical ideas, I do not look to the Bible's words for metaphysical analysis. Biblical narratives about humans and mountains, olive trees and goats, do not explain but presuppose in their hearers some understanding of what such things are. Similarly, the theologian must bring philosophical conceptuality, hunches, and commitments along, as s/he tries to explicate the underlying meanings and answer further questions about what the Bible says. In his *Monologion*, Anselm sets out to prove *sola ratione* the existence of a triune Supreme Nature, Itself the source of all being and well-being. As he reaches various preliminary conclusions, formulated in philosophical language, he slips in biblical phrases as redescriptions of what has been established. By this method of correlation, he signals the reader that what philosophy has just proved is what the Bible was talking about: "the God of Abraham, Isaac, and Jacob, and the God of the philosophers is the same!" Later on, the great disputations of medieval school theology set theses from Aristotle's *Categories* up against Christian *auctoritates*, in argument after argument, until an equilibrium is reached, in which metaphysics is made to learn from Scripture, creeds, and councils, before it ultimately clarifies and specifies belief.

Returning to the topic of Christology in particular, I agree with Hick that New Testament documents do not attribute explicitly Chalcedonian conceptuality to Jesus. If they did, would the Fathers have taken some 400 years to arrive at the definition? Likewise, the Jewish theological rubrics Gospel authors are struggling to resystematize are not metaphysical in nature. Yet, it is precisely their loose integration, and their underdetermination of questions raised by *fides quaerens intellectum* – most pressingly, the one the Gospels themselves raise, viz., who is Jesus, and what is his relation to God? – that "cries out" for alternative conceptualities to integrate the desiderata and embed them in some wider explanatory schemes. Historically, philosophy stepped in to answer that call.

My proposal to include philosophical beliefs and commitments in the database of theology makes urgent the distinction between the role of ecclesiastical authority in dogmatizing – in defining doctrines as binding on all believers (in my terminology, unbudgeably entrenched) – and that of theologians in offering explanations. Just as what is explicit in the Bible underdetermines answers to many questions both *fides quarens intellectum* and unbelieving objectors may raise, so conciliar definitions are usually demanded by particular polemical contexts, focus on what they take to be certain and important, and are appropriately minimalist in scope. Because philosophical claims are inherently controversial, we should expect a variety of explanations of the same doctrinal claim. Thus, medieval school theology proved the ripe time for the Chalcedonian definition – that in Christ there are two distinct and unconfused natures and one person – to receive extensive technical philosophical attention. Among others, Aquinas, Bonaventure, Scotus, and Ockham brought their own distinctive philosophical commitments to bear. None of them thought the Church had any business *dogmatizing* the philosophically contentious items that divided them. At the same time, those many rigorous theoretical developments of the doctrine furnished *gravitas* and texture, and (to those on the outside) exhibited the dogma as philosophically defensible.

From where I stand, my proposal to include philosophical beliefs and commitments in the database of theology has the further happy consequence of falsifying the dichotomy between "Christology from above" (which assumes Christ's Divinity and lets *a priori* assumptions interpret New Testament claims to draw an idealized portrait of His human being and earthly career) and "Christology from below" (which holds itself responsible to begin with history, or at any rate the New Testament record). Throughout the twentieth century, most attempts at "Christology from below" eventually smuggled in their own *a priori* assumptions, both because the historical Jesus is an artifact of historiography and because *a priori* soteriological assumptions secure various features of Christ's earthly character in advance. I want to be frank about beginning with both, the better to argue that a Christology that is metaphysically high but materially low-to-medium lends coherence to both kinds of data.

2 | Posing the problems: beginning with Job

1. Rubrics, manifold and shifting

Good theories exhibit elegant simplicity by virtue of having one (type of) explanatory posit do many different jobs and thereby occupy a variety of theoretical roles. In patristic and medieval Latin school theology, God is taken to be the ultimate explainer of both the being and the goodness of everything. Augustine, Anselm, and Aquinas add truth to the list of what needs to be explained; following Aristotle, Aquinas identifies God as the unmoved mover, the first efficient cause of any and every change. In the order of discovery, Christology begins with another set of *explananda* – with the fact that the human condition generally and Divine–human relations in particular are non-optimal. It attempts to analyze their nature, to trace their source, and to identify their remedy. Christian soteriology (which probes how we are to be saved from what ails us) concludes that God was in Christ exercising the Savior's role.

1.1. Overlapping rubrics

Beginning with the Bible, Christian tradition has conceptualized these twin non-optimalities in different, contrasting, and complementary ways. (1) *In terms of purity versus defilement*: The God of Leviticus declares, "You must be holy as I am holy!" (Leviticus 2:19). But humans are unclean, defiled. Christ is both priest and victim, the one pure sacrifice offered for us once and for all on the cross, that spotless oblation presented daily on that altar eternal in the heavens.

(2) *In terms of honor versus shame*: God is a being a more worthy of honor than which cannot be conceived, possessed of maximal honor of virtue. Human beings generally, God's chosen people in particular, are collectively worthless clients; even the upright are regularly shamed and put to shame by enemies. God's own performance as a patron also *seems* shameful, because Divine servicing of clients is regularly characterized by apparent neglect and unbearable delays. Divine policy is to get glory for Godhead by vindicating the faithful only *after* the worst has already happened: e.g., by raising Jesus on the third day after crucifixion to sit in glory at God's right hand. (3) *In terms of bondage versus ransom*: The children of Israel were slaves in Egypt, and, except for brief periods, subject to big-power domination. Adam's race is enslaved to sin, in bondage to principalities and powers, and at death locked in the spirit prison run by Satan himself. Jesus came to give His life as a ransom for many. (4) *In terms of divorce or estrangement versus reconciliation*: God divorces Israel, His unfaithful bride, won't even speak to her for times and seasons, only to relent, send more prophets to renew the conversation, even His only begotten Son to renew love's appeal. (5) *In terms of sin and satisfaction*: Adam's sin makes his whole family liable for a debt we cannot pay, but the God-man makes satisfaction for the sins of the world. (6) *In terms of ignorance and teaching*: Humans are lost in darkness, but Christ is the Light of the world; the Way, the Truth, and the Life; the Word Who teaches us by what He says and by Who He is. Alternatively, philosophers of religion often sort non-optimalities between (7) *"moral" minuses versus "natural" evils*, on the basis of whether their causes are moral agents (as in genocide or theft) or merely impersonal forces of nature (as in AIDS, cancer, or heart disease).

1.2. Focus on freedom

Western theological majority reports – as asserted in Augustine and refined by Anselm and later medieval western school theologians as well as (and perhaps most emphatically) by Protestant reformers – and late twentieth-century Anglo-American philosophy of religion alike root human non-optimality problems in *sin*, construed as the rebellion of relatively competent agents against God, and identify our psycho-spiritual disarray, our estrangement from God, our vulnerability to a generally hostile environment, and the certainty of death as natural and/or punitive consequences of the sin of free creatures.

Such ancient and honorable "free-will" approaches enjoy certain advantages. (1) There is biblical inspiration for them: sin is the Bible's favorite diagnosis for why things are not right with us and not right between us and God, although the trope of Adam's fall occurs less frequently in the primary canon of Scripture (Genesis 2–3; Romans 5) than traditional soteriology and the reformed creeds would lead us to believe. (2) So far as positive theological motivation is concerned, free-will approaches usually commend the dignity of human nature: e.g., when they locate God's reason for making free creatures in a Divine desire to allow creatures to be as Godlike as possible, to open the way for us to imitate Godhead with respect to a distinctive measure of self-determination. Anselm explains that God *is* justice, and God is self-determined with respect to justice. God gave rational creatures the power of self-determination so that they/we could freely choose to uphold justice and hence be Godlike not only with respect to *justice* but with respect to being *self-determined* to justice.[1] Of course, the capacity for self-determination opens the side-effect possibility that angels and humans would elect to desert justice. They did, setting in motion our tragicomic tale. (3) Negatively, Augustine and other free-will defenders celebrate the fact that – because of this capacity for self-determination – created agents have enough independence to allow us to *blame* our present disarray on someone other than God. God endowed us with the capacity for self-determination and the opportunity to exercise it, in order that we should better

---

[1] See Anselm, *De Casu Diaboli*, chs. 12–14; Schmitt I.251–259. (That is, the F. S. Schmitt edition, vol. I, pages 251–259.)

ourselves. The opposite choice is neither God's end nor a chosen means to God's end; neither sin nor the evil resulting from its punishment is necessary for the perfection of the universe. Rather it is a known but unintended side effect of making creatures capable of self-determination; not something God *does*, but something God *allows* created agents to do. However non-optimal, we brought our present condition on ourselves and have only ourselves to blame!

Surely, sin *is* a problem. Most people middle-aged and older can feel the point of Julian of Norwich's comment that sin, being a sinner, is the worst scourge with which a human being can be tormented.[2] Nevertheless, I believe that attention to a different category – to what I have called horrendous evils[3] – will show that sin is a severe symptom and disastrous consequence of an even deeper problem. Taking my cue from the book of Job rather than stories of Adam's fall, I want to explore what shape Christology takes if the Savior's job is to rescue us, not fundamentally from sin, but from horrors!

2. Horrendous problems

Horrors are the stuff of human crisis. But since they are not the usual starting point for philosophy of religion or Christology, it is worth pausing to spell out precisely what I have in mind. *Defining the Category:* Many attempts have been made to conceptualize evils of the very worst sort. I begin with the *existentialists'* category of personal meaning, and define "horrors" as "evils the participation in (the doing or suffering of) which constitutes *prima facie* reason to doubt whether the participant's life could (given their inclusion in it) have positive meaning for him/her on the whole." Paradigm horrors

---

[2] Julian of Norwich, *Revelations of Divine Love*, trans. Clifton Wolters (London: Penguin Books, 1966), ch. 39, 120.

[3] Most notably in my book *Horrendous Evils and the Goodness of God*.

include the rape of a woman and axing off of her arms, psycho-physical torture whose ultimate goal is the disintegration of person-ality, schizophrenia, or severe clinical depression, cannibalizing one's own offspring, child abuse of the sort described by Ivan Karamazov, parental incest, participation in the Nazi death camps, the explosion of nuclear bombs over populated areas, being the accidental and/or unwitting agent in the disfigurement or death of those one loves best. Participation in horrors furnishes *reason* to doubt whether the par-ticipant's life can be worth living, because it engulfs the positive value of his/her life and penetrates into his/her meaning-making structures seemingly to defeat and degrade his/her value as a person. Nazi con-centration camps aimed not merely to kill but to dehumanize their victims, by treating them as worse than cattle to break down their personalities and to reduce their social instincts to raw animal aggres-sion and self-preservation. Organizing and running such institutions also degraded the Nazis, who caricatured human nature by using their finest powers the more imaginatively to transgress the bounds of human decency. Insofar as taboos are hedges erected to main-tain minimum standards necessary for human community, taboo violations degrade their perpetrators by exhibiting their unfitness for human society. They appear subjectively to degrade by socially disorienting their victims, exploding role expectations at the most fundamental levels.

This criterion is *objective but relative to individuals*. Nature and experience endow people with different strengths, so that one read-ily bears up under what crushes another. Since horrors are defined in terms of the *prima facie* loss of the possibility of positive personal meaning, and since personal meaning is partially framed by social symbols and roles, what counts as horrendous may to some extent vary from society to society[4] (e.g., in ancient Greece, pederasty was publicly accepted between a mentor and his boy protégé; in some

---

[4] Thanks to Tatyana Lifintseva for pressing this point.

aboriginal cultures, it was the father's duty to introduce his daughter to sexual intercourse gently; both practices are taboo in modern western societies). I do not take the horror-participant's own estimates of what is horrendous to be incorrigible: witness the curmudgeon or habitual complainers who know how to make the worst of a good situation, and the callous and unrepentant who think nothing of destroying others for material or political gain. But – *pace* Job's friends – the victim's estimates of how bad the suffering is are among the most significant data to be considered. So are sensitive and honest reflections on the twisting effects of perpetrating various evils. The bottom line is that participation in horrors is supposed to give both participants and onlookers *prima facie* reason to believe that the participant's life is thereby deprived of the possibility of positive personal meaning.

I do not equate horrors with outrageous injustices (Ivan Karamazov's preferred classification) because, first of all, not all horrors are injustices (e.g., the enthusiastic father who innocently but nonnegligently runs over his son, or a person's slow degrading death by cancer). Even where horrendous actions and conditions are unjust, injustice doesn't get to the bottom of what's bad about hunting dogs ripping up a small boy before his mother's eyes, or a mother's eating the corpse of her already dead son, or formerly friendly neighbors chopping each other up with machetes. For the same reasons, I do not define horrors in terms of "cold-bloodedness" (a category Tolstoy chose to express his moral revulsion at public executions). Nor do I confine the horrendous to the massive collective sufferings of war, genocide, slavery, and severe classist economic oppression, because I want to include the excruciating torment of individuals – e.g., the Bible's Job, those with cerebral palsy, schizophrenics, victims of Tay-Sachs disease – whose societies are in general peaceful, prosperous, and relatively just. Rather, the heart of the horrendous, what makes horrors so pernicious, is their life-ruining potential, their power *prima facie* to degrade the individual by destroying the possibility of positive personal meaning.

2.1. Horrendous observations

It doesn't take much insight to recognize that human history is
riddled with horrendous evil. In fact, it is comparatively easy for
human beings to cause (be salient members in causal chains leading
to) horrendous evils. A moment's inattention behind the wheel can
turn a star athlete into a paraplegic, a brilliant mathematician into
a brain-damaged vegetable. Moreover, an individual's capacity to
produce suffering (horrendous and otherwise) unavoidably exceeds
(both quantitatively and qualitatively) his/her ability to experience
it. Pol Pot's psychic capacity was not large enough to suffer each
and all of the tortures he inflicted on millions. Seventeen-year-old
male soldiers lack the empathetic capacity to experience anything
like enough to match the mother's anguish as her baby is bounced
on sharp bayonets. Yet, because – where suffering is concerned –
capacity to conceive follows capacity to experience, our ability to
cause horrors unavoidably exceeds our powers of conception. Just as
the totally blind are cognitively deficient about color no matter how
many color facts they know, because of their inability imaginatively
to represent colors to themselves, so also we cannot *fully* grasp how
bad are the evils of which we have had no experience. Since incorrigible "ignorance diminishes the voluntary," it follows that we cannot
be fully morally responsible for the horrors we perpetrate. I am not
saying that white segregationists who set German Shepherd police
dogs on African Americans or fire-bombed churches or lynched and
shot activists did not know enough about what they were doing to
be seriously wicked. My claim is that there is a vast surplus left over,
that Martin Luther King, Jr., was right that, in a very important
sense, horror-perpetrators "know not what they do" (Luke 23:24;
Acts 3:17)! Grimmer still, virtually every human being is complicit
in actual horrors merely by living in his/her nation or society. Few
individuals would deliberately starve a child into mental retardation.
But this happens even in the United States, because of the economic
and social systems we collectively allow to persist and from which

35

most of us profit. Likewise complicit in actual horrors are all those who live in societies that defend their interests by warfare and so accept horror-perpetration as a chosen means to or a side effect of its military aims. *Human being in this world is thus radically vulnerable to, or at least collectively an inevitable participant in, horrors.*

2.2. The impotence of free-will approaches

Traditional free-will approaches – with their move to shift responsibility and/or blame for evil away from God and onto personal creatures – are stalemated by horrendous evil. Human radical vulnerability to horrors cannot have *its origin* in misused created freedom, because – even if one accepted the story of Adam's fall as historical (which I do not) – the way it is told, humans were radically vulnerable to horrors from the beginning, even in Eden. The framework within which the primal ancestors made their choices was such that obedient choices meant persistence of the *status quo*, while disobedient choices would result in the horrendous disarray such as humans have experienced ever since. Even if Adam's and Eve's choices are supposed to be somehow self-determined, the fact that the consequences amplify far beyond their capacity to conceive and hence to intend – viz., to horrors of which *ex hypothesi* they had no prior experience and of which they could therefore have no adequate conception – is not something for which humans are responsible. Rather it is a function of the interaction between human agency and the wider framework within which it is set, and *God* is responsible for creating human beings in such a framework!

2.3. The lameness of moral categories

Moreover, moral categories do a poor job of handling horrors. My examples illustrate how playing a salient role in horror-perpetration is not tightly correlated with an individual's moral guilt or innocence. In a world such as this, not only do bad things happen to good people; morally innocent people sometimes perpetrate horrors on others, sometimes even those they love the most (e.g., women who took thalidomide drugs during pregnancy on then up-to-date medical advice and bore children without arms and legs). No amount of conscientious caution can guarantee human beings horror-free lives. Again, even where the horror-triggering action is within our power to avoid, God would do us no honor by leaving it "up to" us whether that potential for horror is actualized or not. Suppose a terrorist threatened to torture and behead ten people unless we always put our pencil down exactly one inch from our desk's edge – something it is, strictly speaking, within our power to do. Imposing such disproportionate consequences on our actions puts us under too much pressure and so does not exalt but crushes human agency. Even where the horror-perpetration is morally wrong, moral wrongness barely scratches the surface of what's so bad about it, and the agent is not in a position to shoulder full moral responsibility for it because its badness is unavoidably beyond his/her powers fully to conceive. In any event, retributive justice is stalemated insofar as imposing horror for horror among merely human beings deepens the tragedy by multiplying the ruin. Torturing and beheading terrorists who torture and behead will only degrade those who organize and carry it out. It can do nothing to set things right. I insist – in the spirit of Ivan Karamazov – that, once horrors have happened, it is too late for justice!

2.4. Non-optimality problems, reformulated

My contention is that *the fundamental reason why the human condition generally and Divine–human relations specifically are non-optimal is that God has created us radically vulnerable to horrors, by creating us as embodied persons, personal animals, enmattered spirits in a material world of real or apparent scarcity such as this.* Sin is a symptom and a consequence, but neither the fundamental *explanans* nor the principal *explanandum*. The real roots of our non-optimality problems are systemic and metaphysical. (1) There is a metaphysical mismatch within human nature: tying psyche to biology and personality to a developmental life cycle exposes human personhood to dangers to which angels (as naturally incorruptible pure spirits) are immune. The fact that human psyche begins in groping immaturity and dependence, stumble-bumbles by trial and error towards higher functioning, only to peak and slide towards diminishment – makes our meaning-making capacities easy to twist, even ready to break, when inept caretakers and hostile surroundings force us to cope with problems off the syllabus and out of pedagogical order. Likewise, biology – by building both an instinct for life and the seeds of death into animal nature – makes human persons naturally biodegradable. Human psyche is so connected to biology that biochemistry can skew our mental states (as in schizophrenia and clinical depression) and cause mind-degenerating and personality-distorting diseases (such as Alzheimer's and some forms of Parkinson's), which make a mockery of Aristotelian ideals of building character and dying in a virtuous old age.

(2) There is a metaphysical mismatch between human nature and the material world as we have it, one in which the necessities of life and flourishing seem and are difficult of access and in short supply. If human psyche and biology, personality and animality, mind and body, are odd couples that run interference with one another, scarcity triggers fear and animal aggression and drives us into Darwinian struggles for existence in which only the fittest survive!

(3) There is also the metaphysical mismatch between Godhead and humanity, the enormous gap between Divine and human personal capacities. God's ways are higher than our ways – vastly more so than adult outlooks are above toddlers'. What we are and what Divinity is make communication difficult and trust hard to win.

Metaphysical mismatches are metaphysically necessary, in the first instance, a function of what things *are* and not of what anyone does. Yet, it is *God* Who decided to include such mismatches in the world as we have it. We may ask: whatever for?

3. Cosmological hypothesis

Such soteriological reflections drive me to a partial hypothesis about *God's creative motives and cosmic purposes*: viz., to the conclusion that God must love material creation with a love that dual-drives towards *assimilation* and *union*. On the one hand, God wants matter to be as Godlike as possible while still being itself. Like any good parent with its offspring, God wants as far as possible for creatures to be like God and still possess their own integrity. So God makes chemicals and stuffs dynamic, plants and animals vital, human beings personal. Human nature crowns God's efforts to make material creation – while yet material – more and more like God. On the other hand, God's passion for material creation expresses itself in a Divine desire to unite with it, not only to enter into personal intimacy, but to "go all the way" and share its nature in hypostatic union.

Attributing such an *assimilative* aim to God has the merit of furnishing a partial (if doubtless superficial) explanation of why God would create us in a material world such as this. At the same time, it has the defect of putting Divine intentions behind a project that is *prima facie* self-defeating. Creating a material world such as this and letting material creation "do its thing" has resulted in the evolution of embodied persons who are radically vulnerable to horrors. Put the other way around: personifying matter makes it more Godlike, perhaps of as Godlike a material kind as possible. But setting embodied persons in a material world such as this – one in which material creatures are allowed to "do their thing" – makes the embodied persons radically vulnerable to horrors, which *prima facie* deprives their lives of positive meaning. Letting matter such as this evolve into the most Godlike kind tends to get individuals whose lives are *prima facie* ruined. This raises the question why – if God loved material creation so much – God didn't settle for natural kinds that exhibit lower grades of Godlikeness but whose specimens are not so vulnerable to functional ruin. Why didn't God content Godself with pebbles and streams, mountains and frogs?

Happily, God's *unitive* aim already contains the seeds of a solution, insofar as it purposes Divine sharing of created nature in hypostatic union. If human nature proverbially straddles the divide between matter and spirit, God can share the nature of all creatures by uniting Godself to a particular human nature, and so enter creation as a particular human being. God Incarnate shares not only our nature but also our plight in a material world such as this, the Divine Word also becoming radically vulnerable to horrors.

God's unitive aim drives towards personal intimacy with material creation. But because God's assimilative aim is *prima facie* self-defeating, Divine intimacy with human persons – among other things – takes the distinctive form of identification with us in horror-participation, which *prima facie* defeats the positive meaning of God's human career. Divine solidarity with us in horror-participation weaves our own horror-participation into the warp and woof of our own witting or unwitting intimate personal relationship with God. Because Divinity so mismatches creatures that a metaphysical size-gap yawns between us, Divinity is a good incommensurate with both created goods and created evils. Likewise, personal intimacy with God that is on the whole and in the end beatific is incommensurately good *for* created persons. By catching up our horror-participation into a relationship that is incommensurately good for us, Divine participation in horrors defeats their *prima facie* life-ruining powers.

My proposal is inspired by the following analogy. Soldiers who became fast friends in World War I foxholes might admit that they would never have prospectively willed the horrors of war as means to the end of friendship. Yet the value of the relationship thus occasioned is such that they would not retrospectively will away those wartime bonding moments from their lives. So also victims of horror from the vantage point of heaven, when they recognize how God was with them in their worst experiences, will not wish to eliminate any moments of intimacy with God from their life histories. Soldiers are not only victims, but also often partners in the perpetration of horrors that become unmentionable when they go back home. By dying a ritually cursed death, God in Christ crucified identifies – at least symbolically – with horror-perpetrators whose deeds cast them into outer darkness, outside the bounds of human decency. (From the vantage point of heaven, horror-perpetrators will be able to recognize that their very worst did not cut them off from the love of God; they will be able to take consolation in Divine resourcefulness in compensating their victims, and to wonder at Divine determination to make horrors bear surprising fruits (the way in the Gospels the juridical murder of God by the people of God was turned to the world's redemption); and they will thereby be enabled to live with themselves.)

By defeating the *prima facie* ruinous quality of merely human horror-participation, Divine horror-participation also defeats its own *prima facie* ruinous effect on Jesus' own human career. *This is the one case in which "horror for horror" does make the situation better: when God participates in the horrors that God has perpetrated on us!* Put more concretely and more biblically, because crucifixion renders its victim ritually cursed and so cast into outer darkness, excluded from the people of God and cut off from the God Who goes in and out with them (Deuteronomy 21:23; Galatians 3:13), crucifixion appears decisively to defeat Jesus' claim to be the Messiah. But if Christ comes to save human persons from the ruinous power of horrendous evil, then crucifixion is precisely the sort of thing that would make His mission successful. If God takes God's stand with the cursed, the cursed are not cut off from God after all!

So far, my diagnosis of what ails us and my narrative of God's cosmic aims and soteriological methods participate in an irony worthy of St. Anselm (I hope also of the New Testament)! All the same, I have helped myself to a number of assumptions and distinctions, and I have oversimplified. I now amplify with clarifications and complications.

4. Many and various distinctions!

4.1. *Justifying versus explanatory reasons*

The reason I have offered for human non-optimality problems appeals to God's global and cosmic goals. God created us in a world like this because God wanted to accomplish God's assimilative and unitive aims within a material creation such as this. Mine might seem to be just another in a long line of approaches that try to *justify* Divine permission of evils as a necessary means to, consequence of, or side effect of some excellence in the world as a whole. We recall others: evils in the amounts and of the kinds and with the distributions found in the actual world are necessary for its counting as the best of all possible worlds or for its exhibiting maximum variety with maximum unity (see Leibniz and more recently Nelson Pike[5]); alternatively, such evils are side effects of Divine efforts to optimize the *ratio* of moral good to moral evil produced by personal creatures (see Alvin Plantinga[6]).

Elsewhere, I have repeatedly insisted that merely global approaches are unsatisfactory where horrendous evils are concerned.[7] To say that, for God, desire to produce a world with a certain cosmic excellence is sufficient by itself to override the negative consideration raised by horrors is to imply that God lets cosmic considerations conquer His *prima facie* desires to be good-to created persons. This is because, by definition, horrors are not good-for but *prima facie* ruinous to horror-participants. For all we know, Divine willingness to make a horror-infested world with a certain cosmic excellence might be compatible with maximal Divine Goodness along the dimension of excellence in cosmos-production. But – so far from vindicating – such

---

[5] Nelson Pike, "Hume on Evil," *Philosophical Review* 72 (1963), 180–197.

[6] Alvin Plantinga, *The Nature of Necessity* (Oxford: Clarendon Press, 1974).

[7] M. M. Adams, *Horrendous Evils and the Goodness of God*, chs. 1–2, 7–31. Cf. my "Horrendous Evils and the Goodness of God," *Proceedings of the Aristotelian Society*, Supplementary Volume 63 (1989), 299–310.

willingness exacerbates the problem of Divine goodness-to created persons. Having criticized others, am I not in danger of falling into the same trap?

My hope to avoid it rests on a distinction between *explanatory* and *justifying* reasons. It is one thing to propose a consideration as looming large in Divine calculations about which – if any – world to make. The Bible and traditional theology offer a number of plausible suggestions: the desire to make a very good world that includes a variety of creaturely kinds, the desire to include personal creatures made in God's image, the desire to let creatures "do their thing" (exercise their natural functions) much of the time. Taken only that far, such reasons are offered as *explanatory* reasons – reasons that help to account for Divine choice and/or the state of the world as we find it. It is another to say that such reasons are sufficient by themselves to *justify* Divine permission of evils in the amounts and of the kinds and with the distributions found in the actual world. Put otherwise, it is another to say that such reasons are enough by themselves to show that Divine permission of such evils is compatible with the Goodness of God. (Pike spoke of "morally sufficient reasons" because he conceived of Divine Goodness as *moral* goodness.)

My own view is that talk of theodicy – of *justifying* the ways of God to humankind – is misleading, because God has no obligations to creatures and hence no need to *justify* Divine actions to us. Personal though God is, the metaphysical size-gap is too big for God to be drawn down into the network of rights and obligations that bind together merely human beings. Elsewhere, I have argued that horrors are so bad that no candidate reason-why that we can think of is remotely *sufficient* to exhibit the compatibility of horrors with Divine goodness-to created horror-participants, and that any attempt to construe one or more of them as sufficient underestimates how bad horrors are and caricatures God into something monstrous.[8] Recall, for example, the

---

[8] E.g., in *Horrendous Evils and the Goodness of God*, ch. 3, 53–55.

suggestions that God allowed Nazi soldiers to march children into flaming ditches or into gas chambers simply to follow through on the Divine plan of letting free creatures – including Hitler – determine their own destinies, or merely because it was the price of creating the best of all possible worlds.

Unsurprisingly, then, I do not offer my cosmological hypothesis as a justifying reason. Proposing that God loves material creation permissively does not solve but intensifies the soteriological problem of how and whether God can be good-to the thousands killed by the Boxing Day 2004 tsunami! I forward my cosmological hypothesis as one among other explanatory reasons. I do focus on this hypothesis not because I imagine it to tell the whole story or even a very deep story about Divine motivations. Here Anselm is surely right: even our most beautiful soteriological theories are superficial attempts to describe the abyss of Divine Goodness![9] At one level, my hypothesis of Divine love for material creation seems obvious, bordering on trivial: this material world exists; therefore, its Creator must have wanted it! When the hypothesis is taken to another level and articulated in terms of Divine assimilative and unitive aims, I find it attractive because it promises to integrate my understanding of what ails us and of how God is for us with God's creative cosmological aims. Put otherwise, my cosmological hypothesis promises to describe a cosmos held together by Christ and to exhibit the coherence of Christology!

4.2. Dimensions of Divine goodness

When suffering humanity asks why God doesn't prevent or eliminate evils, the concern is not fundamentally the theoretical one of how the coexistence of God and evil is logically possible, but the existential worry that – because God seems not to have "been there" for us to shield us from horrors – God must hate us, not care about us, or at any rate not be interested in being good-to us. But the Bible

---

[9] Anselm, *Commendatio* to *Cur Deus Homo*; Schmitt II.40, 4–5.

represents God as making human persons a focal interest of Divine projects in creation. Divine love for created persons would mean that God does not have merely global goals (e.g., to produce the best of all possible worlds, a cosmos displaying maximum variety with maximum unity, or a world with as favorable a balance of moral good over moral evil as God could get) and/or does not pursue them at the cost of not being good-to the individual created persons God makes. My cosmological hypothesis integrates God's global goodness (superlative skill at cosmos-production) with Divine goodness-to created persons, insofar as it implies that God cannot achieve Divine purposes with respect to material creation without making sure that the plot resolves into a happy ending for us. Since this world *is* horror-infested, Divine love for created persons must mean that God knows how and intends to be good-to us even after the *prima facie* worst has already happened. My contention is that God cannot be good-to an individual created person unless God guarantees to him/her a life that is a great good to him/her on the whole, *and* unless God makes good on any horror-participation by that individual, not merely within the context of the cosmos as a whole, but within the framework of that individual horror-participant's own life. Evidently, God does impose costs on individuals in this world. My claim is that *Divine love would not subject some individual created persons to horrors simply for the benefit of others or to enhance cosmic excellence.* Divine love would permit horrors only if God could overcome them by integrating them into lives that are overwhelmingly good for the horror-participants themselves.

4.3. Balancing off versus defeat

For God to *make good on* horror-participation is for God to overcome it with some great enough good. But the notion of "overcoming" is ambiguous, because there are different kinds of relations that value-parts can bear to value-wholes. There is the quasi-arithmetical notion of *balancing off*, in which one merely adds to a negatively (positively) valued part a positively (negatively) valued part of greater value. For example, one might balance off a painful hour in the dentist's chair or a conflictual committee meeting with a stunning concert in the evening. By contrast, *defeat* involves a relation of organic unity between the negatively (positively) valued part and the whole, with the result that a significantly smaller negatively (positively) valued part can actually increase (decrease) the value of the whole of which it is a part. For example, in Monet's painting, a square centimeter of ugly bilious green may be just right to depict the light on Rouen Cathedral in early morning, while replacing it with a square centimeter of gorgeous blue would spoil the design. Mere balancing off of horrors does not confer any positive meaning on them, and so would leave open the question of why a God Who loved human beings would not – since horror-participation is *prima facie* ruinous – omit the horrendous segments altogether (e.g., deleting apocalyptic terrors of this present world and proceeding immediately to the bliss that is to come). But meaning-making is distinctive of personal functioning, while horrors make it *prima facie* impossible for human horror-participants to make any positive sense of their lives. My conclusion is that a God Who loved individual created persons would not merely balance off but defeat any horror-participation within the context of the individual person's life.

4.4. How valuable a defeater?

Horrors are so bad that no package of merely created goods will balance off, much less defeat, them. Aharon Appelfeld's novels are particularly powerful in depicting the psychic wasteland of Holocaust survivors surrounded by new families, professional success, and personal luxury. Despite the strength of their survival instinct and their own resourceful ingenuity, the concentration camps had crippled their capacity for making meaningful connections with other people, had violated their sense of personal worth too deeply for ordinary created goods to reverse the trauma of their lives. Their horror-participation had thus stumped their efforts to make positive sense of their lives, because none of the many and impressive things they could conceive of and carry out added up.[10] By contrast, God – metaphysically, what God is – is the incommensurate good, radically outclassing any created goods or evils. Generally speaking, appropriate relationship to good things is good-for us. We are good to children when we feed them nourishing food, provide them with a stimulating education, give them opportunities to view the world's great art. Likewise, appropriately relating us to the right goods is one way for God to be good-to us. Christian tradition affirms that intimate relationship with God which is on the whole and in the end beatific is incommensurately good-for created persons. *My conclusion is that the only currency valuable enough to make good on horrors is God, and the horror-participant's overall and eventual beatific intimacy with God.*

4.5. *Three stages of defeat*

To defeat horror-participation within the individual created person's life, God must weave it into the fabric of that individual's intimate and (overall and in the end) beatific personal relationship with God. But horror-defeat is a process that can be broken down into stages. (1) What Divine horror-participation does is to turn merely human horror-participation into occasions of personal intimacy with God. I call this *Stage-I* horror-defeat. This means that the materials for lending positive meaning to any and all horror-participation are already planted in the history of the world here below; whether or not we recognize it, God has acted to provide it. (2) Because meaning-making is a personal activity, it is not enough for the materials of meaning-making to be furnished. They must be recognized and appropriated. Because we are developmental creatures whose

---

[10] Aharon Appelfeld, *For Every Sin* (New York: Weidenfeld and Nicholson, 1989), and Appelfeld, *The Immortal Bartfuss* (New York: Harper and Row, 1989).

meaning-making capacities are easily damaged and distorted in a material world such as this, because horrors at best stump and at worst shatter our abilities to make positive sense out of our lives, our meaning-making capacities require healing and coaching. I call this *Stage-II* horror-defeat. (3) Finally, the plot cannot really resolve into a happy ending unless the relation of embodied persons to our material environment is renegotiated so that we are no longer radically vulnerable to horrors. I call this *Stage-III* horror-defeat.

4.6. Soteriology, ontologically defined

My approach – which traces our twin non-optimalities to multiple metaphysical mismatches, fundamentally to what things *are* and not in the first instance to what persons do – gives the soteriological problem a fundamentally *ontological* analysis. In this, I am no innovator. There is an ancient and honorable (mostly Platonizing) tradition that defines "evil" in terms of "falling short" or "defecting" from Goodness (or goodness). These metaphors get construed in many ways. (i) Any creaturely nature falls short of Goodness by being changeable and corruptible. Sometimes the further corollary is drawn that such ontological instability makes the eventual defection of the wills of rational creatures inevitable. The evil of sin is thus a by-product or an expression of such ontological falling short. (ii) Individual creatures may also fall short of their creaturely natures, by failing to be perfect specimens (e.g., the three-legged horse, the blind sheep, the sinful human or angel). In this connection, "evil" is defined as "the privation of something a thing naturally ought to have." (iii) According to some, the great chain of being and goodness "bottoms out" with matter, which is evil insofar as it falls the furthest short of Goodness and – of itself – is the most deprived. (iv) Again, evil is *disorder* or a *failure of fit*, whether by overreaching one's natural place (the pride of Lucifer in wanting to seize God's throne), or by falling short of one's natural dignity (when humans descend into bestial behavior), or by failing to take one's proper place in the cosmic whole. Insofar as "evil" signifies the lack of something, it is said that evil is non-being. Insofar as "evil" signifies privation, it is ontologically parasitic on some being that lacks what it properly ought to have. Eastern Christians who appropriated elements of this picture tended to be confident that this ontological problem of evil (with sin as its derivative correlate) would admit of a full and final solution, because Goodness Itself surely *is* what it takes to overpower the non-being of defect or privation! Hence, Origen's and Gregory of Nyssa's bias in favor of universal salvation!

Generally, western patristic and medieval theology was equivocal about (i): sometimes presupposing it and emphasizing the severe ontological degradation of any and every creature ("almost nothing" or "scarcely extant," Anselm remarks[11]); other times insisting that created natures are intrinsically good, but only finite goods. By contrast, western medieval theologians favored (ii), along with its definition of evil as a privation, and for that reason rejected (iii) insofar as matter is not low-grade by virtue of lacking something that properly belongs to *it*. For many, sin itself involved both (ii) a privation (a defective aim) and (iv) a form of disorder – a failure of the creature properly to coordinate its pursuit of goods with Divine standards or commands.

My own diagnosis of human non-optimalities is ontological, but contrasts with these traditional positions. Most notably, on my cosmological hypothesis, matter – material creation generally – must be good because God loves it (i.e., not-[iii])! Likewise, personality must be good because God is personal. Both are good; neither is intrinsically evil. Gnosticism and materialism are both false! Radical vulnerability to horrors arises because human psycho-spiritual powers are not reliably great enough to achieve and sustain an appropriate functional coordination between these two dimensions of human being in a material world such as this. Once again, it is a question of (iv) misfit or disorder. Without being invested in any notion of evil

[11] Anselm, *Monologion*, c.28; Schmitt I.45–46.

as non-being, I make it a minimal measure of Divine omnipotence that God can enable a wholesome integration of human personality into human bodily life.

4.7. Matter, embraced or eschewed?

Historically, with or without the "benefit" of such metaphysical reflections, many spiritual leaders have seen the body and our material environment as enemies from which we should eventually hope to escape. In practice, desert fathers and Franciscan spirituals regarded their bodies as the battle ground with the devils, and strove heroically to crucify their sensory desires, to amputate involvement with them as much as possible. Even theologians who affirmed the resurrection of the body were far from consistent in assigning the body any positive role to play in heavenly beatitude. Once again, my soteriological starting point drives me to the opposite conclusion. *Personal embodiment in a material world such as this is so costly to human beings that it is not enough for it to be a temporary episode to be left behind.* If God is going to ask us to pay the price of *prima facie* personal ruin, then *Divine love for us would lead God to make good on the experiment.* Hence, my hypothesis that Divine commitment to created embodied persons is permanent and universal, *and* Divine commitment to material creation generally is relentless (see chapter 8)!

4.8. Shrunken agents?

Starting with the horrendous predicament of humankind, I have painted a more pessimistic picture of human agency than traditional free-fall approaches draw of Adam and Eve in Eden. Emphasizing the metaphysical size-gap between God and creatures, I insist that human agency could not have enough stature to shift responsibility for the way things are off God's shoulders onto ours. I deny our competence to organize personal animality into a functional harmony, much less to anticipate and steer our way clear of horrors. Nevertheless, my low doctrine of the human condition is balanced with a high doctrine of our place in God's providential plans. Human beings crown Divine assimilative aims by being meaning-makers in God's image. Personal intimacy with us is penultimate within God's unitive aims, and a main benefit of Incarnation is that it enables God to meet us on our level. Moreover, I insist, God will be good-to each created person by weaving up any horror-participation into an unending relationship of beatific intimacy with God. In my judgment, grim realism is not inappropriately derogatory of human dignity, but rather serves to magnify the miracle of God's making good on God's cosmic project by benefiting each and every human being. (And, yes, my focus on horrors does drive me to a doctrine of universal salvation!)[12]

4.9. Incongruous dichotomies

Framing the redemptive task in terms of horror-defeat falsifies traditional dichotomies. It refuses to choose between the *objective* focus on an external transaction accomplished by Christ's suffering and death (as in the Ransom and Satisfaction theories of the atonement) and the *subjective* focus on the transformation of the psycho-spiritual state of human beings as well as reconciliation in Divine–human relations (as in Abelard). Divine identification with human vulnerability to and participation in horrors throughout the course of Christ's earthly career confers a positive aspect on human participation in horrors, whether or not human participants ever come to acknowledge that *objective* fact (= Stage-I horror-defeat). But subjective recognition and appropriation of these meanings is needed for the *prima facie* ruin of the participant's life to be overcome, and wholesome Divine–human relations to be established or restored (= Stage-II horror-defeat). Bringing vulnerability to horrors finally to an end

---

[12] See my "Neglected Values, Shrunken Agents, Happy Endings: A Reply to Rogers," *Faith and Philosophy* 19:2 (2002), 487–505.

will also involve both the objective creation and the subjective recognition of a land of milk and honey (= Stage-III horror-defeat).

Likewise artificial would be the attempt to divide stages of *justification* and *sanctification*. On Protestant Reformation usage, "justification" is a legal category associated with settling the charges against us, while "sanctification" is a cultic category associated with the process of inner transformation of the sinner. But looking at the threefold task of "horror-defeat," we can see that things are not "set right" between us and God until both of the first two stages are well underway, and yet the second already involves a revolutionary remodel of the functional dynamics and inner meaning-making structures of the horror-participant's life.

4.10. Revised job description

If non-optimality is construed in terms of God's setting us up for horror-participation by creating us as personal animals in a material world such as this, then the Savior's job is to be the horror-defeater. Our next question is: Who would Christ have to be, what relation to God and humankind would Christ have to have, to accomplish this saving work?

3 | Sharing the horrors: Christ as horror-defeater

1. Introduction

Christ comes as Savior to solve our non-optimality problems. Like Anselm, I have argued that it takes a God-man to do the job. Like Anselm, I want my Christology to be normed by the so-called Chalcedonian definition, negotiated in 451 BCE. Sarah Coakley translates as follows:

> Following, then, the holy Fathers, we all with one voice teach that it should be confessed that our Lord Jesus Christ is one and the same Son, the Same perfect in Godhead, the Same perfect in manhood, truly God and truly man, the Same [consisting] of a rational soul and a body; *homoousios* with the Father as to his Godhead, and the Same *homoousios* with us as to his manhood; in all things like unto us, sin only excepted; begotten of the Father before ages as to his Godhead, and in the last days, the Same, for us and for our salvation, of Mary the Virgin *Theotokos* as to his manhood; One and the same Christ, Son, Lord, Only begotten, made known in two natures [which exist] without confusion, without change, without division, without separation; the difference of the natures having been in no wise taken away by reason of the union, but rather the properties of each being preserved, and [both] concurring into one Person *(prosopon)* and one *hypostasis* – not parted or divided into two persons *(prosopa)*, but one and the same Son and Only-begotten, the divine Logos, the

Lord Jesus Christ; even as the prophets from of old [have spoken] concerning him, as the Lord Jesus Christ has taught us, and as the Symbol of the Fathers has delivered to us.

So far as its historical origin is concerned, the Chalcedonian definition is a polemical, compromise document, carefully worded to rule out Apollinarianism, Eutychianism, and extreme Nestorianism, while remaining compatible with a variety of conflicting opinions represented by council luminaries. Coakley helpfully itemizes a number of issues on which the so-called Chalcedonian definition does *not* explicitly commit itself:

(1) in what the (a) Divine and (b) human natures consist;
(2) what *hypostasis* means when applied to Christ;
(3) how *hypostasis* and *physeis* (natures) are related to one another (how to solve the problem of the *communicatio idiomatum*);
(4) how many wills Christ has;
(5) W/who the *hypostasis* in Christ is (e.g., whether it is the Divine Word);
(6) what happens to the natures at Christ's death and resurrection;
(7) whether the meaning of *hypostasis* in the Christological context is the same or different from that in the Trinitarian context;
(8) whether the risen Christ is male.

In 681 CE, the Council of Constantinople answered (4), with its rejection of *monothelitism*: if Christ has a Divine nature and a human soul, then Christ has a Divine will and a human will as well.[1] Points (3), (5), (6), and (7) will form the focus of chapters 4 and 5.

Chalcedon *is* clear that the natures are not to be confused, so that Jesus Christ is conceived of as some sort of hybrid – God the Son or some superhuman spirit animating a human body. Rather, besides His Divine nature, Jesus Christ had both a human soul and

---

[1] Sarah Coakley, "What Chalcedon Solved and Didn't Solve," in *The Incarnation*, ed. Stephen T. Davis, Daniel Kendall SJ, and Gerald O'Collins SJ (Oxford: Oxford University Press, 2002), ch. 7, 143.

a human body, because – as Gregory Nazianzen declared – *what is not assumed cannot be restored!*[2] But Chalcedon does not specify (1b) what sort of human nature Christ assumed.[3] Tradition reaching back to Augustine through Boethius but reasserted in the twelfth century by Peter Lombard recognizes four states of human nature: that before the fall, after the fall but before grace, after the fall and under grace, or in its eschatological completion.[4] If each of these is compatible with, as well as accidental to, human nature, Christ could be fully human in any one of them. What sort of human nature did Christ have during His *ante-mortem* career? Theologians triangulate their way into contrasting answers by looking to systematic presumptions, soteriological requirements, and Holy Scripture.

2. Perfectionistic treatments

Medieval Latin schoolmen were heavily influenced by certain strands of patristic theology that sought to make Christ's human nature as Godlike as possible while still allowing Him to accomplish His saving work. (1) These thinkers begin with distinctive *systematic*–what Gore and other turn-of-the-twentieth-century Anglicans would call "*a priori*" – *presumptions*. Some harbored *a presumption against Incarnation*, vigorously voiced by non-Christian (Jewish and Muslim) monotheists and reinforced by a Platonizing appreciation of the metaphysical "size-gap" between creatures and God. In *Cur Deus Homo*, Anselm in effect concedes that Incarnation is *prima facie* metaphysically indecent (why would a being a greater than which cannot be conceived unite itself with what is "almost nothing"?) and therefore something God would undertake only if the fulfillment

---

[2] Kelly, *Early Christian Doctrines*, ch. 11, 297.

[3] See my *What Sort of Human Nature? The Metaphysics and Systematics of Christology: The Aquinas Lecture, 1999* (Milwaukee, WI: Marquette University Press, 1999).

[4] Peter Lombard, *Sent.* III, d. 16, c. 2; Grottaferrata II.105 (= Grottaferrata edition, vol. II, p. 105). Cf. Boethius, *Liber contra Eutychen et Nestorium*, c. viii.

of Divine purposes made it *conditionally necessary* to do so. Given the fact of Incarnation, non-Antiochene patristic and early medieval theologians transmuted the presumption against Incarnation into *a presumption of perfection*, that, other things being equal, the human nature God made God's own would have to be as perfect as it is possible for a human nature to be. Thirteenth-century theologians who took on board pseudo-Dionysius' conception of Goodness as self-diffusing (as having or being a positive tendency to share itself out) arrived at the presumption of perfection another way. For them, the nature of Goodness as self-diffusing outweighed any presumption against Incarnation created by the metaphysical size-gap.[5] But the metaphysical proximity of Divinity to Christ's human nature in Incarnation would set up a presumption that Divine Goodness would flood it with as much perfection as it could hold.

Thus, the presumption of perfection drove these theologians to conclude that Christ has – from the moment of His conception – as much grace as it is humanly possible to receive, fullness of moral and theological virtues and spiritual gifts; beatific vision by which He sees not only God but – as far as possible for a finite human mind – all things in God (i.e., all actuals and all possibles producible by merely created powers). As time went on, Aristotelian authors (e.g., Aquinas and Scotus) applied the principle of perfection to insist that, besides such supernatural knowledge and grace, Christ's human cognitive and appetitive faculties must also be allowed their optimal normal functioning as well. In addition to knowledge supernaturally infused from conception, Christ also "acquires" information through sense experience. Interestingly, school theologians from Lombard forward agreed that the presumption of perfection pushed in the direction of attributing to Christ a glorified, incorruptible body (such as the elect will have in heaven). But presumptions function only to assign burdens of proof; they are in principle rebuttable if other considerations are brought to bear. In weighing these, Lombard says

---

[5] See Aquinas, *Summa Theologica* III, q. 1, a. 1, c.

we must strike the balance of *"what is fitting for Him"* and *"what is useful to us."*

(2) Such utilities were conceptualized and calculated in terms of further systematic considerations – viz., *soteriological roles*, which generate job descriptions and lists of job qualifications which Christ has to meet to be able to accomplish His saving work. Medieval authors included such roles as paying the ransom, making satisfaction for our sins, offering the perfect sacrifice, conquering the devil, being an exemplar of humankind (with pedagogy and participation being among the themes), being head of the Church and as such mediator of grace, being the first of many co-lovers of God, making Divine Love's appeal to Adam's race. They understood *sinlessness* to be precondition of all of these roles, but they let the presumption of perfection raise this to an attribution of *impeccability* (lack of capacity to sin). They admitted the defects – of vulnerability to suffering and death – into Christ's human nature, because His suffering and death were seen as necessary means to paying the ransom, making satisfaction, offering sacrifice, and conquering the devil. The vulnerable, corruptible body was also found to have the secondary, epistemological merit of convincing onlookers of the *reality* of Christ's humanity.

(3) Their third point of triangulation was Holy Scripture. The *quaestio–disputatio* theological method of school theologians encouraged them to consider Scripture one verse at a time (as a premiss in a *pro* or *contra* argument). Their hermeneutical approach to then-standard Christological texts was dictated by the combination of their *a priori* systematic presumptions, their estimates of Christ's saving roles, and their philosophical views about what human perfection naturally involves. (a) *Grace*: Thus, so far as *grace* is concerned, Colossians 2:9 (the whole fullness of God dwells bodily), John 3:34 (the Spirit is given to Him without measure), and John 1:16 (from Him we have received grace upon grace) articulated the expected consequences of the presumption of perfection, while Luke 2:52 (growth) tended to get construed in terms of growing *manifestation*

rather than growing possession. (b) *Knowledge and wisdom*: Scholastics appeal to I Corinthians 2:10–11 (the Spirit of God searches everything and everything was given to Christ in full measure) and Colossians 2:3 (the One Who contains all treasures of wisdom and knowledge) for corroboration, while Luke 2:52 is understood in terms of growing manifestation of knowledge and/or as referring to Christ's *naturally acquired* human knowledge over and above His supernatural endowments. Matthew 11:27/Mark 13:32 (ignorance of the day and the hour) don't come up but would have been handled the same way. (c) *Emotions*: If many patristic authors tried to explain away passages that attribute emotions to Christ – *sorrow* (Isaiah 53:4 [bears our griefs and sorrows]; Matthew 26:38 [sorrowful unto death]; John 12:27 [deeply disturbed]), *fear* (Luke 19:41/Matthew 27:35 [fears approaching the passion]; Mark 14:35 [let this cup pass]; Psalms 22:3/Matthew 27:46/Mark 15:34 [cry of dereliction]), *anger* (Psalms 68:10/John 2:17 [zeal for God's house]; but James 1:20 [anger cannot do God's work]) – medieval school theologians were increasingly willing to allow for emotions so long as there was no question of their being strong enough to upset right reason's rule. (d) *Sin/curse*: Likewise, since impeccability and holiness are dictated by the presumption of perfection and reinforced both by the exigencies of Christ's soteriological roles and by Hebrews 4:15 (tempted without sin), other striking passages – II Corinthians 5:21 (God made Him to be sin Who knew no sin), Isaiah 53 (the Lord put on Him the iniquities of us all), and Galatians 3:13 (became cursed for us)/Deuteronomy 21:23 (cursed be he who hangs from a tree) – are interpreted in terms of Christ's taking the penalty for our sin, or in terms of His enemies mistakenly thinking Him a cursed sinner.

Medieval Christian thinkers had no doubts about Divine power to act "outside" or "beyond" nature – freely and contingently to create or annihilate anything other than Godself, freely and contingently to obstruct the exercise of any created power, freely and contingently to act alone to produce things normally effected in collaboration with natural created powers. Nor would they have hesitated to affirm the authenticity of Gospel miracle stories – of Jesus' exorcizing, healing (the deaf, dumb, blind, and paralytic, hemorrhaging women and withered hands), and raising the dead; of His calming storms and walking on water; of His multiplying loaves and fishes and turning water into wine. But both Bonaventure[6] and Aquinas agreed with Lombard[7] on the metaphysical impossibility of any created nature – including Christ's human nature – being omnipotent. Pausing over the point, Aquinas explains that, because active power follows nature, Christ's human nature has exactly the same natural active power as any other human nature does, and so *qua* human has no more power over His own body or the rest of the material world than any other human being does in itself. When miracles are wrought through the agency of angels or humans, God is the principal agent Who graciously involves the creature by using its agency as an instrumental cause. The only difference is that Christ's humanity is an *internal* instrument for the Divine Word, insofar as that nature belongs to Him, whereas other created natures (including those of angels and saints) are *external* instruments.[8]

Overall, the scholastics painted a portrait of Christ's human nature as highly advantaged in comparison with ours. To be sure, like ours, His is vulnerable to hunger, thirst, and fatigue, as well as to suffering and death. Like ours, His acquires knowledge through natural processes in ever increasing amounts, and experiences human emotions in the face of obstacles. But from the moment of His conception, He enjoys fullness of grace, beatific vision, as much (supernatural) knowledge as a human soul can hold, impeccability and *a fortiori* an unwavering rule of right reason, so that His human condition represents the perfection of lost Eden and future fulfillment of heaven as much or more than it does our present earthly state.

---

[6] Bonaventure, *Sent.* III, d. 14, a. 3, q. 3, c; Quaracchi III.324 (=Quaracchi edition, vol. III, page 324).

[7] Peter Lombard, *Sent.* III, d. 14, sec. 3; Grottaferrata II.92.

[8] Aquinas, *Summa Theologica* III, q. 13, aa. 1–3, c; *De Potentia*, q. 6, a. 4, c.

3. Turn-of-the-twentieth-century British Christology

Broadly speaking, turn-of-the-twentieth-century British liberal theologians deplored the *a priori* character of such patristic and medieval
Christology, with its tendency to make the metaphysical "gap" and
the presumption of perfection decisive. On the contrary, Christology should begin with Holy Scripture, and with then-contemporary
higher critical exegesis of it, which treated the Bible as a *historical*
document. If – like other historical documents – the Bible need not
be taken to be infallible, and if much of the Old Testament cannot be
credited with historical accuracy, still – they thought – the Gospels
are, on the whole, an accurate record of *the historical facts*.[9] Moreover,
they reasoned, if Jesus is *a historical* figure, we must take His humanity with full seriousness, as subject to the same sorts of biological,
psychological, and historical analyses as anyone else's. Christology
should thus proceed *a posteriori*, by sticking close to the latest scientific theories and discoveries and to *the historical facts* that the Gospel
records.[10]

The higher critical results that made the biggest impression
were those that challenged perfectionistic patristic/scholastic attribu-
tions of (near) omniscience to Christ's human soul. Old Testament
criticism called into question numerous points that Jesus' Gospel

9 Charles Gore, "The Holy Spirit and Inspiration," *Lux Mundi*, ch. 8, 315–362, esp. ch. 8,
   327, 337, 361; Gore, *The Incarnation of the Son of God: The Bampton Lectures (1891)*
   (London: John Murray, Albemarle Street, 1893), Lecture I, sec. IV, 18, Lecture VII,
   sec. V, 195–199; Gore, *Dissertations on Subjects connected with the Incarnation*
   (London: John Murray, Albemarle Street, 1895), Dissertation II, 79, 196, 205–206;
   Frank Weston, *The One Christ: An Enquiry into the Manner of the Incarnation*
   (London, New York, Bombay, and Calcutta: Longmans, Green, 1907), Part III, ch. VI,
   135. See P. T. Forsyth, *The Person and Place of Jesus Christ* (London: Independent Press,
   1909), ch. VI, 159–161, 168–169, 172–173, where Forsyth argues that the Synoptics set
   out the facts, while the Pauline epistles furnish their inspired interpretation.
10 Gore, *Dissertations* II, 95–96; Weston, *The One Christ*, Part I, ch. II, 35–37, Part II,
   ch. III, 60, 75.

conversation seems to presuppose: e.g., Mosaic authorship of the Penteteuch, Davidic composition of the psalms, the historicity of creation and flood stories as well as of Jonah's being swallowed and regurgitated alive by a big fish. If Gore explained some of the latter away patristic-style as manners of speaking and audience-accommodation,[11] others remained telling. For example, there were Jesus' own professed *ignorance* of the day or the hour of the end,[12] and His expressions of *surprise* at His parents' reaction to His remaining behind in Jerusalem, at the unbelief of His generation, at the fig tree's barrenness, and repeatedly at the slowness of His disciples! Again, there is the cry of dereliction, with its expression of apparent abandonment and forsakenness.[13] Moreover, Gore noted, Jesus was not an Oxford don: He never enlarged the stock of our knowledge of the natural sciences or history etc.[14]

What these British Christologians did not always acknowledge, however, was how they brought their own, contrasting set of *a priori* assumptions to their analysis of Christ's human capacities and functions. Philosophically, they bought into the themes that the nature of the universe in general and of human being in particular is developmental, evolutionary.[15] Moreover, their soteriological plots tended to be moralistic and moralizing, requiring Jesus to be a moral paragon,

---

[11] Gore, "The Holy Spirit and Inspiration," ch. VIII, 357–361.

[12] Matthew 11:27; Mark 13:32. Cf. Gore, *Dissertations* II, 83–84; Weston, *The One Christ,* Part III, ch. VII, 198–199.

[13] Gore, *Bamptons,* Lecture VI, sec. II, 147–148; Gore, *Dissertations* II, 82–84; Weston, *The One Christ,* Part III, ch. XII, 276, 278–279.

[14] Gore, *Bamptons,* Lecture VI, sec. II, 149–150; Gore, *Dissertations* II, 82–87.

[15] Gore, "The Holy Spirit and Inspiration," ch. VIII, 319–329; Gore, *Bamptons,* Lecture 2, 32–33; J. R. Illingworth, "The Incarnation and Development," in *Lux Mundi,* ch. 5, 181–214. See Forsyth, *The Person and Place of Jesus Christ,* ch. III, 64–67, where Forsyth endorses evolutionary biology and the developmental nature of human individuals, but denies any developmental track for human history which makes later more normative than earlier, because this would compromise the status of Jesus Christ as the final revelation.

Who submits perfectly to the categorical imperative, the moral law of righteousness, and/or – picking up on Johannine themes of mutual indwelling and abiding – exhibits perfect conformity to the Father's will.[16]

With these in hand, they readily subsumed the idea that Jesus was not (virtually) omniscient from the moment of His conception to the idea that His human nature and hence His consciousness and knowledge – like that of every human being – grew from the embryonic stage through infancy and childhood to adulthood.[17] Several biblical texts seemed obviously friendly to this developmental proposal: Luke 2:52 (growth in wisdom); Hebrews 5:8 (learned obedience); Philippians 2:5–11 (emptied himself of the form of God, took the form of a servant). Weston summed up this developmental read as follows: Jesus'

> human ego . . . must develope [sic] on normal human lines, as befits one possessing a normal human soul and body. Thus primarily he will be conscious of himself as a babe; next as a child, though he will, no doubt, have a secret instinct of divinity in a small degree. As he grows in soul his consciousness developes [sic], and he comes to know himself and the Logos as the determination of himself, as the complement of the full conception of himself. This consciousness becomes perfect so soon as his manhood has attained the full measure of its stature and wisdom.[18]

---

[16] R. W. Dale, *The Atonement: The Congregational Union Lecture (1875)* (London: Congregational Union of England and Wales, 1902), ch. IX, 370–429; R. W. Moberly, *Atonement and Personality* (London: John Murray, Albemarle Street, 1901); Gore, *Bamptons*, Lecture I, sec. III, 10–13, Lecture I, sec. IV, 24–25, Lecture II, sec. V, 49, Lecture V, 113–140, Lecture VIII, sec. I, 203.

[17] Gore, *Bamptons*, Lecture VI, sec. II, 145–150; Gore, *Dissertations* II, 80; Weston, *The One Christ*, Part I, ch. II, 32, Part II, ch. IV, 90, Part III, ch. VI, 140, 143–144. See Temple, *Christus Veritas*, Part III, ch. VII, 121–122.

[18] Weston, *The One Christ*, Part II, ch. IV, 90.

Again, he writes,

> the Incarnate state is one of progress at every moment; beginning
> with the life of the unborn child and looking for its consummation
> to the day when He shall mediate to His mystical body the beatific
> vision of Godhead.[19]

Indeed, Weston declares, "He should taste of the unconsciousness or
practical unconsciousness of the unborn child."[20]

Nevertheless, the old presumption of perfection was not dead. On
the contrary, it was in some measure fed by their moralizing soteri-
ologies, so that the claim that Christ's human psychological capacities
were complete from the moment of conception was replaced with
the notion that His development was perfect at every stage. Thus
Gore proclaims,

> In Him first we see man completely in the image of God, realizing all
> that was in the divine idea for man. He was perfect child according to
> the measure of childhood, boy according to boyhood's measure, man
> according to man's standard; and He was perfected at last according
> to the final destiny of manhood in eternal glory.[21]

Among other things, they envisioned, Christ's self-consciousness
grew, with inklings of preexistence as a boy in the temple,[22] emerging
into a more explicit awareness at His baptism and throughout His
ministry.[23] P. T. Forsyth thinks that Matthew 11:27, which ascribes
ignorance of the day and the hour, also is the clearest Synoptic

---

[19] Weston, *The One Christ*, Part III, ch. II, 140.

[20] Weston, *The One Christ*, Part III, ch. VII, 181–182.

[21] Gore, *Bamptons*, Lecture VI, sec. VI, 168; cf. Gore, *Dissertations* II, 79; Weston, *The One Christ*, Part III, ch. VII, 182. See Temple, *Christus Veritas*, Part III, ch. VIII, 147–148.

[22] Gore, *Dissertations* II, 78.

[23] Gore, *Bamptons*, Lecture VI, sec. II, 145–146; Weston, *The One Christ*, Part III, ch. VII, 183–187.

indication of knowledge of preexistence.[24] But Forsyth will also speak of His growing mastery of His vocation[25] and sense of identity which does not come fully clear to His dying hour.[26]

Likewise, their own soteriology drove them to further overreadings in a patristic direction. If New Testament "facts" stand in the way of (near) omniscience in general, they are seen to pose no obstacle either to extraordinary insight or foresight.[27] Moreover, Jesus is not merely an authoritative but an *infallible* moral teacher.[28] Likewise, these self-professed British "empiricists" about Christology follow patristic/scholastic leads in declaring that Jesus is not simply sinless but *impeccable*. Forsyth sees the withdrawal of omniscience as a positive advantage in explaining the reality of His temptations: they seemed real because He did not know He was impeccable![29]

Despite their sensitivity to the higher criticism of the Bible, none of Gore, Weston, or Temple was inclined to doubt the wonder-working aspect of Jesus' earthly career. Gore and Temple worked the miraculous into their analysis of the cosmos into levels of reality, each of which reveals something about God, but each of which finds its full explanation and realizes its maximum potential in relation to the higher level. Thus, if mere nature reveals an order-producing force, miracles outside or breaking through signal a purposive mind wanting to communicate something in particular. Miracles are not cherished to make room for a "God of the gaps," but as signs that God is personal (One Who acts by thought and choice) and as indications

---

[24] Forsyth, *The Person and Place of Jesus Christ*, ch. IV, 111–117.

[25] Forsyth, *The Person and Place of Jesus Christ*, ch. IV, 121–122, 126, ch. VI, 176.

[26] Forsyth, *The Person and Place of Jesus Christ*, ch. IV, 121–122.

[27] Luke 2:49; Mark 4:49, 6:6, 7:18, 8:21, 11:13, 14:37; Gore, *Bamptons*, Lecture VI, sec. II, 147.

[28] Gore, *Bamptons*, Lecture VI, sec. III, 154; Gore, *Dissertations* II, 80, 95–96; Weston, *The One Christ*, Part III, ch. VII, 205–208.

[29] Forsyth, *The Person and Place of Jesus Christ*, ch. XI, 301–302. See Gore, *Bamptons*, Lecture VI, sec. II, 146, sec. III, 154, sec. VI, 166–167, Lecture VIII, sec. IV, 221–222; Gore, *Dissertations* II, 80, 95–96; Weston, *The One Christ*, Part III, ch. VI, 138–139, Part III, ch. VII, 205–208. See Temple, *Christus Veritas*, Part III, ch. VIII, 147–148.

of what kind of character God is.[30] Christ is the apex and completion of this revelatory pyramid: His life and work bring Divine purpose into sharp focus, and His miracles are not meaningless portents
but redemptive acts that advertise how the whole universe subserves
God's moral purpose.[31] Nevertheless, Gore and Weston insist that
Christ acts within the scope of natural human capacities in performing the Gospel miracles.[32] Indeed, it is in Christ that we see the
true measure of human capacities, because it is in Christ that they
are found and function without the effects of sin.[33] Drawn to the
same picture, Temple hesitates: "did He ever make use of powers that
are altogether outside the reach of ordinary men?" "The question is
hard to answer, because we do not know what power would be possessed by a man who was, and always had been, in perfect fellowship
with God."[34]

Overall, the methodological self-advertisements of turn-of-the-
twentieth-century British Christologians lead us to expect sharper
differences with patristic/scholastic accounts of Christ's humanity
than we in fact get. In fact, the chief differences are two. First, Christ's
humanity is conceived of as *developmental*, although perfect for each
developmental stage, with the result that He is not mature enough
to be loaded up with maximal grace, virtue, and knowledge from
the first moment of His conception. Second, He is *denied (near)
omniscience* – supernaturally supplied knowledge of everything that
is, was, or ever will be actual, and of everything possible producible
by created causal powers. Yet they claim not only freedom from error
but *infallibility* in the subject matter of morals; not only sinlessness,
but *impeccability* for His human choice and character. Moreover,

---

[30] See Gore, *Bamptons*, Lecture II, secs. I–II, 31–35; Lecture II, sec. V, 45–46; Temple,
Christus Veritas, Part I, ch. I, 4–19.

[31] Gore, *Bamptons*, Lecture II, sec. V, 48–50.

[32] Gore, *Dissertations* II, 94–95, 165–166, 206, 219–220; Weston, *The One Christ*, Part I, ch.
II, 34, Part II, ch. V, 123–124, Part III, ch. VI, 141–144, Part III, ch. XV, 321.

[33] Weston, *The One Christ*, Part I, ch. II, 30, Part III, ch. VII, 211, Part III, ch. XV, 324–325.

[34] Temple, *Christus Veritas*, Part III, ch. VII, 120.

His miracles are chalked up not to Divine omnipotence, but to His finite human powers. Thus, their account teeter-totters between the systematic desire to be biblical and empirical versus the systematic need to present Jesus in His humanity as moral exemplar and source.

4. Horror-defeater, portrayed

On my soteriology, the Savior solves our non-optimality problems by defeating horrors, not only within the framework of the universe as a whole, but within the context of the horror-participant's own life. I have distinguished three stages of horror-defeat:

Stage I: establishing a relation of organic unity between the person's horror-participation and his/her intimate, personal, and overall beatific relationship with God;

Stage II: healing and otherwise enabling the horror-participant's meaning-making capacities so that s/he can recognize and appropriate some of the positive significance laid down in Stage I;

Stage III: recreating our relation to the material world so that we are no longer radically vulnerable to horrors.

This contrasting soteriological job description paints a portrait of the *ante-mortem* state of Christ's human nature that looks quite different from the one perfectionistic patristic and scholastic thinkers drew.

4.1. Stage-I defeat, systematically considered

Because Stage-I horror-defeat turns on Divine solidarity with human horror-participation, it sets up counterpresumptions that Christ's *ante-mortem* human nature will be as much like ours as possible, and that Christ will identify more with our present condition than with any putative past or future utopic state. First, and most obviously, Stage-I defeat requires that Christ share human *vulnerability to horrors*, which arises from our being personal animals in an environment of real and apparent scarcity. This means that Christ's humanity must be driven by the opposing forces of metabolism (that builds up) and catabolism (that tears down). Like ours, His body must be mortal, tending towards death in such a way that it is not within His *human* powers to lay down His life and to take it up again. He must be urged on by life instincts of hunger, thirst, and sex, and threatened by the built-in seeds of its own demise.

As turn-of-the-twentieth-century British theologians insisted, Christ's human being must also grow from infancy to adulthood through a developmental process. Like us, He had not only to acquire information, but to grow in His ability to conceptualize, to experience paradigm shifts – small-scale and localized as well as comprehensive and dramatic – in his successive worldviews. Obviously, this is incompatible with the perfectionistic patristic/scholastic idea that Christ's human soul had maximal knowledge (as much as it was supernaturally possible for a human being to have) from the moment of conception. *A fortiori*, such ordinary human development is incompatible with His human soul's having from the first moment of its existence as perfect a beatific vision as humanly possible. To share our lot, Christ would have humanly to grow in the knowledge and love of God. P. T. Forsyth insists on what the temptation narratives (Matthew 4:1–11/Luke 4:1–13) in any event suggest, that Jesus struggled to win the right focus for, eventual mastery with respect to, His vocation. Certainly, the systematic desideratum of horror-identification encourages a Lutheran reading of the cry of dereliction (Matthew 27:46; Mark 15:34), which understands the crucified Jesus to have shared in our sense of abandonment by God and of Divine condemnation – which is surely incompatible with simultaneous *beatific* intimacy, and plausibly at odds with any simultaneous face-to-face vision at all.

What the desideratum of horror-participation brings to the fore is that – *pace* turn-of-the-twentieth-century British theologians – the developmental process that Christ goes through must be *messy*.

When His subjective world goes to smash at six months, or at the terrible twos or the Oedipal threes, or at adolescence, He must share our initial incompetence and confusion, the anxiety and tension that goes with floundering around for a new integration. This includes the trial and error of false and rejected solutions, at the cognitive and emotional, moral and spiritual levels. Moreover, fully to embrace our vulnerability to horrors would mean struggle and the not merely apparent but *real* possibility of His not striking an appropriate Eriksonian balance, even of going seriously wrong.

Finally, sharing our vulnerability to horrors means living in a horror-prone environment: in a material world like ours, with real and apparent scarcities that arouse fear and provoke competition; being reared by and living among other human beings who have negotiated their own radical vulnerability to horrors in skewed and neurotic ways. (Yes, this does threaten the idealized portraits of Mary. How could Jesus be tempted in all things as we are if He had a perfect mother?) Like ours, Christ's human words and deeds had to be inserted into an environment in which they could be salient causes in the production of horrors, unavoidably beyond His human powers to anticipate or conceive of. Insofar as Jesus was a historical figure, born into our world, most of these last points are virtually guaranteed.

By themselves, Stage-I counterpresumptions drive in the direction of maximizing the amounts and kinds of Christ's own actual *ante-mortem* horror-participation. But just as patristic and scholastic treatments envisioned Christ's *ante-mortem* career as taking something from each of the four states of humankind, so I want to say that Christ's *ante-mortem* career signals Christ's own participation not only in Stage-I but in Stage-II and Stage-III horror-defeat as well. These desiderata will sometimes rebut Stage-I presumptions to posit differences between Christ's *ante-mortem* human nature and ours, and to set limits on the kind of horrors in which Christ's *ante-mortem* human nature actually participates.

4.2. Christ as horror-participant, biblical testimony

In fact, the Gospels present Jesus as having had a horror-studded earthly career. (1) Most obviously, the Gospels climax in Jesus' horror-participation as a victim, in His crucifixion. Not only was the method of killing degrading because crueler than that normally used to slaughter cattle; it was socially uprooting. Not only was Jesus betrayed, denied, and deserted by His closest followers: Deuteronomic law declared that death by hanging from a tree rendered its victim cursed, cut off from the people of God and from God (Deuteronomy 21:23; Galatians 3:13)! From a Jewish point of view, death by crucifixion clearly defeated Messianic pretensions and turned Jesus' earthly ministry into an evident failure.

(2) Moreover, to hear the Gospels tell it, Jesus' coming also *occasions* many horrors. Matthew's infancy narrative makes Christ's birth *the occasion* of horrors, with Herod's slaughter of the innocents. Even if we grant Raymond Brown's thesis that the infancy narratives are verisimilitudes, narratives that represent the plot dynamics of Jesus' ministry,[35] what they anticipate is the fact that Jesus' ministry, passion, death, resurrection, and Great Commission (Matthew 28:18–20) *occasioned* the martyrdom of His disciples (see Matthew 16:24–26). Likewise, Luke–Acts represents Jesus' coming as *occasioning* the second destruction of Jerusalem – God perpetrating horrors on the people of God, whether (as non-Christian Jews claimed) because he was a false prophet that led the nation astray (Deuteronomy 13:1–5), or (as Christian Jews contended) because Israel did not recognize the hour of its visitation (Luke 19:41–44).

(3) By its very nature, Jesus' prophetic ministry *risked horror-perpetration*, insofar as it was intended to challenge and attack, to bring about or at least occasion the end of basic meaning-making

[35] Raymond E. Brown, *The Birth of the Messiah: A Commentary on the Infancy Narratives in Matthew and Luke* (New York: Doubleday, 1977), Introduction, 25–39.

structures that had organized and made sense of life in Israel. Thus, Jesus violated the Holiness Code and the traditions of the elders, touched lepers and bleeding women, healed on the Sabbath, allowed disciples to thresh grain and ordered the cured to carry beds in violation of Sabbath rules. Likewise, Jesus attacked the Jerusalem Temple establishment and predicted its destruction. Insofar as subjective world-smashing is an ordinary part of human development, it may be painful but it is not usually horrendous for those who are able – with help from family, friends, and social institutions – to reconstruct themselves a wider and better world. Jesus' call to repentance was an invitation to let go of old meaning-making structures and to embrace the new world order He proclaimed.

Nevertheless, insofar as persons structure the positive meaning of their lives in terms of the old world order, their lives "fall apart" and their integrity is violated by bulldozing the framework within which they found meaning and purpose. Consider the "benevolent" slave owner after the American Civil War, "benign" white segregationists in the 1950s, pro-apartheid South Africans in the 1980s, pro-communist philosophers when the Berlin Wall fell, or patriarchy unmasked by feminist critiques. Many former slave owners were not, many divorced sexist males are not, able to "get it together" to see things a new way. In the course of resisting, their behavior may turn more perverse and their character may become more caricatured.

(4) The Gospels represent Jesus' ministry as *actually* provoking His enemies to *prima facie* ruinous levels of self-betrayal: the Pharisees who were most bent on preparing Messiah's way actually handed the Messiah over to be crucified. However "morally" responsible Jesus' enemies may be held for their own actions, His ministry remains a salient cause in their *prima facie* ruin. Moreover, the Gospels suggest, this provocation was deliberate and strategic, for it is the prophet's job not only to announce the coming of the new, but to bring judgment on the old. When the religious establishment refused really to "hear" His preaching and teaching or to welcome His healing and exorcizing,

Jesus moved to expose their hearts' secrets by getting them to "act them out" on Him.

(5) Again, the Bible records (and secular documents confirm) that Jesus lived in the first-century CE Roman empire. Insofar as He willy-nilly participated in the benefits of Roman law and order, roads and information services, taught disciples to render to Caesar what is Caesar's (and hence to pay taxes), throughout His life and hence long before His crucifixion, He joined every other subject in collective complicity in the horrors wrought by Rome.

Thus, the Gospels give us a Jesus who was not only a victim, but also an occasioner and a perpetrator of horrors. What Scripture does *not* show is Jesus perpetrating horrors with malicious intent or outside a Divinely purposed framework within which those very horrors may be defeated.

4.3. Intimations of Stage-II and Stage-III defeat

For most merely human horror-participants, the fulfillment of Stages II and III comes beyond the grave; *a fortiori* it is not fully accomplished within the scope of Christ's *ante-mortem* human career. Nevertheless, the Gospel portrait allows us to ground eschatological hope for Stage-II and Stage-III defeat in Christ's life and ministry, death and resurrection. Christ's preaching and teaching the civilities of the Reign of God are outward and visible signs of the Inner Teacher's rearing us adopted children up into the mores of God's family; exorcisms (the healing of the mentally ill and spiritually broken) are a downpayment, signaling Divine power and intention to follow through with Stage II – to heal and enable our meaning-making capacities and so to rescue us from permanent personal ruin. Johannine discourses on the mutual indwelling of Christ and the Father offer their relationship as a paradigm of the Divine instruction and Divine–human collaboration involved in Stage II. Thus, Jesus says, I say only what the Father gives me to say, do only

CHRIST AND HORRORS

what the Father gives me to do: I-not-I-but-the-Father issue these words and these commands etc. (see chapter 6).

Likewise, Jesus' healings of the hemorrhaging woman, of the lame, maimed, blind, deaf, mute, and leprous; His resurrection of Jairus' daughter, the widow of Nain's son, and Lazarus; His nature miracles (walking on water, calming winds and waves, turning water into wine, multiplication of loaves and fishes); and His own resurrection from the dead: all of these are downpayments on and signal Divine power and intention to follow through with Stage-III horror-defeat – with cosmic re-creation that will place us in a non-toxic relation to our material environment, one that will bring an end to the power of matter to ruin personal meaning.

4.4. Limits and underdeterminations

Overall, Christ's soteriological role as horror-defeater combines with His Gospel career to set the following limits on how much and in what ways He identifies with us. First, Christ could have only those human faults and psychological peculiarities compatible with such clarity of Godward orientation that people could reasonably take Him to speak and act on God's behalf in His prophetic ministry of teaching, preaching, and healing. Second, He could participate only in those horrors that could beset a self-conscious, highly integrated servant of God.

Thus, if Jesus perpetrates horrors, it is not in the spirit of Hitler. By word and example, the Gospels' Jesus teaches God's love for the world and Divine mercy on the marginal. He calls disciples to a lifestyle based on love of God and neighbor, the forgiveness of enemies, and compassion for the weak. His "platform" was diametrically opposed to Hitler's or Stalin's reign of terror and ruthless disregard for personal worth.

New Testament accounts of Jesus' career stand in the way of numbering Him with the homicidal maniacs, the pathological people-haters, or the agoraphobic. Synoptic emphasis on Jesus' violations of the Holiness Code and His penchant for boundary-blurring suggest that His was not a compulsive personality. Yet, the Synoptic career does not require Him to have attained the optimal Eriksonian balance at every developmental stage, nor to have arrived at the threshold of His ministry free from neuroses. Biblical prophets, John the Baptist, St. Paul, voiced God's message, despite their eccentric and abrasive sides. Because New Testament documents do not focus on Jesus' psychological condition, much less include Freudian transcripts of fifty-minute hours, we are not in a position to say.

New Testament portraits of Jesus' teaching role contradict any thought that He had Down's syndrome and make it extremely unlikely that He was a paranoid schizophrenic. Yet, it leaves open whether He was dyslexic or beset with other "learning disabilities." Contrary to patristic/medieval and turn-of-the-twentieth-century British consensus, Jesus' New Testament roles as teacher, preacher, and healer do not by themselves require sinlessness or moral infallibility. St. Paul enters all those roles, despite his self-declared status as "the worst of sinners," as one who persecuted the Church of God. In our own day, Martin Luther King, Jr., and Mother Teresa of Calcutta were neither sinless nor morally infallible. But they shed bright light on what sort of kingdom God has in mind.

Role-wise, it is John's presentation of the relation between Jesus and the Father as that of *exemplary mutual indwelling* that sets the highest standards – I do only what the Father wills me to do, say only what the Father wills me to say; I-not-I-but-the-Father act, I-not-I-but-the-Father say these things to you. For now, it is enough to note that the role – by itself – does not force maximization. If – as turn-of-the-twentieth-century British Christologians claimed – Jesus did not reach this state of explicit functional collaboration with the Father until the peak of His career, His arrival would still be compatible with a messy developmental process to reach that goal. Given the metaphysical size-gap between Divine and human consciousness, mutual indwelling cannot be a matter of literal identity between Divine and human ways of seeing things, and so – insofar as we always will something under a description – cannot involve lit-eral sameness of willed objects. Mutual indwelling across the "gap" will have to mean harmony humanly aimed-at through the filter of limited understanding and affective scope. Moreover, St. Paul also affirms mutual indwelling as a goal (I-not-I-but-Christ) and can claim it as a fontal source of his ministry (Galatians 2:18–20) with-out the implication that perfect conformity to Christ has penetrated into every detail of his life (something that he would deny and that the epistles themselves might otherwise belie). Role-wise, one could give (as John probably did not) the harmony-claim limited scope, as applying only to (what P. T. Forsyth calls) Jesus' mastery of His voca-tion, without implying that the dictates of right reason were never violated in any respect!

4.5. Construing the proof texts

Traditionally, portraits of Christ's human nature are sketched not only from systematic considerations, role definitions, and overar-ching biblical plots, but also with an eye to certain key Scriptural verses. My own view is that these texts have been both misread and overread. When replaced in their own context, they are relevant, but their import is different, less decisive, less singularly salient, than theologians have typically made out.

(1) For both patristic/scholastic perfectionistic treatments and turn-of-the-twentieth-century British authors, Luke 2:52 raised the question of growth. In fact, read in context without presumption-of-perfection blinders, the text can be seen to take growth for granted; the emphasis of the story has been rather on how *precocious* Jesus' progress towards wisdom is (Luke 2:46–50). With Raymond Brown, I am happy to take this vignette as a verisimilitude pointing to the authoritative wisdom exhibited in His ministry (see Luke 7:35).

(2) Hebrews 4:14–5:10 is an inspiration for my counterpresump-tion of identification; Jesus is tempted as we are, prays with loud cries and tears to be saved from death, learns obedience through suffering,

so that He is able to sympathize with our weakness. Apart from the presumption of perfection, there is no reason to import into this text the idea that these struggles were not real but apparent, or that there was for Him no real chance of any defection from the will of God.

(3) Hebrews 4:15 (tempted as we are yet without sin) is cited as a fully explicit affirmation of Christ's sinlessness. Yet, the focus of the epistle is not sin in general, but apostasy in particular. The whole letter "cheerleads" its recipients to persevere by holding up the example and the surpassing worth of Christ. Thus, the thrust of the passage might be the more limited one: "Christ was tempted, had to struggle to maintain His loyalty in the face of death, but He didn't betray His calling. You shouldn't either!"

(4) Nowadays, a similar reading is often given of the temptation narratives (Matthew 4:1–11; Luke 4:1–13), where Jesus struggles with the devil to maintain and/or win an accurate vocational focus. The issue is not (as Tillich would say) sins, but Sin, the temptation to renounce or pervert the Godward orientation of His life. The Synoptic contrast between Jesus and the disciples is that in the hour of trial He perseveres while they divorce and desert their vocations, not that unlike them Jesus never sassed His mom!

(5) What about Matthew 27:46/Mark 15:34/Psalm 22:3 (the cry of dereliction)? In my judgment – pace Jürgen Moltmann, who was avowedly indebted to turn-of-the-twentieth-century British Christologians – the passion narratives underdetermine how we are to take these verses. The dying Jesus quotes psalms of lament in all three Synoptics. Is this because liturgical memory verses are sometimes the only prayers the human mind can deliver up when pressed up "against the wall"? Are we to imagine that He uttered only the mentioned verse, or is this literary economy for His having been reciting whole psalms? Just as the presumption of identification and exemplary indwelling pull in opposite directions, so also the passion narratives of Matthew and Mark on the one hand and John on the other. Focussing on mutual abiding, John gives us a Socrates-Jesus,

striding into His (crucifixion) glory with deliberate calm, taking thought to fulfill the Holy Script to the letter. Luther's reading of Matthew and Mark fits very well with the conceptualization of Jesus' saving work as horror-defeater. My own systematic commitment – to let the role of horror-defeater dominate – motivates me to construe mutual indwelling as not requiring equanimity, as being compatible with loud cries and tears and real struggle, a loss of confidence in one's grip on Divine purpose, and even a lack of any vivid sense of the presence of God.

4.6. Wonder-working power?

Neither my patristic/scholastic nor my turn-of-the-twentieth-century British theologians doubted that Jesus performed signs and wonders. But by the time we reach *The Myth of God Incarnate*, British theologians feel free to dismiss the miraculous almost out of hand. In between, Bultmann's program of demythologization took hold, Troeltschian historiography ruled past miracles out *a priori*, and Hegelian sensibilities that the laws of nature are themselves the best expression of Divine policy mingled with a Kantian respect for the autonomy of science to stuff mid- through third-quarter-of-the-twentieth-century Bible commentaries with tiresome declarations that miracle stories can't be true.

In my judgment, their self-confidence is philosophically parochial, worse yet, betrays a lack of self-consciousness that philosophical choices have been made. They fail to notice, for example, that instrumentalism with regard to natural science is an intellectually respectable option. They simply assume that scientific explanation is comprehensive, whereas arguably creation, re-creation, and Incarnation all lie outside its scope.

My own philosophical choices reveal different patterns of entrenchment. I join the great medievalists – Aquinas, Scotus, and Ockham – in giving Divine omnipotence wide scope: to be able to bring about whatever does not involve a contradiction; to be able to supply the efficient causal contribution of any and all created efficient causes and so to act alone to produce whatever effects God can produce in collaboration with them. Thus – *pace* Hegelians, Tillichians, or Rush-Rees Wittgensteinians – I see no *philosophical* obstacle to God's performing miracles. Nor do I share Maurice Wiles' sense that miracle-working would show an appalling inconsistency of purpose (for God to create a natural order and not let it "do its thing") or that miraculously to relieve some but not all *ante-mortem* suffering would be so immoral that it would be better for God not to intervene at all.[36]

On the contrary, the defeat of horrors requires of God multiple exercises of supernatural power: at Stage I, the miracle of Incarnation; at Stage II, the miracles of life after death and of psycho-spiritual healing; at Stage III, the miracle of environmental transformation, and of rendering our bodies invulnerable to disease, atrophy, and decay. Jesus' Gospel miracles would not be *required* for the God-man to play His role in Stage-I horror-defeat, any more than they would be for the jobs outlined by Ransom, Satisfaction, Penal Substitution, or Moral Influence theories. Rather (as above) they signal Divine power and intention to accomplish Stage-II and Stage-III defeat.

My own understanding of human nature renders moot the question of whether Christ performed the miracles out of His merely human or out of His Divine powers. *Mutatis mutandis* I follow Augustine, Anselm, Bonaventure, and Henry of Ghent in thinking that (recognized or unrecognized) Divine collaboration is always required even for *normal* human (especially, thinking and evaluative) functioning. My somewhat different philosophical reason is that – as I see it – personal animality is not competent by itself to organize spirit and matter into a smoothly functioning unit (I will return to this point in chapter 6). But if Divine power is involved

---

[36] See my "Evil and the God Who Does Nothing in Particular," in *Religion and Morality*, ed. D. Z. Phillips (London: Macmillan Press and New York: St. Martin's Press, 1996), 107–131; Comments and Responses, Voice F, 310–321, esp. 310–316.

in normal human functioning, it is *a fortiori* in any miracles. Like Aquinas and turn-of-the-twentieth-century British Christologians, I see no philosophical reason why Divine power could not have collaborated with other human beings to do such works. But at least in the case of walking on water, this might have been *semantically* misleading, insofar as the deed is supposed to recall Psalm 77:19, and to evoke the association that the only One Who can trample the waves is God!

5. Concluding diagnosis

The perfectionistic tradition begins with metaphysical reasons for making Christ's human nature as Godlike as possible and so for radically minimizing His human limitations to what would be needed to accomplish His saving work – for Anselm, a human nature descended from Adam and the ability to die if He chose to. Aquinas finds metaphysical reason both to attribute maximal supranatural upgrades in grace and knowledge, and to ascribe to Christ a full range of natural human cognitive and appetitive functions, including naturally acquired knowledge and emotions. But this means that normal human functioning and growth are added into a soul already equipped – *ab initio* and permanently – with as much supranatural knowledge of God and creatures as a human soul is capable of, likewise with maximal grace and virtue.

Turn-of-the-twentieth-century British Christologians have philosophical commitments (to an evolutionary picture of reality and a developmental understanding of human nature) that drive them to deny that Christ is equipped with maximal knowledge and mature virtue at birth and through childhood. And they have biblical reasons to deny that Christ enjoyed near omniscience during His ministry.

Different as these approaches are, they share the conviction that sin is the main soteriological problem, and that One Who saves us from sin must be sinless. This leads British Christologians to insist on Jesus' moral perfection, only relativized to developmental stage.

Naturally, I agree that Christ solves the sin-problem, but I do not identify this as the primary way of conceptualizing His soteriological job. I see the sin-problem in terms of dysfunction that is derivative from the metaphysical mismatches God has set up in creation: between the personal and the animal dimensions of human being, between human being and our material environment of scarcity, and between human and Divine personal capacities (see chapter 2). But *Divine* power working on the inside will be required to help us pull ourselves into functional coordination (see chapter 6) and *Divine* power will be required to renegotiate our relation to our material environment into something non-toxic (see chapter 8). Consequently, I understand the sin-problem as something Christ decisively deals with mainly through His *Divine* nature, which is sinless. Christ's human nature allows Christ to join us in horror-participation. This identification with us in horrors is essential to Stage-I horror-defeat, and means that Christ's *ante-mortem* career will not fully anticipate Stage-II and Stage-III defeat. The result is that we do not need to take on a commitment to Christ's utter human sinlessness. We are free instead to admit that Jesus had to outgrow parochial racism under the tutelage of the Canaanite/Syrophoenician woman (Matthew 15:21–28/Mark 7:24–30) and to acknowledge that He might have been harsh with His blood relatives!

Overall, then, my soteriology can tolerate a Christology that is materially low to medium. The exigencies of Stage-I horror-defeat, requiring as it does Divine solidarity with human horror-participation, disallow a Christology that is materially maximally high!

4 | Psychologizing the person: Christ as God-man, psychologically construed

1. No clear meaning?

A God-man can't have explanatory value without being logically or metaphysically possible. Embracing Chalcedon – the claim that in Christ there is one person but two (Divine and human) natures – medieval theologians recognized that explanations would be needed; "faith seeking understanding" shouldered the task of philosophical articulation. Already Boethius, in his theological treatises, draws on Aristotelian metaphysics to define "person" as "an individual substance of a rational nature." Although in *Cur Deus Homo* Anselm recognized Incarnation to be one of the most difficult mysteries, he struggled through succeeding drafts of his *Epistola de Incarnatione Verbi* to offer an intelligible account that gets it (at least superficially) right. In the twelfth century, Peter Lombard took on the issue in Book III of his *Sentences*. Following Lombard's syllabus, the school theology of the thirteenth and fourteenth centuries raised the standard of debate to a high level of philosophical sophistication, and spawned not one, but a whole family of attempts to modify Aristotelian metaphysics to accommodate the datum of a God-man. Thus, it is *prima facie* surprising to find 1970s *Myth-of-God-Incarnate* authors – most notably, John Hick, Maurice Wiles, and Don Cupitt – rendering the verdict that Christian theological tradition has never assigned the Chalcedonian definition any clear meaning.[1]

---

[1] Maurice Wiles, "Christianity without Incarnation," in Hick, *The Myth of God Incarnate*, ch. 1, 5; Cupitt, "The Christ of Christendom," 135; Hick, *Metaphor of God Incarnate*, ch. 1, 3, ch. 4, 45; see Hick, "An Inspiration Christology for a Religiously Plural World," esp. 17, 19, 34–35.

Yet this declaration does not come out of nowhere. The way to it was paved by the previous century of British Christological thinking. At least since *Lux Mundi*, theologians had evacuated Chalcedon and other conciliar pronouncements of philosophical content, the better to reinterpret them within the framework of more up-to-date conceptualities, only to cry "mystery" when problems with their own formulations proved great.[2] *Myth-of-God-Incarnate* authors dashed cold water on this pious gesture. Thus, what began with a modernizing dismissal of Greek philosophy climaxed in the conclusion that the doctrine of Incarnation is merely mythological and metaphorical. In this chapter, I want to examine this fascinating, turn-of-the-twentieth-century thought experiment in enough detail to appreciate its appeal and to establish its trend. My conclusion will be that it is a *failed* experiment, and that a return to metaphysics is required!

2. Turn-of-the-twentieth-century problematics

For Anglicans in the last quarter of the nineteenth century, the problems of integrating faith with reason were multiple, and of mounting urgency. Their strategic hope was to steer a *via media* – what John Stewart Lawton calls a "right-wing liberal" course[3] – between more radical biblical scholarship and Protestant theological movements of Germany, and the (in their view) authoritarian Church of Rome. They themselves boasted that Anglican reason was neither fettered by authority nor scornful of it, but rather *schooled* by Scripture and tradition. Likewise, they engaged contemporary learning neither to arm themselves for polemical pot-shots, nor to submit themselves "slavishly" to the deliverances of "the sciences," but, with critical

---

[2] Gore, *Dissertations* II, Part III, sec. 3, 216–218; Weston, *The One Christ*, Part III, ch. VI, 167; William Temple, "The Divinity of Christ," in *Foundations: A Statement of Christian Belief in Terms of Modern Thought* (London: Macmillan & Co., 1913), ch. V, sec. 3, 252.

[3] John Stewart Lawton, *Conflict in Christology: A Study of British and American Christology from 1889–1914* (London: SPCK, 1947), ch. 5, 16.

appreciation and discerning expectation, they looked to discover what light it might shed on God and how the legitimate findings of science might be housed under the roof of their overarching theological commitments.

As Anglican *liberals*, they wished to be responsive to the findings of then-contemporary biblical scholarship that treated the Scriptures as historical documents. "Right-wing" liberals that they were, they were minded to conform Christology to Holy Scriptures. "Right-wing" *liberals* that they were, they were ready to let then-modern exegesis instruct them. We have seen (in chapter 3) how they took passages about Jesus' growth in wisdom and stature, His learning obedience through suffering, His being tempted in all things as we are, His ignorance of environmental incidentals, the authorship of various Old Testament books, of the day and the hour of the parousia, as *"historical" facts* about Jesus' earthly career.

As "right-wing" Anglican liberals, they shared the Tractarians' allegiance to the historic creeds and pronouncements of the ecumenical councils, as well as their respect for patristic theology. This meant a commitment to uphold Chalcedon's formula of one person with two natures.[4] Yet as Anglican *liberals*, they were sensitive to objections that such language weighed down the doctrine of the Incarnation with the millstone of Greek metaphysics, whose allegedly "static" picture of the universe was so at odds with then-contemporary (nineteenth-century) philosophy, with its emphasis on "dynamic" process, progress, and evolution. They sought to make Archbishop Frederick Temple's mid-nineteenth century dream come true: of a Christian theology reconceptualized in terms of the then-budding-and-blossoming "science" of *psychology*, and so – as the subtitle of *Foundations* was later to advertise – to restate "Christian belief in terms of modern thought."[5] Appearances to the contrary,

---

[4] Weston, *The One Christ*, Part III, ch. VI, 135–136.
[5] See Temple, "The Divinity of Christ," sec. 2, 226, sec. 3, 259–260.

they declared, Chalcedon and other relevant conciliar statements do not commit one to Greek metaphysics. It is not the Church's business to enter the philosophical fray, much less to *dogmatize* temporary and transient philosophical systems. The fathers were borrowing what language their intellectual environment made ready to hand not to make *positive* claims, but rather to issue *negative* prohibitions as to what may not be *said*. The conciliar decrees do not advance positive philosophical or theological doctrines, but function as hedges or fences of the pasture-ground[6] within which theological formulation is to occur.[7] For them, the Chalcedonian definition did not merely *underdetermine* Christology; it was a semantically empty vessel, which they were free to fill by reconceptualizing Christology within the framework of then-contemporary psychology, and – as it eventually turned out – seemingly more up-to-date philosophical ideas, both of which emphasized developmental models.

With issues thus refocussed, they committed themselves to the twin theses that

(T1) there is one and only one subject of consciousness or psychological center in Christ (the psychological reading of "person" in Chalcedon);

and that

(T2) there is one and only one subject of consciousness or psychological center behind the career of Jesus described in the Gospels.

Their question became: who or what is it?

---

[6] Gore's phrase: *Dissertations* II, Part II, sec. 8, 171.

[7] Gore, *Bamptons*, Lecture IV, sec. I, 80–81, sec. IV, 96, sec. V, 104–108; Gore, *Dissertations* II, Part II, sec. 8, 166–171, Part III, sec. 2, 212–214; Temple, "The Divinity of Christ," esp. 230–232.

Their "right-wing" instincts took them straight back to the fathers to discover two main types of answers they had allegedly given. The Alexandrian or Cyrillene approach identified the subject of Christ's earthly career as the omniscient and omnipotent Divine Logos. Some Alexandrians sponsored a fusion of Divine and human natures and were thought to endorse a Word/flesh Christology. Insofar as Cyril himself acknowledged a human soul in Christ, he seemed to make it as Godlike as possible (and so very much unlike ours). Leading the "perfectionist" approach to Christ's human nature (see chapter 3), Cyril construed New Testament talk about growth and temptation and ignorance in terms of the Logos' holding back the manifestation of His Divinity for economic reasons. By contrast, the Antiochene school insisted on the true humanity of Christ. At the same time unwilling to sacrifice His Divinity, Antiochenes seemed to find in Christ two centers of consciousness, vastly differing in scope. Exegetically, theirs was the "divide-and-conquer" strategy of sorting New Testament passages between those that pertain to the human and those that pertain to the Divine nature of Christ.

"Right-wing liberal" Anglicans joined the Antiochenes against the Alexandrians/Cyrillenes in valuing the reality of Jesus' human nature, and of attributing to Him a genuinely human consciousness. At the same time, against the Antiochene but like (their reading of) the Alexandrian/Cyrillene position, they were explicitly and adamantly opposed to any idea of two distinct centers of consciousness behind the Gospel descriptions of Jesus' earthly career[8] (see [T2]). Once "person" was taken psychologically, positing two subjects of consciousness in Christ seemed tantamount to Nestorianism! Against the Alexandrians/Cyrillenes, they wanted to insist that center of consciousness that is the subject of His Gospel career operates within the constraints of human nature (whether its normal capacities or

---

[8] Francis J. Hall defends this exegetical strategy *against* the kenoticists in his sharp book *The Kenotic Theory* (New York and London: Longmans, Green, & Co, 1898), ch. 1, 46–47.

within the capacity of human nature for receiving further Divine enabling). Within these parameters, they pressed their question: if there is only one center of consciousness behind the Gospel career, which is it? A Divine one squeezed down to human size? Or a human one stretching up towards heaven?

3. Kenotic Divinity

Initially, "right-wing liberal" Anglicans explored the first answer, because they took from the creeds and the conciliar documents a commitment to the Divinity of Christ. The subject whose consciousness underlies the Gospel career is *God the Son*. But how can we make sense of the idea that God the Son was born ignorant, grew in wisdom, was tempted in all things as we are, learned obedience through suffering, and remained ignorant of numerous past (Old Testament authorship) and future (the day and the hour) facts? One daring answer – inspired by Philippians 2 – was that God the Son somehow veiled or emptied himself of (so that there was a *kenosis*, an emptying out) various Divine perfections during His earthly career.

3.1. Protestant precedents

Francis J. Hall and John Stewart Lawton sketch how this proposal found its startling precedent in various developments in continental Lutheran and Reformed theology.[9] In the course of eucharistic controversies, Luther seems to have defended the doctrine of the real presence of the Body and Blood of Christ in the eucharist by arguing that Christ's human nature is (potentially) *ubiquitous* because the union of the natures in one person licenses a *communicatio idiomatum* or sharing of the predicates with respect to Christ's *natures*

---

[9] Hall, *The Kenotic Theory*, "Historical Introduction," 12–14, ch. 1, 40–43, ch. 13, 230. See Gore, *Dissertations* II, Part II, sec. 9, 180–182.

(see chapters 5 and 10)! Patristic authors had appealed to a *communicatio idiomatum* to explain the truth of "God died" or "This babe sustains the world." But in such cases the *communicatio* was supposed to be grounded in the fact that the same person (the Divine Word) is the metaphysical subject of both natures. Thus, the subject term of the sentence may pick out that person with a description taken from one of its natures ("God" from the Divine nature or "babe" from the human nature) and the predicate may assert of that person a description taken from the other nature ("died" from the human nature or "sustains the world" from the Divine nature). To hold that predicates from both natures are not only shared with the person to whom both natures belong, but also that *the natures* share each other's predicates would be to confuse the natures – contrary to what Chalcedon requires.

Debate focussed, however, not on the *a priori* incompatibility of the two natures, but on the doctrine's *a posteriori* "fit" with Holy Scriptures. The worry was about how Christ's human nature – thus deified – managed to appear human at all during His earthly career. The school of Tübingen taught that during the Incarnation the Divine properties possessed by Christ's humanity underwent a process of veiling (*krypsis*). The school of Giessen held that the Divine properties possessed by Christ's humanity were temporarily abandoned by Him (*kenosis*): but this is an abandonment by the human nature of the properties of the Divine nature, not an emptying out of the Divine nature itself. Thomasius explicitly saw himself as reversing the direction of Luther's *communicatio*, to stress that the Divine nature takes on the limitations of the human.

3.2. *Varieties of kenosis*

Nineteenth-century theologians took the spotlight off the natures and turned them back onto *the person* of the Divine Word, but applied the kenotic strategy to explain how God the Son could be circumscribed within the confines of the Gospel career. This approach came in many versions, most of which remained – from a philosophical point of view – conceptually muddy and underdeveloped.

There was what we may call "total absolute kenosis" (advanced by Gess and Godet), according to which, in the Incarnation, God the Son *abandons* the whole of the Divine nature or state or mode of being and is reduced to the human mode of being instead.[10] Alternatively, there was what we may label "partial absolute kenosis,"[11] according to which God the Son abandons some of the Divine perfections but not others. These latter thinkers distinguish between the "internal, ethical" attributes (such as truth and love), and the "external, physical" attributes (most notably, omnipotence, omniscience, and omnipresence). The physical attributes are necessary for the cosmic functions of a creator, while the moral features play a role within the Godhead itself. Shedding omnipotence, omniscience, and omnipresence is supposed to make it possible for God the Son to act within the necessary limits as the subject of His humanity. At the same time, His retention of the Divine "inward" or "moral" attributes and His exercise of them during His earthly career is supposed to enable Him to be the true light of the world.[12] Certainly, both positions were homiletically attractive, insofar as – à la Philippians 2 – they give metaphysical weight to the idea that the Son of God sacrificed much for our sakes.

3.3. *Critiques of absolute kenosis*

These theological proposals had philosophical implications, indeed, seemed to constitute radical departures from traditional (patristic and scholastic) Christian doctrines of God. Total absolute kenosis

---

[10] See Gore's *Dissertations* II, Part II, sec. 9, 184–188; Hall, *The Kenotic Theory*, "Historical Introduction," 15–20.

[11] Sponsored by Thomasius, Franz Delitzsch, and A. M. Fairbairn in *The Place of Christ in Modern Theology* (New York: Scribner, 1894); noted by Hall in *The Kenotic Theory* "Historical Introduction," 1; see Lawton, *Conflict in Christology*, ch. 5, 119–121, 133–143.

[12] See Weston, *The One Christ*, Part II, ch. V, 104.

entails that *the Divine essence is not essential to everything that possesses it*, and that an individual can retain its identity and persist through the change from being Divine to being human and/or vice versa. If partial absolute kenosis retains the traditional claim that Father, Son, and Holy Spirit could not exist without being God, it insists that not all of the perfections formerly thought to be essential to Godhead were genuinely necessary to It. So-called physical attributes are allegedly the permanent but contingent possession of the Father and Holy Spirit, and are contingently had, then abandoned, then repossessed by the Son. Thus, it seems, *with respect to some perfections, Godhead essentially includes a capacity for them but not their actuality.*

Moreover, if God the Son does change with respect to these properties, and does become the subject of suffering, it follows further that *Godhead does not essentially include immutability or timelessness or impassibility either.* Likewise, in traditional theology, God is the ultimate explanation of being and goodness in the universe. But if the Divine persons aren't Divine necessarily (as total absolute kenosis implies), or if the Divine persons have omnipotence, omniscience, and omnipresence not essentially but contingently (as partial absolute kenosis entails), then what explains whether they are or aren't, whether they do or don't? Certainly, they cannot any longer qualify as ultimate explainers on traditional explanatory models.

Again, where partial absolute kenosis is concerned, the criterion for sorting "internal versus external," "losable versus unlosable," perfections seemed inadequate. Don't omnipotence and omniscience play a role within the Godhead (the life of the Trinity)? Don't, shouldn't, moral attributes come into play in God's relation to creation?[13]

Likewise, critics worried how God the Son – once He had absolutely abandoned His Divine nature, or at least its physical attributes of omnipotence, omniscience, and omnipresence – would be able to

---

[13] See Weston, *The One Christ*, Part II, ch. V, 120–122; Temple, "The Divinity of Christ," sec. 1, 213–215.

get them back. With omnipotence, it would seem that, if He had the ability to re-endow Himself with it, He never really lost it.[14] It seems not to have occurred to them that – on the assumption that losing and reacquiring such perfections is possible for Divinity – the other Divine persons would have the ability to bring God the Son back to His former exalted state. All of which brings us to the point that absolute kenosis (whether total or partial) seemed to its critics to constitute a radical theological departure insofar as it *entails a Social Trinity*.[15] According to absolute kenosis, God the Son, during His earthly career, loses the "physical" attributes *in order* to have more limited experiences than God the Father and God the Holy Ghost are having during the period of His Incarnation.

From a philosophical point of view, radical revision is not necessarily a damning criticism. Many of these consequences point in directions one might have expected nineteenth-century *liberal* theologians to go, once they dismissed ancient and medieval philosophy *in order* to reconceptualize in terms of more modern ways of thinking. One might have expected them to take a few more pages from nineteenth-century German philosophy where such ideas were given more systematic development. But these theologians were not philosophers and did not take philosophical responsibility for their claims.

From a theological point of view, revisions in the concept of God are not universally barred, but demand to be tested for consistency, coherence, explanatory power, and fruitfulness. As Coakley points out, Chalcedon does not specify the contents of either the Divine or human natures in Christ. The above arguments against absolute kenosis expose the entrenchment of certain claims about the Divine nature within the critics' systems of belief. In the end, what most *right-wing* liberal Anglicans could not swallow was the theological

---

[14] Thomas V. Morris, *The Logic of God Incarnate* (Ithaca, NY, and London: Cornell University Press, 1986), ch. 4, 91.
[15] See Morris, *The Logic of God Incarnate*, ch. 4, 92–93.

implication – explicitly drawn by some adherents of absolute kenosis – that, during His earthly career, God the Son takes leave of His cosmic functions, so that the Augustinian dictum "one action, one will *ad extra*" is broken; and likewise that the Incarnate Son abandons His role within the (western) Trinity in the procession of the Holy Spirit from the Father and the Son.[16] "Right-wing" liberal Anglicans mocked the idea of absolute abandonment of Divine attributes and of cosmic and Trinitarian roles as downright mythological, and declared that such radical departures from mainstream tradition would have to be justified by explicit positive support from Scripture – which absolute kenosis lacked.[17]

4. Modified kenosis

4.1. "Spheres" of operation

However problematic *absolute* kenosis proved to be, the notion of kenosis itself was attractive and seemingly biblical. Could *via media* "right-wing" liberal Anglicans win through to a modified kenosis that would – in effect – have it both ways? Charles Gore first floated the idea in his Bampton lectures, then developed it in Dissertation II, and took most of the ecclesiastical heat from its critics; Frank Weston made it the objective of his impressive book-length study, *The One Christ*. Gore and Weston cherished the advantage of denying God the Son any exercise of the so-called physical attributes throughout His earthly career as described by the Gospels, while insisting that His Trinitarian and cosmic roles were in no way affected thereby. Both moved therefore to *relativize the kenosis*, by distinguishing two "spheres": it is in the sphere of Incarnation that God the Son does

---

[16] See Gore's *Dissertations* II, Part II, sec. 9, 188.

[17] Gore, *Dissertations* II, Part II, sec. 9, 188–189; Weston, *The One Christ*, Part II, ch. V, 115, 119–121.

not manifest omnipotence, omniscience, or omnipresence, while in the cosmic or eternal sphere these attributes remain fully in play as His roles of conspirator and creator require.

Gore's earlier and messier version continued to speak of the Son's *abandoning* the physical attributes, but only *temporarily* for the period between birth and ascension, and *locally* within the sphere of Incarnation. Yet, if Gore's New Testament Christ is non-omniscient, He never loses consciousness of His eternal Sonship. Moreover, if Gore never "cashes" the metaphor of spheres, he does speak of them as if it were important for them to be sealed off from one another, lest the unlimited Divinity of the cosmic sphere break out and redocetize or rescholasticize the humanity of the Incarnate Lord![18]

Weston shoulders the burden of developing his version in more detail. First, he explains that by "state" or "sphere" he means a system of relationships, and that, in the Incarnation, we are to think of a single Ego, the Divine Word, as the term of two sets of relationships,[19] which are differentiated in terms of the self-consciousness on which they are based:[20]

> The universal state is merely the sum of universal relationships proper to the eternal Son, Godward and manward, *being based upon His eternal self-consciousness as God.* The Incarnate state or sphere is the sum of those particular relationships which, being alien from Him, He assumed Godward and manward, Himself *basing them upon His self-consciousness as God-in-manhood.*[21]

By contrast with Gore, Weston insists that the spheres are not sealed off from one another;[22] nor does entering the second involve God

---

[18] See Hall, *The Kenotic Theory*, "Historical Introduction," 21–39.

[19] Weston, *The One Christ*, Part III, ch. VI, 147, 149.

[20] Weston, *The One Christ*, Part III, ch. VI, 161–162.

[21] Weston, *The One Christ*, Part II, ch. V, 130; see Part III, ch. VI, 146–148.

[22] Weston, *The One Christ*, Part II, ch. V, 130, Part III, ch. XV, 322.

the Son in *abandoning* any of the Divine perfections.[23] Rather, they are linked by a continuous act of the Divine will in the universal sphere (i.e., an act of will based on the Son's consciousness of Himself as unlimited in His Divinity)[24] to exercise *self-restraint* and to operate within limited capacities of a human nature, both physical and psychological.[25] Likewise, where Gore sees "abandonment in the sphere of Incarnation" as temporary, Weston holds the traditional view that, once the human nature is assumed, it is never laid aside. He concludes that the Divine Son's act of self-restraint (based on the Son's self-consciousness of Himself in His unlimited Divinity), once begun, is permanent and will continue throughout all eternity.[26]

Weston further clarifies that, in the sphere of Incarnation, God the Son has no contact with anything in the universe (including Himself) except through "the medium [i.e., the capacities and faculties] of His manhood";[27] and that – because those human capacities grow and develop from embryonic unconsciousness through infantile and childlike up to adult level in his thirtieth year – the scope of His self-restrained functioning begins narrower and widens through His earthly career.[28] Weston cautions: the Incarnation Itself was not gradual; nor did God the Son wait to identify Himself only with a fully adult human condition. Rather God the Son identified Himself with that human nature from its beginning, but the amount of self-restraint involved in doing so gradually decreased.[29] Likewise, in the sphere of Incarnation, the Son is conscious of Himself, not as

---

[23] Weston, *The One Christ*, Part II, ch. V, 112–113, 116–118.

[24] Weston, *The One Christ*, Part II, ch. V, 116–118, 130, Part III, ch. VI, 145, Part III, ch. XV, 320–324.

[25] Weston, *The One Christ*, Part II, ch. V, 130, Part III, ch. VI, 135–139, 148.

[26] Weston, *The One Christ*, Part III, ch. VI, 174–177, Part III, ch. XV, 321, 323.

[27] Weston, *The One Christ*, Part III, ch. XV, 321.

[28] Weston, *The One Christ*, Part III, ch. VI, 141, 143–144, Part III, ch. VII, 181–187, Part III, ch. XV, 321.

[29] Weston, *The One Christ*, Part III, ch. VI, 144, Part III, ch. XV, 321.

unlimited Logos, but as God in manhood, and that only to the degree that the evolving human consciousness allows.[30] He is not conscious of any self that is too great to be mediated by the human soul that He has joined to Himself.[31] Nevertheless, in the Victorian manner, the "consciousness and power" of "His manhood" is "flawless, sinless, perfectly developed, and always united to the eternal Son" at every stage (see chapter 3).[32]

Several times, Weston draws the consequence that his modified-kenotic Christ takes dual perspectives on Himself:

> Looked at from above, as from the standpoint of the Logos Him-self, His consciousness as man must surely bear the marks of self-sacrificing love, of powerful self-restraint . . . the result of the self-emptying of the Son; of His determination to accept *within certain relationships*, the fashion of a man and the form of a slave . . . so to relate Himself to the Father and to men that *within these relationships* He could not know Himself as unlimited Son of God.[33]
>
> Looked at from below, from our standpoint, His consciousness as man is that of the perfect Son of Man, who at every moment, in ever-growing clearness, realizes in and through manhood His divine Sonship; *who knows Himself as God at every moment just in the measure that such self-knowledge can be mediated by the soul as it passes from perfect infancy to perfect childhood, from perfect childhood to perfect youth, and from perfect youth to perfect manhood* .[34]

Speaking of baby Jesus, Weston once again uses the "above"/"below" imagery:

[30] Weston, *The One Christ*, Part III, ch. VI, 152–153.
[31] Weston, *The One Christ*, Part III, ch. XV, 321.
[32] Weston, *The One Christ*, Part III, ch. XV, 322–323.
[33] Weston, *The One Christ*, Part III, ch. VI, 156.
[34] Weston, *The One Christ*, Part III, ch. VI, 156–157.

> Looking from above, the acceptance of practical unconsciousness is seen to be the momentary expression of the will of the living unlimited Logos . . . for there is no wall between the unlimited and the incarnate Logos . . .
>
> Looking from beneath we see the Incarnate almost unconscious because the soul is not yet able to mediate self-knowledge.[35]

Embryonic consciousness serves to dramatize what is in any event a contrast between the practical consciousness needed for activity in the Trinitarian and cosmic as opposed to the Incarnational sphere.

4.2. Difficulties

Gore and Weston are committed to

(T1) there is one and only one subject of consciousness or psychological center in Christ (the psychological reading of "person" in Chalcedon);

and

(T2) there is one and only one subject of consciousness or psychological center behind the career of Jesus described in the Gospels.

But modified kenosis emphasizes that

(T3) there is a vast gap between the contents of consciousness on which intra-Trinitarian and cosmic functions are based, and the consciousness that mediates activity in the sphere of Incarnation,

and

(T4) Christ is simultaneously operative in both spheres from the Incarnation onward.

---

[35] Weston, *The One Christ*, Part III, ch. VI, 160.

Weston acknowledges that his principal problem is the difficulty of conceiving the coexistence of the full Divine and the limited human consciousness in a single person, once "person" in the Chalcedonian formula has been given a psychological construal, so that the unity of person requires "a single consciousness in Christ."[36] Put otherwise, (T2) combines with "right-wing" liberal Anglican readings of the Gospels to motivate (T3). But how is the conjunction of (T3) with (T4) compatible with (T1)?

4.3. Christological analogies?

Weston responds by looking for analogies that will make his portrait of Christ *psychologically* more imaginable. Each analogy shows a single human agent in a dual relationship to his environment, where each sphere of relationships is sufficiently distinct as to require a personal center of activity. The first case seems more to capture the perspective "from above." *(1) Analogy of St. Francis de Sales, who came to act as the confessor of his own father and mother*: "As son of his parents, he was famous for his loving affection and filial devotion and his constant interest in all that made up their lives." As confessor he was "unable to exercise filial love or to make use of his wider knowledge of their lives but was related to them only through the medium of his priesthood." Therefore, he was subject of two relationships with them, and in the second he was restrained in the exercise of his sonship. But it was "as son that Francis willed to act as priest to his parents and as son that he put aside all such knowledge of them as priesthood could not mediate."[37]

The next three analogies seem rather to picture the view "from below." *(2) Analogy of the African king, defeated by a neighboring tribe and reduced to a state of slavery in his own house*: "He is a king; and in his own mind, as he dwells in thought upon his surroundings,

---

[36] Weston, *The One Christ*, Part III, ch. VI, 157–160.
[37] Weston, *The One Christ*, Part III, ch. VI, 151.

he knows himself as king and ruler of men. But *within the sphere of his servitude* he has to realize himself as *a king in slavery*. Not as a mere slave, for he *is* a king; but as a king in slavery. And everything in his accustomed environment he must relate to himself in a new way. To himself as a king in slavery he relates all that once was related to him as a king. He has in a sense a limited self-consciousness; not a second one, for he is one and the same person throughout."[38]

(3) *Analogy of the favorite son of a commanding officer as a soldier in his father's regiment*: "His self-consciousness as son of his father belongs to the sphere of his full, proper life; but within the particular narrow relationships set up by his enlistment he is the subject of a limited consciousness, knowing himself only as a son in conditions of military service. And it is only in the measure that the limited consciousness is allowed to prevail over the wider that his military life is really effective and tolerable. He is one single person; he has no dual consciousness; but the content of his self-consciousness as a soldier is less than the content of his consciousness as son, free in his father's house."[39]

(4) *Analogy of the king's son as workman*: Suppose "a king's son were to will, for purposes of his father's policy, to leave his palace and to dwell a workman among workman; to pass through all the troubles and vicissitudes of the life of a manual labourer, and to refuse to receive anything from others that he could not naturally receive and use as a working man. Those who recognize him and in their hearts bow before him are forbidden to acknowledge him or to help him in any way. Imagine a time of distress, and the king's son numbered among the unemployed and chosen to be one of their leaders. He goes with them into the king's presence; he is as they are in the king's sight; and the answer that he receives is that nothing can be done for any one of them. Outside the palace he shares the grief, the distress, and the hunger of the unemployed; and none may help him apart

---

[38] Weston, *The One Christ*, Part III, ch. VI, 154.
[39] Weston, *The One Christ*, Part III, ch. VI, 155.

from the whole body of weary sufferers. As the days pass the distress deepens; and finally a riot ensues in which he is severely handled and lies at death's door in the prison infirmary. He is recognized but must be treated only as an unemployed workman, now a prisoner awaiting trial. Yet all the while he is a king's son. However, he is resolved only to know himself as king's son in conditions of manual labour. The law of self-restraint that he imposed upon himself when in his father's palace must hold."[40]

None of these analogies shows a single person operating out of both sets of relationships at once the way God the Son is supposed to do within the universal sphere and the sphere of Incarnation. Neither does any of the analogies capture both sides of the God the Son's alleged self-awareness. (1) Francis de Sales is represented as one person who is the center of two current relationships at once; he uses his wider-scope consciousness for one role and his narrower-scope consciousness for the other, but his narrower-scope consciousness is not sealed off from his wider-scope consciousness. But Francis de Sales does not relate to his parents as son and as priest simultaneously. Moreover, within the sphere of Incarnation, the Son is not supposed to have consciousness of everything that omniscience knows, the way Francis de Sales – even while functioning as priest – still *knows* everything he knows about his parents *qua* son; he just doesn't act as priest on the non-overlapping wider-scope knowledge. Hence, this example seems to model the Incarnation "top-down."

(3–4) The analogies of the son in his father's regiment and son gone to join the workers show one person in two roles, but who has renounced relating to the father out of the son-role in order to relate to him merely as recruit or as common workman. He can remember relating the old way, but his decision (to enlist, or to be in solidarity with commoners) brings that pattern of relating to an end. Likewise, (2) the African king-in-slavery was a king-in-power and had one set of relations to the house in the past, but now is a king-in-slavery and

---

[40] Weston, *The One Christ*, Part III, ch. VI, 164.

has a different set of relations to the house. He can remember the old, but his enslavement brings that way of life to an end. Weston also talks of the sons and the king-in-slavery trying to forget the old, in order to make the new pattern of relationships more tolerable. Just as Weston's Son within the sphere of Incarnation knows Himself to be God, but doesn't know Himself as functioning out of Divine knowledge and power, so the sons and king-in-slavery know themselves to be sons or king but do not know themselves as functioning out of those roles. But with the sons and the king, this is because they do not function out of these roles any longer at all. By contrast, Incarnation does not – for Weston – mean abandonment of the Logos' cosmic and intra-Trinitarian roles. So these analogies furnish more of a "bottom-up" picture.

Weston concedes that none of the analogies gives him a psychological model that does everything he wants, even though each is of some help heuristically. He concludes, "the Holy Spirit has not given us a revelation concerning the conception of a single person as the center of two sets of relationships *at the same moment*. He has, however, revealed to us the actual relationships themselves."[41]

4.4. *Kenosis and ownership*

The from-above/from-below contrasts make Weston's position sound (unintentionally) close to that of Thomas Aquinas, according to which God the Son is essentially Divine, essentially possesses Divine consciousness, and essentially engages in Divine functions. But God the Son wills also to join a particular human nature to Himself and operate through it as through an internal instrument (much as a human being does things with his/her hand or foot). Insofar as God the Son is operating through the human nature, His activities are – by definition – circumscribed by its capacities (just as a human

---

[41] Weston, *The One Christ*, Part III, ch. VI, 168.

being can kick but not grasp things with its foot). Yet, just as a human being can kick with its foot while grasping with its hand, so God the Son can use His omnipotence and omniscience with the Father to co-produce the Holy Spirit and to sustain the created order in being, while thinking lesser thoughts and doing limited things through His human nature. Thus, speaking of the relation of the two spheres, Weston comments, "looked at from above, this isolation has no existence in the eternal order; for the person who constitutes each set of relationships is one and the same, the eternal Son of God, to whom such relations [i.e., those that pertain to the sphere of Incarnation] are additional to those that are universal [i.e., that pertain to the universal sphere]."[42]

Here – as John Stewart Lawton notes[43] – there is no real *kenosis* – God the Son does not *empty* Himself of anything. Nor is there any *self-restraint* – God the Son does not refrain from exercising His full powers as needed in Trinitarian and cosmic contexts. Rather, there is the *addition* of another sphere and another mode of operation. (I can use a hand only to do what hands can help do!)

Moreover, since the (patristic and scholastic) duality of natures has been replaced by a duality of spheres, we have to ask what – for Weston – holds them together. It cannot just be that God the Son's universal-sphere consciousness is omniscient and so includes His Incarnation-sphere consciousness among its objects, because omniscience includes the consciousness of every other finite person among its objects as well (cf. the Collect for Purity of Heart), and yet they are not *His own*. One-way cognitive access cannot account for the unity involved in the Incarnation, because God has at least one-way cognitive access to everything! If it is that the Ego (i.e., God the Son) operates through those human capacities as instruments, this would not be sufficient for Aquinas, who thinks

---

[42] Weston, *The One Christ*, Part III, ch. VI, 149.
[43] Lawton, *Conflict in Christology*, ch. 5, 150–155.

God operates through all creatures as instruments (as an artisan through his hatchet). Rather it has to be that God the Son operates through those capacities as *internal* instruments, in such a way that the powers in question are *His own*. And it seems that something more than psychological conceptuality, something rather in the neighbor-hood of scholastic metaphysical notions, would be needed to concep-tualize such "ownership."[44] Similarly, more metaphysical, not psy-chological, machinery will need to be supplied if Weston thinks of the Ego as something detachable from any and all of the streams of consciousness that *de facto* belong to it and as contingently attaching itself to one or more streams.[45]

5. Elevating the son of man

In bringing Christ down, absolute and modified kenotic theories stress the gap between the (cognitive and conative) contents of the Father's Divine consciousness and that of the personality at the center of Jesus' earthly career. By contrast, in *Foundations: A Statement of Christian Belief in Terms of Modern Thought*, William Temple explains the Divinity of Christ in terms of identity of conscious contents, most especially, sameness of will. Like kenoticists, Temple deplores the influence of Greek philosophy on Christian theology,[46] even lodges the charge that talk of natures is static and materialistic (!) rather than dynamic and spiritual![47] Temple celebrates what he takes to be a shift in Latin ecclesiastical documents from metaphysical to legal conceptuality, which focusses on persons with rights and duties. And,

---

44 See Hick, *The Metaphor of God Incarnate*, ch. 5, 51–56, who criticizes Morris' "Two-Minds Theory" (spelled out in *The Logic of God Incarnate*, ch. 4, 102–107) on the grounds that one-way cognitive access cannot account for the unity involved in Incarnation.

45 See Lawton, *Conflict in Christology*, ch. 10, 275–276.

46 Temple, "The Divinity of Christ," 231.

47 Temple, "The Divinity of Christ," 232–233.

already in Augustine, he finds a happy psychologizing focus on the will.[48]

Writing in *Foundations* almost a quarter of a century after *Lux Mundi*, Temple seems confident in approaching patristic theology with a freer reconstructive hand. On his reading, the Greek fathers construed (what I have called) the non-optimality problem metaphysically. The difficulty is that, due to sin, human nature is perishable and corruptible. The solution is to "commingle" the imperishable Divine with human nature. Thus, according to some Greek fathers, Christ did not assume an individual human nature (one as opposed to others) but that universal humanity which we all share. Uniting it to the power of the Divine Word makes human nature imperishable once more. The rest of us share in this benefit by participating in that humanity which is joined to Christ.[49]

In *Foundations*, Temple proposes a point-by-point replacement of this metaphysical with a modern *moral* interpretation. Morally speaking, what is non-optimal about the human condition and Divine human relations can be summed up in the problem of evil – the problems of pain and of sin, respectively. The moral solution is that Christ reveals the character of God as humble, self-forgetting, and self-sacrificing love.[50] By contrast with kenoticists, Temple insists that "the self-humbling and self-emptying and the self-forgetting sacrifice are" not just a temporal and transitory expedient, but are "themselves part of the *eternal* glory of God."[51] This solves the problem of pain, because it reveals God as a fellow sufferer who is afflicted in all of our afflictions and whose real sympathy for our suffering redeems it.[52] This solves the problem of sin (which Temple equates with selfishness) because the cross reveals God as suffering love of

---

[48] Temple, "The Divinity of Christ," 233–237.

[49] Temple, "The Divinity of Christ," 223–226, 231, 233.

[50] Temple, "The Divinity of Christ," 218–219.

[51] Temple, "The Divinity of Christ," 219.   [52] Temple, "The Divinity of Christ," 220.

enemies, and because – Temple is convinced – it is a fact of human psychology that "selfishness must always yield to love, if only the love is really understood."[53]

Christ is able to reveal the character of God through a union of wills, not of natures. Paul of Samosata was condemned for saying this, because he was operating with an inadequate faculty-psychology, which represented the will as only one faculty among others and so made will appear less real than substance.[54] Temple's "more adequate" modern psychology identifies will with the individual person, the entire active personality, as the only substance there is in human beings.[55] Because – on this scheme – "sameness of will" is tantamount to "sameness of person," Temple appeals to the former to explain how and in what sense Christ is Divine.[56]

What is the criterion for sameness of will? Temple begins by assuming that *sameness of content, sameness of intentional objects,* will suffice: "Christ is identically God," that is, "the whole content of His being – His thought, feeling, and purpose – is also that of God."[57] This is the *idem velle, idem nolle* of ancient friendship, which drove Cicero to the hyperbole that fast friends are like one soul in two bodies! Temple thinks this is the correct "moral" interpretation of the indwelling of John's Gospel, and ought to supplant the metaphysical reading of it given by Gregory of Nyssa.[58] But surely it is hyperbole to say that harmony of wills makes for *identity* as opposed to *equivalence* of agency. After all, in considering the Divinity of Christ, Temple asks after the relation of Christ's to *the Father's* will, and traditional theology never counts them *the same person!*

In the very next breath, Temple distinguishes a will's *subjective function* from its *contents.* "Christ's Will, as subjective function, is of course not the Father's Will, but the content of the Wills – the

[53] Temple, "The Divinity of Christ," 220–221.
[54] Temple, "The Divinity of Christ," 226–229.
[55] Temple, "The Divinity of Christ," 226, 247–248.
[56] Temple, "The Divinity of Christ," 247–250.
[57] Temple, "The Divinity of Christ," 249.   [58] Temple, "The Divinity of Christ," 259.

purpose – is the same."[59] "Christ is not the Father; but Christ and the Father are One. What we see Christ doing and desiring, that we thereby know the Father does and desires."[60] Equivalently, Temple distinguishes *formal* from *material* aspects of the will: "formally (as pure subjects) God and Christ are distinct; materially (that is in the content of the two consciousnesses) God and Christ are One and the Same."[61] Having posited these distinctions, Temple hastens to blur them: trading on an equivocity of "the subject is nothing apart from its object," Temple seems to assume that there is a distinction only of reason between the subject and its act, and a distinction only of reason between the act and its content, and thence to infer that the content is the whole substance of Christ, so that "Christ is identically one with the Father in the content of His Being."[62]

In the end, however, the content of Christ's Being *is* just the content of His will. For Temple in *Foundations*, the Divinity of Christ is reduced to His willing the same contents as God does. His passing concession – to scholastics and kenoticists alike – that a finite human consciousness cannot see and will exactly the same as the Divine, that it will be enough if the wills align on certain spiritual matters, only re-emphasizes that Temple does not really have subjective identity in view.[63] Continuing to "moralize" the patristic "metaphysical" model, Temple identifies Christ's Humanity as the exemplar of what human being was meant to be, a "moral" exemplar insofar as Christ's will is perfectly conformed to the Father's.[64] Christ's revelation of Divine love draws us into a like conformity (i.e., of willed contents and purpose), so that we become more and more divinized thereby. Our personalities are subjectively exclusive: "We are subjectively ourselves and not He. We do not surrender to Him our freedom." But "gradually He becomes all-inclusive" as we come to will the same content as

[59] Temple, "The Divinity of Christ," 248.
[60] Ibid.   [61] Temple, "The Divinity of Christ," 249.
[62] Temple, "The Divinity of Christ," 250.
[63] Temple, "The Divinity of Christ," 250–252.
[64] Temple, "The Divinity of Christ," 254, 259.

He wills.[65] And so we are left with a plurality of subjectively distinct human beings, being drawn towards willing (in a manner relevant and possible) the same content as the subjectively distinct God the Father wills.

Significantly, in *Foundations*, Temple never speaks of God the Son, but only of the relationship between the will of Christ and that of the Father. That essay thus creates the impression that the Divinity of Christ simply consists of the individual Jesus' human will being aligned with the Father's in an exemplary way. Temple's logic thus leads us to a *left-wing* liberal Christology, not so distant from that of Hick, who sees Jesus as a human being who is exemplary in the spiritual dimension of personal other-centeredness or God-centeredness or Reality-centeredness, and who thereby became the leader of a (until recently) highly successful religious movement. The principal difference between Temple and some *Myth-of-God-Incarnate* authors would be his failure to appreciate the extent to which Jesus' personality and conception of His soteriological role would be shaped by the thought worlds of Second Temple Judaism.

6. Assessing the thought experiment, restriking the posture

For my part, I join "right-wing" *liberal* Anglicans in cultivating a critical appreciation of (lower and higher) biblical criticism (see chapter 1). Likewise, I welcome the conceptualities of psychology – particularly developmental psychology and object-relations theory – to the table of theological formulation. Like these turn-of-the-twentieth-century Anglicans, my own approach makes persons (agents who act by thought and will) fundamental both philosophically and theologically. I understand Divine Being to be personal. Among creatures, I take ordinary-sense human persons as fundamental, so much so that I insist that, to be good-to us, God

---

[65] Temple, "The Divinity of Christ," 253–254.

has to make good on the worst evils within the contexts of those individual participants lives. Like turn-of-the-twentieth-century British Christologians – for that matter, like *Myth-of-God-Incarnate* authors – I take the genuine deliverances of the physical sciences seriously, and want to hold that true religion can have nothing to fear from them. Unlike the *Myth-of-God-Incarnate* authors, however, I am an Anglo-Catholic, who holds the creeds and deliverances of the ecumenical councils to be normative in the sense of being systematically entrenched. The result is that, like the kenoticists, I want to begin by identifying the second person of the Trinity, God the Son, as the individual who led the human career of Jesus. And I want to recognize that his human being here below was much more like ours than patristic and scholastic portraits allow (see chapter 3).

Unlike most of these theologians, however, I am a philosopher, a sceptical realist, who takes metaphysics seriously. I therefore join Eric Mascall in dissociating myself from their project of trying to make psychological and moral categories do the work that metaphysical notions were meant to do.[66] My own view – which our incomplete survey supports without being sufficient to prove – is that, however worth trying, that experiment has failed. Worse yet, its century-long majority-report status in British theology has actually undermined Christian confidence in Christology, and led to the disarray that *The Myth of God Incarnate* sets before our eyes. My own remedy is a return to metaphysics; my own preference is for the medieval metaphysics my turn-of-the-twentieth-century Anglicans were so eager to expel (see chapter 5)!

In this story, (what has come to be) the hermeneutical dogma – that Chalcedon and other conciliar formulae do not make positive claims but function negatively to rule out what may not be said – has proved pernicious, enabling as it did the dismissal of metaphysics from Christology. Happily, it holds no entitlement to our allegiance,

---

[66] Eric Mascall, *Christ, the Christian, and the Church* (London: Longmans, Green & Co., 1946), Preface, vi, ch. II, sec. V, 39–42, ch. III, sec. II, 54.

because it represents a confused and confusing response to worthy and misguided concerns. Like most of the great medieval school theologians, I would agree with turn-of-the-twentieth-century Anglicans that the Church should not overdogmatize; that conciliar formulae are and ought to be minimalist; in particular that ecclesiastical authority should not put its weight behind what ought to remain philosophically optional. It does not follow from this, however, that conciliar pronouncements make no positive theoretical claims, but rather that these positive claims are indeterminate and radically underdetermine theological explanatory theory. This means that they are themselves compatible with a variety of theoretical elaborations, which it is the job of theologians to produce and to test for their consistency, coherence, fruitfulness, and explanatory power. Medieval school theology's discussions of Trinity, Incarnation, the sacraments, gave rise to many competing explanations. Their *quaestio et disputatio* method sharpened articulation and produced theological systems of compelling texture and weight. In our own day, all too often, allergy to dogmatizing has led to theological irresponsibility which eschews detailed formulation and refuses to take responsibility for the coherence of its philosophical presuppositions.[67]

As a sceptical *realist*, however, I also stand firmly opposed to the historicism that encouraged turn-of-the-twentieth-century Anglicans to evacuate conciliar pronouncements of Greek philosophy because they deemed it out of date. To be sure, the theoretical formulations and philosophical intuitions of persons will vary with the times in which they live. Certainly, historians may describe the fact that the liveliness of theoretical options varies over time. But if there are philosophical fads, the *truth* of metaphysics is independent of current convention. It is unphilosophical either to dismiss a system as outdated, or to embrace one because it is newfangled, without examining it for consistency, coherence, and explanatory power – in

---

[67] See Jürgen Moltmann's comment that every German is a Lutheran and a Hegelian, and excuse dismissing the responsibility to be metaphysically clear.

Christology, without inquiring how it aids and abets, hinders or obstructs, us from saying what we want to say about Jesus. Corollary to this, to a philosopher with sleeves rolled up to give a coherent formulation of entrenched data, theoretical liveliness is and ought to be a function of what promises the best contribution to the explanatory job. That is why philosophical tendencies are perennial in nature: one spirals round and round trying to nuance and compensate for strengths and weaknesses. I have no objection to trying out other conceptualities to see how well they work. My plea is rather not to dismiss the metaphysics of substance and supposit just because it has Aristotle's name on it.[68]

---

[68] Incidentally, it is amusing to find the American theologian Shubert Ogden dismissing Greek philosophical categories as "incredible" while replacing it confidently with process philosophy (Ogden, *The Point of Christology* [Dallas: Southern Methodist University Press, 1992], ch. 7, 127–147). At the superficial level this is remarkable. Aristotle's metaphysics of substance and accidents – of things that have some losable and other unlosable features – is virtually a commonsense position, by comparison with pan-psychism, much less the view that everything is a society of actual occasions, which are mini-minds that receive data and respond with an integration of it, and do so instantaneously!

5 | Recovering the metaphysics: Christ as God-man, metaphysically construed

Central to my "Chalcedonian" approach to Christology is the insistence that it is *God* who becomes human. Positively, from the viewpoint of my cosmological hypothesis, Incarnation is key to satisfying God's unitive aims in creation. Negatively, Divine solidarity is key to the solution of human non-optimality problems: Stage-I defeat requires that it is *God* who participates in horrors. Both ways identify *God* as the One of Whom we affirm that He was born of the Virgin Mary; that He walked and talked; spat and touched; ate, drank, and slept; that He was crucified under Pontius Pilate, suffered, died, was buried but rose on the third day.

Yet, common sense joins with philosophy and *Myth-of-God-Incarnate* theologians to press Mary's question: "how can this be?" (Luke 1:34). By way of an answer, I shall outline two accounts of the metaphysics of Christology: one offered by Richard Swinburne in his book *The Christian God*; and the other inspired by a family of formulations defended by thirteenth- and fourteenth-century medieval Latin school theologians. Like all theories, each has its costs and benefits. My own preference is for the second, but I believe that either is sufficient to rebut the mythographers' charge that the notion of a God-man is unintelligible.

1. Doctrinal desiderata

First, a brief reminder of the historical parameters of the discussion is in order. Chalcedon laid it down that

(T1) in Christ there are two distinct natures – one human and one Divine;

and

(T2) in Christ, there is a real unity of natures in a single person or supposit;

while Ephesus made their corollary explicit:

(T3) in Christ, there are two wills – one human and one Divine.

Already in the first quarter of the sixth century, Boethius took it for granted that "person" or "supposit" (*suppositum, hypostasis*) means the same thing in the doctrine of the Trinity (one God, three persons) as in Christology (two natures, one person), because the second person of the Trinity (i.e., God the Son, the Divine Word) was supposed to be the One Who became Incarnate. Boethius' definition –

(D1) a person is an individual substance of a rational nature;

and its implicit companion understanding:

(D2) a supposit is an individual substance –

had the authority of a classic by Anselm's time. Thirteenth-century medieval Latin school theologians had reached consensus on the following interpretive theses:

(T4) in the Incarnation, human nature is assumed by the Divine Word;

(T5) the Divine Word is its own supposit/person and hence the single person or supposit in Christ;

(T6) the Incarnation of the Divine Word is a contingent matter of Divine free choice;

(T7) the Incarnation of the Divine Word is reversible (having become human, the Divine Word could cease to be human) but will in fact never be reversed.

Yet, both Boethius' definition and medieval Latin school theology's metaphysical developments of these doctrines found their philosophical roots in Aristotelian philosophy, to which we now turn.

2. Aristotelian background

Metaphysics is inherently controversial. But in the *Categories*, Aristotle aims to articulate the commonsense view that there are things, which are characterized by features, some of which are more permanent than others.

Seeking to order such intuitions, he distinguishes substance from accidents, and primary substances (e.g., Socrates, Beulah the cow, Brownie the donkey) from secondary substances or substance-kinds (e.g., man, cow, donkey).

  (i) The secondary substance or substance-kind is "*said of*" the primary substance and is that through which the primary substance is constituted as the very thing it is (e.g., Beulah the cow is made the very thing she is by bovinity; Socrates, the very thing he is by humanity).
 (ii) Accidents "*exist in*" primary substances and characterize them in ways that the primary substance could exist without (e.g., Socrates is pale in winter but becomes tan in summer, was once, but in adulthood is no longer, shorter than his mother, etc.).
(iii) Primary substances neither exist in (like accidents) nor are said of (like secondary substances) anything, but are the ultimate subjects of the properties.

Aristotle took the substance- and accident-kinds with which he was concerned to be *natural* kinds, not nominal essences – kind-terms (like "desk" or "bachelor") that are the products of human linguistic conventions. Human and whiteness are *real* essences: what-it-is-to-be human or white is what it is prior to and independently of human attempts to conceptualize and talk about the world.

Medieval interpreters, harmonizing across Aristotle's works, read him as an *essentialist* – that is, as holding that

(T8) for each primary substance *x*, there is a secondary substance-kind *K* that pertains to it *per se* and is essential to it, in the sense that *x* could not exist without being a *K*.

Because the necessary connection is not between concepts (as in "a bachelor is an unmarried, post-pubescent male") but between the thing (Socrates or Beulah) and the kind (humanity or bovinity), the connection is said to be necessary *de re*. Because such essential substance-kinds constitute the primary substance as the very thing it is, Aristotle also held:

(T9) for each primary substance *x*, there is *only one* secondary substance-kind *K* that pertains to *x* through itself and is essential to it, in the sense that *x* could not exist without being a *K*.

It is impossible for any substance individual to have two substance-kind natures *essentially*, for that would involve its being constituted as the very thing it is twice-over!

How, then, can one individual be both Divine and human? If the Divine Word is constituted as the very thing It is by Divinity (together with the person-distinguishing property of Filiation), how could it take on human nature as its own? This problem remains commonsensical. What Beulah *is* is a cow. Surely, Beulah could not *also* be a donkey; nor could *Beulah* be a donkey instead!

Unmodified Aristotelian essentialism raises a problem for how a substance individual could have two substance-natures *essentially*, in such a way that it could not exist without them. Unmodified Aristotelian essentialism rests here, because it doesn't envision any other way for a substance individual to have or be characterized by a substance-kind.

But the doctrine of the Incarnation does not assert that the Divine Word possesses two substance-kinds *essentially* (and so does not run afoul of [T8] and [T9]). Rather it maintains that the Divine Word is essentially Divine, couldn't exist without being Divine, but contingently begins to be human (in c. 4 BCE). The doctrine of the Incarnation holds that

(T10) it is possible for a primary substance x that is essentially of substance-kind K also to possess/be/come to be of substance-kind K' (where K is not the same as K') contingently and non-essentially.

Nowadays, this is terminologically confusing because substance-kinds are often referred to as essences, setting up an equivocation between contemporary-sense essential possession (x possesses K essentially = def x couldn't exist without possessing K) and essential possession as possession of a substance-kind as one's own (x's being K where K is a substance-kind). But the former usage of "essential" refers to *the way* the property is possessed (in such a way that the thing couldn't exist without it), while the latter refers to *the type* of property possessed (a substance-kind property rather than an accident). Commentators needlessly worry that if the Divine Word does not possess human nature in the way we do – i.e., contemporary-sense essentially, in such a way that we could not exist without being human – then the Divine Word isn't fully or perfectly human – i.e., doesn't really possess all of what goes into being a human being.[1] What the doctrine requires is that the Divine Word – while essentially Divine – contingently come to possess human nature in such a way as to be characterized by such features. So far as I know, no one (not even the total absolute kenoticists of chapter 4) has envisioned the Divine Word's possessing human nature essentially in such a way that the Divine Word couldn't exist without being human. Most Christian theologians would agree: not only is this false; it makes no sense!

[1] Richard Cross, *The Metaphysics of the Incarnation: Thomas Aquinas to Duns Scotus* (Oxford: Oxford University Press, 2002), ch. 8, sec. 2, 205; Allan Bäck, "Scotus on the Consistency of the Incarnation and the Trinity," *Vivarium* 36:1 (1998), 86 and 95.

Even if Incarnation does not require the idea that one substance individual has two natures contemporary-sense *essentially* (in such a way that it could not exist without them), mere characterization is enough to make the so-called Contradiction Problem arise:

1. Jesus is God (Chalcedonian definition).
2. Jesus is a human being (Chalcedonian definition).
3. God is omnipotent, omniscient, perfectly good, eternal, immutable, impassible, infinite (partial analysis of what it is to be God).
4. Human beings are rational animals and so generable and corruptible, mutable and capable of being causally affected and suffering; finite and so of limited power and knowledge (partial analysis of what it is to be a human being).
5. Therefore, Jesus is infinite and finite, immutable and mutable, omnipotent but limited in power, omniscient but limited in knowledge, immutable and impassible, ingenerable and incorruptible but susceptible of growing in wisdom and stature and suffering death on a cross – which is multiply contradictory.

Faced with statements apparently of the form "x is F and x is not F," one may choose between two basic strategies for removing the contradiction and eliminating the assertion that genuine contradictories are true of the same subject in the same respect eternally or at one and the same time. One is to argue that it is *not really the same subject x* that is the proximate subject of contradictory properties, so that really the situation is that x is F but y is not F, or that z is F and y is not F (where x is not identical with y, and y is not identical with z). The other is to argue that *the predicates* only appear but *are not really contradictory*, so that it is not a matter of x's being F and not F, but of x's being F and not G. Obviously, one can also combine the two strategies, insisting that same-subject and same-property affirmed and denied are both only a matter of appearance.

In Christology, however, these strategies represent complementary risks and temptations. The first – arguing that different subjects are Divine and human, respectively – seems to flirt with Nestorianism. The second – maintaining that the predicates are not really contradictory – may redefine Divinity and humanity in ways that no longer capture what Chalcedon intended (a problem charged against some versions of partial absolute kenosis discussed in chapter 4).

3. Swinburne on dividing God's mind

3.1. Metaphysical presuppositions

Like Aristotle, Swinburne posits a distinction between substances or concrete individual things that have properties, and properties (whether monadic or relational) that are universals that can be instantiated in many things and that exist only as instantiated by concrete individual substances.[2]

While agreeing with Aristotle that not all essences are *nominal*, Swinburne nevertheless takes a page from Descartes in supposing that there are only two basic (Swinburne calls them "minimalist") *natural* kinds – material substance and soul substance. These minimalist natural kinds are *essential* to the individuals that in fact instantiate them, in the sense that those individuals could not exist without instantiating them (some *de re* necessities are allowed). Thus he explains that each substance essentially belongs to a minimal essential kind;[3] that each substance that is a material substance is essentially a material substance and so essentially a space-occupier and essentially possesses no features to which anyone has privileged access,[4] whereas each substance that is a soul is essentially a soul and essentially possesses features to which one individual has privileged access.[5] Nor could a *res cogitans* be essentially a *res*

---

[2] Richard Swinburne, *The Christian God* (Oxford: Oxford University Press, 1994), ch. 1, 7–8.

[3] Swinburne, *The Christian God*, ch. 2, 33.   [4] Swinburne, *The Christian God*, ch. 1, 9.

[5] Swinburne, *The Christian God*, ch. 1, 16–17.

extensa, or vice versa. Swinburne would have no trouble accepting (T8) and (T9).

By contrast, Swinburne insists that many of Aristotle's favorite biological kinds (such as "cow" or "oak tree"), artifact kinds (such as "desk" or "bed"), and phase terms (such as "sapling" or "child") that we use in describing the world are only nominal essences, words that have meanings established by linguistic conventions. Swinburne insists that no one set of conventions is exclusive or exhaustive; the real world of matter and souls could be linguistically and conventionally carved up by nominal essences in many different ways.[6] Swinburne finds no problem in endorsing (T10) where the second, contingently possessed substance-kind K' is a *nominal* essence.

Significantly for Christology, Swinburne counts human being among the nominal essences: he claims that "human" is a word for whose use our criteria are vague and malleable in different directions.[7] Swinburne denies that the property of being human is essential to things that have it, because – quite apart from Christology – he thinks it is intelligible that an individual should persist through the change of being transformed from a human being into a gorilla.[8] Moreover, Swinburne insists that (psychological-sense) person is only a phase term and hence not essential to the individuals it truly describes (by Swinburne's criteria, according to which personality requires a certain complexity of current mental life, some Alzheimer's patients were persons but are no longer). Likewise, souls, while essentially souls, may be able to change from one kind into another – from human into non-human or into some very powerful disembodied spirit.[9]

By contrast, Divinity is an *essential* kind: any individual who is God couldn't exist without being God,[10] where to be God is to be

---

[6] Swinburne, *The Christian God*, ch. 1, 12–13, 15–16.

[7] Swinburne, *The Christian God*, ch. 1, 30–32.

[8] Swinburne, *The Christian God*, ch. 1, 27–32.

[9] Swinburne, *The Christian God*, ch. 1, 32.

[10] Swinburne, *The Christian God*, ch. 6, 148–149.

an inevitably everlasting person who does not essentially depend on a body to exist or function, who is the omnipresent creator and sustainer of any universe there may be, and who is perfectly free, omnipotent, omniscient, and perfectly good.[11] For Swinburne, a Divine individual is thus a high-powered and essentially permanent kind of soul (of *res cogitans*)!

Importantly, however, Swinburne does not understand Divinity to include essential immutability and impassibility (and so would not accept step [3] of the Contradiction argument as it stands). It is metaphysically possible for souls of the Divine kind to change or to be causally interactive. Divine self-determination is preserved so long as Divine souls control whether and how they change and are acted upon.

3.2. *Three-souled God, Social Trinity!*

With this metaphysical apparatus in hand, Swinburne gives explicit endorsement to the Social Trinity that kenotic theories had assumed *en passant*. For Swinburne, the three Divine persons are three numerically distinct souls of the Divine essential kind, each instantiating the universal Divinity, each inevitably everlasting[12] but individuated from one another by relations of origin (the Father causes the Son; Father and Son cause the Holy Spirit).[13]

Looming large for Swinburne is the metaphysical challenge that Divine omnipotence poses to these claims. Scotus argues that a plurality of necessarily existent, essentially omnipotent, and essentially free beings is logically impossible. Omnipotent power is necessarily efficacious, and freedom (as self-determining power for opposites)

---

[11] Swinburne, *The Christian God*, ch. 6, 126–137. There are some problems with Swinburne's accounts of God's ontological or metaphysical necessity, but they need not detain us now.

[12] Swinburne, *The Christian God*, ch. 8, 181–182.

[13] Swinburne, *The Christian God*, ch. 8, 176–177.

can will whatever it wants. If there were two such beings (A and B), it would be possible for A to will S for time T and B to will not-S for time T and so for contradictories to be simultaneously true. If B were not essentially free, the problem could be solved by A's always causally determining what B wills, or vice versa. If B were not essentially omnipotent, then the problem could be solved by A's making B not to be omnipotent any longer, or vice versa. If B were not necessarily existent, the problem could be solved by A's making B cease to exist. But if B is supposed to be necessarily existent, essentially omnipotent, and essentially free, the contradiction cannot be avoided.

Medieval formulations of the doctrine of the Trinity hoped to evade the omnipotence problem metaphysically, by appeal to their claim that there is one and only one concrete thing – viz., the Divine essence – that is omnipotent, and that it is numerically unmultiplied in the three Divine persons. Since they all share numerically the same power-pack, they also share numerically the same thoughts and actions *ad extra*. Here Swinburne has begged to differ, taking the Trinity to be constituted of three Divine souls, which he identifies with three concrete individual essences. Turning the Trinity into three numerically distinct individual souls that share no metaphysical constituents is the first division Swinburne effects in God's mind!

Instead, Swinburne seeks to handle the omnipotence problem by appeal to his own distinctive-action theory, according to which freedom is not a self-determining power for opposites, but an unobstructed orientation towards what is reasonable. Reason aims at maximizing or equal-besting the apparent good. That some course is the best constitutes overriding reason to do it; that each of some set of alternatives is "equal best" constitutes overriding reason to implement one of them; that an action is overall bad constitutes overriding reason not to do it; that it is good (bad) constitutes some reason for (against) doing it. Rational agents do (refrain from) what they have overriding reason to do (not to do) unless obstructed by non-rational forces.[14]

If there were a plurality of Divine individuals, each would know that it would be wrong for them to contradict and so to frustrate one another. Hence, Divine omniscience, perfect goodness, and perfect freedom (in Swinburne's sense) would mean that necessarily, if there is a plurality of Divine individuals, they will devise some cooperative scheme: either elect someone chief, or vote, or divide the labor. Much the western theological minority report that it is, Swinburne thinks division of labor would be best.[15] Thus, for Swinburne, there can be a plurality of Divine individuals, because perfect goodness combines with omniscience to limit what omnipotence can choose, while perfect freedom necessarily conforms!

3.3. Word–flesh Christology, modified

Swinburne has affirmed that Divinity is an essential kind. However cooperative the Divine individual souls constituting the Social Trinity must be, one corollary is clear: if they are – as Swinburne claims – neither immutable nor impassible, then the Divine persons can to some extent think different thoughts, perform different actions, and have different experiences from one another. By contrast, Swinburne declares that human being is a nominal essence, a conventional sortal with fuzzy boundaries. However vague and variable the concept, Swinburne finds human being as we know and speak about it susceptible of a mind–body dualist analysis: the core of human being is a human soul that is normally connected with a human body and so capable of having sensations, thoughts, and purposes, a structure of beliefs and desires, and limitations on its powers and knowledge imposed by the human body.

[14] Swinburne, *The Christian God*, ch. 3, 68–71.
[15] Swinburne, *The Christian God*, ch. 8, 172–175.

How could a Divine individual, Who is essentially Divine, become human as well? Not by acquiring *another* soul, Swinburne insists, because two souls would mean two concrete individual substances and his metaphysics has no way appropriately to unite them – to make them belong to one another in such a way that the Divine individual could be characterized by the numerically distinct human soul's characteristics.[16] If Incarnation is to be metaphysically possible, it must be that a Divine individual soul – while remaining Divine – can become human (come to fall under the conventional sortal "human being") as well.[17]

In effect, Swinburne forwards a modified Word–flesh Christology: it is a *Word–flesh* Christology because the Divine Word (the second person of the Trinity) is the only soul Christ has; it is a *modified* Word–flesh Christology because the Divine Word is understood to be mutable and passible in such a way as to be able to become human as well as Divine. For God to become human, a Divine individual soul would have to take a human body from our gene pool and permit Itself to become causally interactive with that body in the way human souls normally are. The Divine individual soul would not thereby lose the cognitive contents, the thoughts and preferences, that It has by virtue of Its essential Divine attributes. Since It is *essentially* Divine, and since omniscience, omnipotence, and perfect goodness are essential to Divinity, that would be metaphysically impossible. Rather, the Divine individual soul would allow Itself to acquire a further range of contents – sensations, feelings, beliefs, and desires – by virtue of Its connection with the human body. As on Weston's theory, Incarnation would mean not kenosis, but an *extension* of Its normal modes of operation. Besides the Divine way of thinking and acting, the Divine individual would have a human way of thinking and acting.[18]

[16] Swinburne, *The Christian God*, ch. 9, 196–197.
[17] Swinburne, *The Christian God*, ch. 9, 194.
[18] Swinburne, *The Christian God*, ch. 9, 196–198.

Metaphysically, what Swinburne offers is one soul substance with two ranges of consciousness: a divided mind. Swinburne credits Freud with helping us to see how an agent can have two systems of belief that are to some extent independent of one another, so that, in performing some actions, the agent is acting on one system of belief and not guided by beliefs of the other system; and conversely. All desires and beliefs are accessible to the agent, but s/he refuses to admit to consciousness those beliefs that are relevant to the action but on which s/he is not acting. While Freud proposed this model to account for our widespread and systematic self-deception, Swinburne reckons that soteriological motives for Incarnation would furnish God the Son with good, non-neurotic reasons for dividing His mind. The partition would be created and enforced by a conscious decision informed by the comprehensive Divine consciousness, which would have access to everything. But there would be a vast gap between the range of consciousness out of which the Divine Word operates as God and that out of which He functions as human – all the more so, because Swinburne wants the human consciousness to correspond to a plain-sense reading of New Testament accounts of Jesus' earthly career. The human range would have to house ignorance, growth, temptation, experiencing infirmities, learning obedience through suffering. The human range would have limited access to the comprehensive contents of the Divine mind.[19]

Moreover, Swinburne envisions the Divine Word acting out of Its comprehensive consciousness to exercise some editorial control over the contents of Its narrower human consciousness. Imagining perfect goodness to be bound by obligations and duties, Swinburne reckons that Christ's human belief-set should include enough to guarantee reliable knowledge of His human duties and of the doctrinal content His earthly ministry was supposed to convey, but might not be enough to rule out temptations to the lesser good. Likewise, the Divine Word's human affections should not sum to a balance of

19 Swinburne, *The Christian God*, ch. 9, 201.

desire to do wrong. Its human beliefs and affections might render It liable to do less than the best action, however, and leave Its human consciousness fearing It might succumb to temptation.[20]

Looking back to Weston's modified kenotic theory (see chapter 4), recall how his quest for psychological models was frustrated partly because he insisted on claiming not only that there is one and only one subject of consciousness or psychological center behind the career of Jesus described in the Gospels, but also that there is one and only one subject of consciousness or psychological center in Christ at all; and partly because Weston's human cases didn't show one person operating out of two centers of relationship at once! Swinburne's strategy is explicitly to abandon the first to insist that Incarnation involves not one, but two psychological centers of thought and action. Otherwise, Swinburne's account stands as one good way to capture metaphysically the rest of what Weston wanted to say.

3.4. The contradiction problem

Swinburne offers us an individual soul that is – à la (T10) – essentially and everlastingly Divine but that begins contingently to be human. Swinburne supposes this to be metaphysically possible because the predicates "Divine" and "human" are not really incompatible. The same individual soul can have both a comprehensive consciousness and a limited system of beliefs and desires which are the interactive product of its connection with a human body. A soul that has such a set of beliefs and desires is thereby human. A soul thus interacting with the body is a human being. Swinburne thus denies that "x is human" entails "x has limited knowledge and power"; rather "x is human" entails "x includes a limited system of beliefs and desires and puts limited power to act behind them." Again, Swinburne

---

[20] Swinburne, The Christian God, ch. 9, 198–199, 204–208.

insists, "*x* is human" does not entail "*x* is *merely* human" but only "*x* has a human way of thinking and acting."[21]

Swinburne's Christology depends on his mind–body dualist account of what it is to be a human being, on his understanding of Divinity as mutable and passible (and hence on a revision of [3]), on his contention that souls might change and come to be of a nominal-essence kind that they weren't before (e.g., humans into gorillas; Divine into human), and on his claim that some souls might be of two kinds at once (notably, Divine *and* human). Are these philosophical interpretations adequate to the Christological intentions of Chalcedon (two natures; one person) and Constantinople (two wills)?

Swinburne insists that Divinity hasn't been diluted, because a mutable and passible Deity can do all of the explanatory work his inductive cosmological arguments require. (Swinburne gives a strong defense of this claim in his other books, but space does not permit a rehearsal of that case here.)

What about Christ's humanity? Does Swinburne not demote humanity when he says that God's being human does not involve a separate soul? Isn't his account reductive with respect to Constantinople's contention that Christ has a human as well as a Divine will? Swinburne protests that he has accommodated patristic desiderata and intentions. When the fathers worried that unmodified Word–flesh Christology denied a human soul to Christ, what they were concerned about was depriving Jesus of any human psychological life. When the fathers insisted on two wills, they meant to say that He has a human way of acting in which His choices and desires are informed by a human way of thinking. Swinburne insists that they could not have been wedded to the idea of Christ's literally having two concrete individual souls in which to house the two distinct ranges of consciousness, because – on Swinburne's metaphysics – that would be tantamount to Nestorianism.[22] Does not Swinburne's claim – that

---

[21] Swinburne, *The Christian God*, ch. 9, 197–198.   [22] Ibid.

the Divine soul becomes human as well – run counter to Chalcedon by confusing the two natures? Swinburne would defend his negative answer the same way. Housing the human range of consciousness in numerically the same soul as the Divine consciousness does not swallow up or fail to preserve the properties of the human nature. He has avoided Apollinarianism or monophysitism by including a distinctly and distinctively human psychological life within numerically the same soul.

4. Medieval metaphysics, Aristotle revised again!

4.1. Real distinction and characterization

Like Aristotle but contrary to Swinburne, medieval Latin school theologians take human being for a real, not a nominal essence, one that is – in all non-miraculous cases – contemporary-sense essential to the primary substances that have it (e.g., to Socrates, to Plato, and to each of us). That meant that for them – unlike Swinburne – their endorsement of (T10) carried with it the claim that a given *natural* kind might be essential to some, but only contingently characterize others.

Not only do they treat natural kinds as susceptible of *real* definitions. They *reify* the natures by treating them as really constitutive of the things to which they belong. They read Aristotle to be claiming

(T12) a primary substance (e.g., Socrates) is necessarily identical with the individual substance nature (Socrates' humanity) that is contemporary-sense essential to it.

Their endorsement of (T10) drove them to draw a further distinction that never entered Aristotle's mind, to complicate Aristotle's contrast between primary and secondary substances by positing two types of concrete individual substance things: primary substances (e.g., Socrates or Beulah the cow) and individual substance natures

(Socrates' humanity; Beulah's bovinity). They needed to claim that it was possible for something that is not essentially human (preeminently, a Divine person, the Divine Word, Who is essentially Divine) to unite itself to a really distinct concrete individual human nature in such a way as to be characterized by it and to be the ultimate subject of the actions and passions that are done and suffered through it.

Faced with an analogous problem – how to unite really distinct Divine and human souls – Swinburne throws up his hands, insists that it is impossible. If the only type of union available between really distinct substance things were aggregation, then Swinburne would appear to be right. Mere aggregation can unite any really distinct things into a whole (e.g., the Taj Mahal and the honey bee in the hive), but the union would be too loose for Christological purposes, because it does not support any literal sharing of attributes (*communicatio idiomatum*) – any literal denomination or *naming* of one part *from* another (e.g., the Taj Mahal is not truly said to be a honey-maker, nor is the bee truly called a beautiful building).

Medievals recognized three ways in which one thing might be named from or denominated from something:

(a) *per se* denomination: the Divine Word is Divine *per se* and Socrates is human *per se*; the Divine Word couldn't exist without being Divine, and Socrates couldn't exist without being human;

(b) *per accidens* denomination: Socrates is white *per accidens*. Socrates is really distinct from whiteness and is contingently white in the sense that Socrates could exist without being white;

(c) *extrinsic* denomination: Socrates is older than Plato and shorter than Aristotle and uglier than Alcibiades.

By [T9] the Divine Word as essentially Divine could not be human *per se* and essentially. But extrinsic denomination seems too loose to reflect human nature's actually belonging to the Divine Word as Its own. Accordingly, Scotus and Ockham take as analogy denomination *per accidens*.

Medieval Latin Aristotelians reify not only substance natures, but some or all accident natures, qualities chief among them. Yet, from their Aristotelian point of view, white Socrates is not a mere aggregation of Socrates and whiteness; whiteness *inheres* in Socrates. Likewise, they want to say, the Word made flesh is not a mere aggregate of Divinity and humanity; the individual human nature is *assumed* by the Divine Word.

But what is the metaphysical difference between mere aggregation and inherence? Medieval Latin Aristotelians cite three features:

(a) co-location: Socrates and his whiteness are in the same place at the same time;

(b) potency-actualization: the whiteness actualizes a potency for being white in Socrates;

(c) ontological dependence: the whiteness essentially depends on Socrates for its existence in a non-efficient-causal way.

(a) does not seem relevant to angels (as essentially immaterial substances) and their inherent accidents. Likewise, it is of no help in understanding the Divine Word's relation to the human nature, because the Divine Word is either nowhere (because immaterial) or everywhere (by virtue of Divine knowledge and power) and no more where the human nature is than where everything else is.

Medievals ruled out (b) on the philosophical ground that the Divine Word as simple cannot be a subject of inherence. They also excluded it on philosophico-theological grounds. Philosophy tells us that, when whiteness actualizes a substance's potency for being white, it affects how it is qualified; and when a substantial form actualizes matter's potency to receive it, it affects the substance-kind to which its subject belongs. Medievals reasoned that human nature is a substance-kind. If it actualized the potency of some subject to receive it, it would affect the substance-kind to which its subject belonged. Since the Divine Word is essentially Divine, such potency-actualization would result in a metaphysically impossible and theologically impermissible confusion of natures! Likewise, the other way around, if the Divine Word were supposed to inhere in the human nature![23]

Scotus concludes that the most relevant relation is (c), an accident's ontological dependence on its subject. Scotus emphasizes that this relation is not to be identified with (although it bears some analogies to) efficient causal dependence. All creatures are efficient causally dependent on all three persons of the Trinity as their first efficient cause. But not all creatures are assumed by the Divine persons.[24] Likewise, a subject (e.g., the intellect) may be an efficient partial cause of some of its accidents (e.g., an act of understanding), but this is a different relation from the ontological dependence the accident has on it as its subject. Scotus declares that ontological dependence of a broad-sense property thing on a subject is sufficient for characterization. Even if whiteness did not actualize a potency in Socrates, Socrates would be the subject on which the whiteness ontologically depended and that would be enough to make it true that Socrates is white. Likewise, ontological dependence by the assumed human nature on the Divine Word is sufficient for the Divine Word to be contingently denominated from the human nature.

Even if the Divine Word had no potency to be actualized by the individual human nature, it might seem that, if the Divine Word is first not-related and then related, the Divine Word undergoes a change – contrary to Divine simplicity and immutability. To avoid this, Scotus invokes the doctrine of non-mutual relations. Sometimes the truth of "aRb" requires a relation thing R in a and a co-relation thing R' in b (e.g., where this wall is similar in color to that wall). But other times it is enough if a is the term of a relation-thing R' that inheres in b (i.e., if $bR'a$). Scotus imagines that the Divine Word (a) will be the term of such a dependence relation (R') that inheres in

---

[23] Aquinas, *Sent.* III, d. 5, q. 1, a. 2, c; Parma VII.68B (= Parma edition, volume VII, page 68, column B); Scotus, *Op.Ox.* III, d. 5, q. 1, n. 2; d. 6, q. 1, n. 9; Wadding VII.1.121, 176 (= Wadding edition, vol. VII.1, pages 121 and 176).

[24] Scotus, *Op.Ox.* III, d. 1, q. 1, n. 7; Wadding VII.1.12; III, d. 1, q. 1, nn. 9–10; Wadding VII.1.15–16; III, d. 1, q. 2, nn. 5–8; Wadding VII.1.36–38.

the assumed human nature (*b*) without any corresponding *R*-thing inhering in It (*a*), and that this will be enough to make "the Divine Word assumes the human nature" true.[25]

---

[25] Scotus, *Op.Ox.* III, d. 1, q. 1, n. 4; Wadding VII.1.7.

Richard Cross complains that this is to treat essential dependence as a one-place predicate (*The Metaphysics of the Incarnation,* ch. 9, 207, 213). But this doesn't follow. Scotus is embracing a non-uniform account of the truth conditions for "*aRb*":

  (i) Where each of *a* and *b* could exist without being related, then "*aRb*" requires a relation thing *R* in *a*, and a co-relation thing *R'* in *b* (e.g., this wall's being similar in color to that wall).

 (ii) Where *a* couldn't exist without being *R* to *b*, even if *b* could exist without being *R'* to *a*, *R* is really the same as but formally distinct from *a* (e.g. the creature's relation of dependence on the Creator).

(iii) Where "*aRb*" can come to be true if there is a change without any change in *b*, then it suffices that *R* is in *a* and *b* is the term of *R*.

All of these metaphysical analyses treat *R* as a two-place predicate, which has a term as well as a foundation of inherence. They differ as to whether a co-relation property *R'* has to exist in the term of *R* and in whether *R* is really distinct from *a* or from its foundation in *a*. See my *William Ockham* (Notre Dame, IN: Notre Dame University Press, 1987), ch. 7, 215–276.

Cross also suggests that treating assumption as a non-mutual relation which the Divine Word is first not the term of, and then the term of, without any real change in the Divine Word Itself, is to count assumption among the merely external relations (like "shorter than" or "to the right of"). Because no real change in the Divine Word is involved, this would – Cross claims – skate too close to Docetism (the heresy that Christ was not really Himself human but only appeared human) (*The Metaphysics of the Incarnation*, ch. 9, 215).

But, once again, Scotus regards relations as two-place predicates, as involving both a *foundation* which is or is in one of the relata and a *term*. Suppose Socrates and Plato are similar in being white. According to Scotus, Socrates' similarity inheres in its foundation (Socrates' whiteness), but it is "towards" Plato who is the term of that relation, with the result that Socrates is similar *to* Plato. By contrast, whiteness inheres in Socrates but is not *towards* anything; that is why it is a one-place predicate! Likewise, the assumed human nature is the foundation of a real relation of ontological dependence, which inheres in the human nature but is *towards* the Divine Word. Cross' criticism refuses to take seriously Scotus' idea that being the term of a relation of ontological dependence would be enough for characterization (so that it is true to say *both* that the assumed human nature depends on the Divine Word *and* that the Divine Word supports or sustains or supposits the human nature) even if no co-relation really inhered in the term itself.

Although this idea of non-mutual relations was widely accepted among medieval Aristotelians, anyone who – like Swinburne – denied immutability and impassibility to be essential to Godhead could allow that the Divine Word acquires a new relation of assuming when it assumes the human nature. Nor would this necessarily renew their worry about the fusion of natures, for it is one thing to suppose that human nature inheres in by actualizing a potency in Divinity or Divinity inheres in by actualizing a potency in humanity. It is another to suppose that Divinity is first not inhered in and then inhered in by the co-relative of the ontological dependence relation in the human nature – that is, by the relation of sustaining or supporting or suppositing the human nature.

What is key is that the ontological dependence relation that Scotus identifies be sufficient for characterization. Scotus says that it is: the ontological dependence of whiteness on Socrates suffices for the truth of "Socrates is white," and the ontological dependence of the human nature on the Divine Word would suffice for the truth of "The Divine Word is human" and be enough to license the further credal predications: "born of the Virgin Mary, suffered under Pontius Pilate, was crucified, dead, buried, but rose on the third day."

4.2. *Characterization and contradiction*

No sooner is characterization secured than the contradiction problem raises its head. Indeed, it might seem that Christology is trapped in a dilemma: either the Divine Word and the human nature are united enough for characterization – in which case the Divine Word is the subject of contradictory properties simultaneously, or they aren't united enough for characterization – in which case Nestorianism seems to follow.[26]

Limited denomination? Traditional Christology requires that the Divine Word and the human nature be joined in such a way that

---

[26] Cross, *The Metaphysics of the Incarnation*, ch. 8, 192–199.

the Divine Word can be characterized from it. But the traditional tag – *communicatio idiomatum* or sharing of the predicates – was recognized early on not to mean that whatever is truly predicable of the ontologically dependent thing is truly predicable of that on which it ontologically depends. (i) This is trivially true, since the ontologically dependent thing is ontologically dependent on its subject, but the subject is not ontologically dependent on itself as on a subject. (Ontological dependence is not a reflexive relation: a thing may be independent, but nothing can be ontologically dependent on itself!) Likewise, the assumed nature is really distinct from the Divine Word, but the Divine Word is not really distinct from Itself. (ii) More substantively, neither the essence nor the definition of the ontologically dependent thing would be truly predicated of its subject. Whiteness is essentially a color and a quality, but Socrates is not essentially or otherwise a color or a quality. What is true is that by virtue of the ontological dependence of whiteness on Socrates, Socrates is denominated from these, so that Socrates is colored and Socrates is qualified. (iii) Again, the origination properties of the ontologically dependent thing are not thereby truly predicated of the subject on which it depends. Socrates' whiteness may begin to be at t_m, but it does not follow that Socrates begins to be at t_m. But Socrates is denominated from this origination property, so that it is true that Socrates begins to be white at t_m.[27]

All the same, these more technical observations do not seem to address the cases most important for Christology: that the Divine Word walked and talked, touched and spat, was ignorant of the day and the hour, suffered within the frame of a finite consciousness, was

---

[27] This might be enough to defuse the worries raised by Morris about the putative contradiction between "God is eternal" and "The human nature begins to be at c. 4 BCE." Morris' own strategy is to extract origination properties from the substance-kind essences and relocate them in the individual essences. But Morris' move runs counter to Aristotelian intuitions according to which it is the substance-kind that explains the individual's origination (or lack thereof) and duration (*The Logic of God Incarnate*, ch. 3, 56–62, ch. 4, 71–72).

possessed of a mind that could be "blown," whose meaning-making functions could be brought at least temporarily to a halt by the pain and degradation of crucifixion.

Qualifying the assertions: One ancient and honorable way to handle the Contradiction Problem is to explain that it is *qua* Divine that God the Son is eternal but *qua* human that He is born of a virgin, *qua* Divine that God the Son is omniscient but *qua* human that He does not know the day or the hour. Recent philosophers[28] cast suspicion on these moves, however. Without further metaphysical underpinnings it is easy to reduce to an absurdity. Why could we not equally well claim that "*x* is a round square" is not contradictory even though it implies that "*x* is a figure without angles and *x* is a figure with four right angles," because really "*x qua* round is without angles and *x qua* square has four right angles," and angleless pertains primarily to round while four-times-right-angled pertains primarily to square?

Medievals probed how the "*qua*" should be understood to function and distinguished three principal ways. (1) *Reduplication*: Strictly, they held that in statements of the form "*x qua G* is *F* " the "*qua G*" functions to give the reason why the predicate *F* attaches to the subject *x*. Accordingly, such propositions were expounded by something like the following: "*x* is *F* and *x* is *G* and all *G*s are *F*." Thus, "Socrates *qua* human is rational" is true, while "Socrates *qua* white is rational" is false, because all humans but not all white things are (necessarily) rational. *Qua*-propositions reduplicatively construed are of no help with the Contradiction Problem in Christology, however, because "*x qua G* is *F* " entails "*x* is *F*." On a reduplicative analysis, "The Divine Word *qua* Divine is omniscient" and "The Divine Word *qua* human is ignorant of the day and the hour" entail "The Divine Word is omniscient and yet ignorant of the day and the hour."

(2) *Specification*: Less properly, the *qua*-clause is taken to qualify the subject term *x*, by "distracting" it from standing for the whole

---

[28] Morris, *The Logic of God Incarnate*, ch. 2, 38–39, and Cross, *The Metaphysics of the Incarnation*, ch. 8, 205.

and making it stand instead for the named part (the *G* in "*qua G*") of which the predicate *F* is literally true. Consider the ancient example "the Ethiopian is white with respect to his teeth." Taken specifica-tively, "with respect to his teeth" distracts the subject term – "the Ethiopian" – from standing for the whole Ethiopian to standing instead for his teeth, which are literally and truly white. Likewise, in "Christ *qua* Divine is omniscient," the subject term stands for His Divine nature or for the Divine Word which is really the same as the Divine nature, while in "Christ *qua* human does not know the day or the hour" the subject term stands for His humanity. When the qualification is taken specificatively, the inference "x *qua* G is F; therefore x is F" is invalid. Contradiction is averted: it will not fol-low from "the Ethiopian is white with respect to his teeth" that the Ethiopian is white; and it will not follow from "Christ *qua* Divine is omniscient and Christ *qua* human does not know the day or the hour" that Christ is omniscient and Christ is not omniscient.

To apply the specificative analysis to the Christological proposi-tions is to treat Christ as a whole made up of really distinct parts, which can serve as really distinct subjects of the contradictory prop-erties. The trouble here is the same as that for mere aggregation: the specificative interpretation threatens to remove contradiction at the expense of characterization, for it is not generally true (indeed is very often false) that a property truly predicable of one part is truly predicable of another part or of the whole of which it is a part. Yet, *God*, the Divine Word, is supposed to be the One Who is not only omniscient, but ignorant of the day and the hour![29]

This difficulty did not escape medieval attention. Aquinas and Scotus both distinguish two kinds of cases. (i) Sometimes a predicate *F* applies to a part *P* where the predicate *F* is the type of predicate that could also apply to other parts or to the whole *W* of which *P* is a part. For example, the table leg might weigh two pounds, but weight is a property that pertains to the other legs, to the table top, and to

---

[29] Cross, *The Metaphysics of the Incarnation*, ch. 8, 192–199.

the whole table. Thus, one can't infer from the fact that the table leg weighs two pounds that the whole table weighs two pounds. (ii) But there are other cases in which a predicate F applies to a part P (a) where P is the precise or only part of W to which F could apply, or (b) where P is the principal part by virtue of which F would apply to the whole.

For an example of (ii.a), hair is the only part of Socrates that could be literally blond. Aquinas says, because of this, Socrates' having blond hair makes it at least figuratively true that (the whole) Socrates is blond. Analogously, since Christ's human soul is His only part that could be ignorant of the day and the hour (because the Divine Word is *essentially* omniscient), it is at least figuratively true that (the whole) Christ is ignorant of the day and the hour. This way, we can have *figurative* characterization without contradicting the literal truth that Christ is omniscient.[30]

For an example of (ii.b), Aquinas and Scotus identify the heart or the chest as the principal subject of health. Aquinas is willing to say that Socrates is figuratively healthy because his heart/chest is healthy. But Scotus is willing to allow that – if the heart/chest were really the principal or only relevant part – we might even say that Socrates is *literally* healthy because his heart/chest is healthy.[31] Scotus does not find this much help with the Christological characterization problem, however, because neither the human nature nor the human soul is Christ's principal part. These observations would not allow us to infer from "Christ *qua* human is ignorant" or "Christ *qua* human is a creature," that Christ is ignorant or that Christ is a creature.[32] Likewise, with "an Ethiopian is white with respect to his teeth": "whiteness" is apt to pertain to other body parts (e.g., skin) as much as to teeth, so that whiteness in the teeth is not sufficient

---

[30] Allan Bäck, "Scotus on the Consistency of the Incarnation and the Trinity," 86. Aquinas' example is "curly" but that doesn't work as well in English (*Summa Theologica* III, q. 16, a. 8).

[31] Scotus, *Op.Ox.* III, d. 11, q. 2, n. 6; Wadding VII.247.   [32] Ibid.

to make it appropriate to call the Ethiopian as a whole white. By contrast, skin might seem to be his principal colored part, by virtue of whose blackness it would be appropriate to say that the Ethiopian is black.[33]

(3) *Qualifying the predicate term*: The remaining alternative is to let the *qua*-clause qualify the predicate term. Scotus says that the *qua*-phrase distracts the predicate term: on this analysis, the predicate in "the Ethiopian is white with respect to his teeth" is not "white" but "white-toothed."[34] Likewise, in "Socrates is blond with respect to his hair" the predicate is not "blond" but "blond-haired." In "Christ *qua* human is a creature," the predicate would be "created human," and "Christ *qua* human is a creature" would not entail "Christ is a creature."[35] In general, "the Divine Word is *F-qua*-Divine and not-*F-qua*-human" seems both to keep characterization and to avoid contradiction! Was this not the desired result?

In his book *The Metaphysics of Christology*, Richard Cross remains dubious. On this analysis, where the *qua*-clause is taken to qualify the predicate term, it turns out that, in "the Ethiopian is white with respect to his teeth" and "Socrates is white," different predicates are asserted of the Ethiopian and of Socrates, for the Ethiopian is said to be white-toothed, while Socrates is said to be white *simpliciter*. Likewise, Christ or the Divine Word will be said to be humanly ignorant, while Peter and Paul are ignorant *simpliciter*. Christ or the Divine Word will be denominated from the assumed nature, but the same predicates will not be true of the Divine Word as of mere humans. Cross charges that this is theologically inadequate, because Chalcedon asserts that "our Lord Jesus Christ . . . is the same (*homoousios*) with us as to His manhood."

Cross worries that two-natures Christology is locked in yet another destructive dilemma:

[33] Scotus, *Op. Ox.* III, d. 11, q. 2, n 4; Wadding VII.1.246.
[34] Scotus, *Op. Ox.* III, d. 11, q. 2, n. 3; Wadding VII.1.246.
[35] Scotus, *Op.Ox.* III, d. 11, qq. 2–5; Wadding VII.1.246–247.

Either [a] the *qua*-phrase distracts the subject or [b] it qualifies the predicate.

If [a] it distracts the subject [to the human nature itself], then [c] the human-nature predicates aren't predicated of the same subject as the Divine-nature predicates [viz., the Divine Word].

If [b] it distracts the predicate term, then [d] the Divine Word doesn't have the same predicates predicated of It through Its human nature as we do through our human nature.

Each of [c] and [d] fails to conform to the requirements of Chalcedon.

Both ways [e] the simple literal predication of the human nature property of Christ and/or the Divine Word is ruled out – which also fails to conform to the requirements of Chalcedon.[36]

My own reply is that Chalcedon's demand that Christ be *homoousios* with the Father with respect to Godhead and *homoousios* with us as to His manhood does not require the simple predication of the human nature or the predicates that flow from it. It takes a brief metaphysical excursus to grasp what I have in mind.

Metaphysical refocussing: Arguably, semantics presupposes metaphysics; putative truth conditions vary with ontological commitments. Metaphysical revision might dictate a change in the semantics as well. Medieval Latin school theologians have modified Aristotle by endorsing

(T10) it is metaphysically possible for a primary substance x that is essentially of substance-kind K also to possess/be/come to be of substance kind K' (where K is not the same as K') contingently and non-essentially.

For them, the flip side of this claim is that

(T13) it is metaphysically possible for any creatable substance nature to be ontologically dependent upon something else as its subject.

[36] Cross, *The Metaphysics of the Incarnation*, ch. 8, 204–205.

In the *Categories*, Aristotle advances individual substance things as necessarily primary substances, the ultimate subjects which it is metaphysically impossible to subject to (in the sense of ontologically dependent upon) anything else. Aquinas, Scotus, and Ockham concede that Aristotle not only captures the way things for the most part are. He gives a correct analysis of the metaphysical default position: apart from Divine intervention, individual substance natures will be primary substances and no creature has power to subject them to (make them ontologically dependent upon) anything else. But they reasoned that the case of Incarnation reveals something about individual substance natures that Aristotle was in no position to know: viz., that each and all of them has the metaphysical possibility of being subjected to (made ontologically dependent upon) something else by Divine power. Ockham went on explicitly to draw the conclusion that not only Divine persons, but each and every created individual substance (e.g., Socrates, Beulah the cow, Brownie the donkey, Fido the dog), has the metaphysical possibility of being an "alien" supposit for a created individual substance nature of another kind.[37]

My suggestion is that these metaphysical revisions complicate our semantics. Once it is claimed that not only Aristotelian accidents but individual substance natures can be ontologically dependent, once it is admitted that alien supposition is possible, then one has

---

[37] For a more detailed discussion, see my "The Metaphysics of the Incarnation in Some Fourteenth Century Franciscans," in *Essays Honoring Allan B. Wolter* (Franciscan Institute Publications, 1985), 21–57, and "What's Metaphysically Special about Supposits?" *Proceedings of the Aristotelian Society* Supplementary Volume 78 (2005), 15–52. For Scotus and Ockham, these claims did not eliminate but revised Aristotle's substance/accident distinction. What for Aristotle were metaphysical necessities – that individual substance things are ultimate subjects that cannot depend on anything as on a subject, while accidents are inherent and cannot exist without depending on something as on a subject – became for Scotus *natural* aptitudes – individual substances have a natural aptitude to be unsubjected ultimate subjects and accidents have a natural aptitude to inhere in another as in a subject – and for Ockham metaphysical defaults which could not be obstructed by any created power but only by Divine power.

to relativize the predicates to the substance nature in question: not just "*x* is *F*" but "*x* is *F qua N*." Where *N* is the nature that *x* cannot exist without, then "*x* is *F qua N*" collapses into/entails "*x* is *F*." But where *x* is an alien supposit of *N*, "*x* is *F qua N*" does not entail "*x* is *F*." Suppose God caused Socrates to assume a bovine nature. From "Socrates is rational *qua* human" we could infer "Socrates is rational *simpliciter*" because Socrates is essentially human. But from "Socrates is not rational *qua* bovine" we could not infer "Socrates is not rational *simpliciter*" because Socrates is not essentially a cow but only an alien supposit of the bovine nature. Socrates would really share the same substance-kind – bovinity – with Beulah. Both Socrates and Beulah would be cud-chewers *qua* bovine. But Socrates would not share with Beulah the predicate "cud-chewer *simpliciter*" because of the way Socrates possesses bovinity.

Likewise, "the Divine Word is omniscient *qua* Divine" entails "the Divine Word is omniscient" because the Divine Word is essentially Divine. But "the Divine Word knows neither the day nor the hour *qua* human" does not entail "the Divine Word is ignorant *simpliciter*," because the Divine Word is an alien supposit of the human nature. This result is not un-Chalcedonian, however, because the difference between valid and invalid inferences from the *secundum quid* to *simpliciter* propositions does not reflect *the content* of the human nature predicated but the different *ways* in which Socrates and Christ have their human natures. Chalcedon requires us to attribute a real human nature – a real human body and a real human soul – to Christ. But Chalcedon also requires us to attribute them to Christ in a different way from the way we attribute them to Socrates. Qualifying the predicates captures the point that the subject *is* characterized or denominated by the nature for which it is an alien supposit. Since it is not characterized *simpliciter*, you do not get contradiction – which is the very result we want.

If one asks what I mean by "*qua*" when I say "*x* is *F qua N*," I mean that *N* is the nature by virtue of which *x* is *F*. But "by virtue of which" is ambiguous between two meanings, both of which I intend.

In some cases, N is the nature by virtue of which x is F because N entails F: e.g., "Socrates is rational *qua* human" "the Divine Word is omniscient *qua* Divine." In some cases, N is the nature by virtue of which x is F because N entails the real possibility of F. In Aristotelian metaphysics, the substance nature makes a thing of such a kind as to have accidents from various determinable ranges and not to be able to have accidents of other kinds: e.g., being an angel makes something the kind of thing that can have thoughts and choices; being a body makes something the kind of thing that can be colored. Being human makes the Divine Word the kind of thing that can eat figs, but it doesn't settle the question of whether He will actually eat figs during His earthly life.

One further point requires clarification. My soteriological plot requires *God* to perform human actions and to suffer human pain and grief in roughly the ways that the Gospels describe. It is easy to imagine, however, that since the Divine Word is essentially God the assumed human nature is like a ventriloquist's puppet which the Divine Word operates through Its Divine thought and will. Divine determinism is, of course, an ancient and honorable if controversial position in philosophical theology. Certainly, medieval Latin school theologians agreed that God creates and sustains all creatures, and concurs in the exercise of their active and passive causal powers. Certainly, the Blessed Trinity will do for Christ's human nature whatever the Blessed Trinity does for any other creature – create, sustain, and concur. What is important for present purposes is to see that our medieval Aristotelian account of hypostatic union does not, by itself, imply the determination of the Divine Word's human agency by Its Divine agency, or that the Divine Word is related to Its human agency only through the mediation of Its Divine agency. This is easier to see by considering the different example of Socrates' assuming (becoming the alien supposit for) an individual bovine nature. When Socrates chewed cud or swatted flies with his tail or became agitated at the swishing of the matador's red cape, his human nature would not *ipso facto* be engaged at all, for his human nature included no power to mobilize such bovine activities before, and acquires none with the hypostatic union. Socrates' acting and suffering through his bovine nature would be unmediated by his human nature. Socrates is the ultimate subject of bovine acting and suffering because of the ontological dependence that the individual bovine nature bears to him.[38]

5. Concluding pros and cons

In my judgment, both of the metaphysical theories just sketched – Swinburne's and the medieval modified Aristotelian one – allow for characterization without contradiction. Both bring out of the theoretical storehouse what is new and what is old.

5.1. Form over content

Distinctive of medieval Aristotelian accounts is that they establish the union between the Divine Word and the assumed human nature *metaphysically*. They do not make the union depend on anything about the content of the two substance natures. In particular, they do not make hypostatic union depend on how Godlike the human nature is or on the moral character formed or moral track record of actions performed or the cultural lifestyle lived through it. Christologies that make Jesus' status as Christ depend upon or *consist in* His being the bearer of exemplary God-consciousness (Schleiermacher) or of new being (Tillich), or His being a moral paragon or the quintessence of self-sacrifice to which a turn-of-the-twentieth-century Englishman might aspire (Temple), make systematically driven assumptions about Jesus' human nature that run beyond our evidence. They are empirically vulnerable to historical studies of

---

[38] Cross wrestles with this problem in a difficult set of reflections in *The Metaphysics of Christology*, ch. 10, 218–229.

Second Temple Judaism which might unveil Jesus' New Testament roles as something culturally much more remote from us than we thought. Medieval Aristotelian accounts explain how the metaphysical connection they envision is possible between any Divine person (some say any substance supposit) and any creatable individual substance nature, whatever its content may be. This versatility also makes the relation of hypostatic union (cashed as ontological dependence) reusable, and I intend to reuse it to account for the real presence of Christ's Body and Blood in the eucharist (see chapter 10).

Medieval Aristotelian accounts preserve flexibility by not requiring us to adopt any particular solution to the mind–body problem as it applies to human being. Given their doctrine of non-mutual relations, they do not make hypostatic union depend on Divine mutability or passibility either. Even if the real relation of assumption that inheres in the assumed nature has a corresponding co-relation (a relation of supporting or sustaining or suppositing) that inheres in the Divine Word, the resultant account of hypostatic union would not require the Divinity to be mutable or passible with respect to other more interesting non-relational properties. Thus, medieval Aristotelian accounts of hypostatic union afford the theologian systematic flexibility to let his/her conclusions about the contents of Divine and human natures be determined by other systematic desiderata, by Scriptures and the results of their historical and text-critical analysis, by reason, and by experience.

Medieval Aristotelian accounts are also strong in preserving Divine and human natures complete and *distinct without confusion*. They do not make the human soul an aspect of the Divine mind, but house it in something created and really distinct from Godhead. They assign the Divine Word a complete human nature, including both a human body and a human soul, both a human intellect and a human will. By itself, the metaphysical connection leaves it open whether and how much control the Divine agency exercises over the human agency and so in no way jeopardizes the two-wills requirement. The exact interaction between them is something for other systematic desiderata, for Scripture and ecclesial pronouncements, to decide.

Medieval Aristotelian theories do reify *individual* properties – both substance and (at least some) accident properties. Medieval Latin Christology did not require the further move of reifying universal properties, because – whatever their philosophical differences regarding the problem of universals – all agreed that it was an individual human nature, not universal human nature, that Christ assumed. Likewise, they embrace *de re* necessities. They see primary substances or substance supposits (e.g., Socrates or Beulah) as constituted by the substance properties that they have essentially. And they understand really distinct accident things (e.g., whiteness) to bear relations of ontological dependence to primary substances or substance supposits, by virtue of which the former characterize the latter (e.g., Socrates is white). So far, rightly or wrongly, they take themselves merely to be following their mentor, Aristotle.

Medieval Aristotelian theories are metaphysically innovative, insofar as they recast the Aristotelian distinction between substance and accidents, to allow individual substance natures to exist without being ultimate subjects but instead to be subjected (via an ontological dependence relation) to alien supposits. Concrete individual substance things still have a natural tendency (Scotus) or metaphysical default (Ockham) towards existing as ultimate subjects. Accidents still have a natural tendency or metaphysical default towards existing in individual substances as ultimate subjects. Not always, but for the most part, things are as Aristotle would have predicted, because these natural tendencies or defaults are obstructable only by Divine power.

5.2. *Content over form*

Swinburne's theory carries different metaphysical baggage. He begins with the ancient and honorable and philosophically familiar: with a *res cogitans/res extensa* metaphysical dualism and a mind–body dualist account of human nature. But his position packs in significant metaphysical innovations as well. Salient for Christology are his claims that many soul kinds (e.g., human and gorilla) are merely nominal essences that pertain to individual souls inessentially; kinds that individual souls can have one after another and that Divine souls can have at the same time as being Divine. Companion to these are his theological innovations, most prominently his rendering of a Social Trinity in which the Divine essence is numerically multiplied in the three Divine souls; and his understanding of Divinity as mutable and passible in a special way. Not only are Divine souls able to take the place of human souls in causing the functions of human bodies the way unmodified Word–flesh Christology claimed (a view that was condemned for confusing the natures by making Christ a hybrid). Divine souls are also able to *become human* by becoming causally interactive with human bodies in such a way as to acquire a human range of consciousness distinct from the comprehensive Divine consciousness. This way, the human suffering of Christ involves suffering in the Divine soul's human range of consciousness. Swinburne relies on his Social Trinity, on the fact that the three Divine souls share no metaphysical constituents, to avoid patripassianism. And he relies on the Divinely enforced segregation of the Divine Word's human range of consciousness from His comprehensive range of consciousness to keep the natures unconfused.

5.3. Systematic preferences

My focus on horrors leads me to agree with Swinburne that the Divine nature is mutable and passible, although ever exercising self-determination over whether and how it changes.[39] Taking a page from Hartshorne, I want to say that Divine omniscience involves God in feeling all our feelings, while Divine love for the world expresses Itself in the Trinity's experiencing God-sized grief and

---

[39] For a fuller discussion of this point, see my *Horrendous Evils and the Goodness of God*, ch. 8, 168–174.

frustration over human horror-participation. Such Trinitarian sympathy would mean that Godhead changes and is very likely acted upon. But it would not suffice for Divine solidarity with humans in horror-participation, for, however ghastly the things that we and God experience, the Divine mind cannot be "blown" by them; Divine meaning-making capacities cannot be stumped by them. God's comprehensive consciousness recontextualizes them in a field that includes joy and delight in the Divine perfections, in the Divine persons' love for one another, in cosmic excellences beyond our ken (see the YHWH speeches in Job 38–42:6). Even in the midst of horrors, Divine imagination already sees a way around them, Divine power is mobilizing ways and means to make good on them, not only globally but within the frame of each and every individual horror-participant's life. As Anselm says, Divine Wisdom doesn't start what it can't finish, and Divine Power always finishes what it starts. Put otherwise, even if Divinity is mutable and passible, the Divine Persons in Their Divine nature are not vulnerable to horrors. For God to share the horrors, God has to become a kind of thing that can be radically vulnerable to horrors. And this will require a finite range of consciousness with limited powers to cope. That is why I have claimed that Stage-I horror-defeat is accomplished by Incarnation.

Centerpiecing horrors disinclines me to mind–body dualism where human being is concerned. Swinburne's dualism makes us essentially souls, only contingently embodied and only contingently of the human kind. My diagnosis of human radical vulnerability to horrors traces our non-optimality problems to our being personal *animals, enmattered* spirits, *embodied* persons, in a material world of real and apparent scarcity. My cosmological hypothesis about God's creative purposes sees the evolution of human being as a contribution towards satisfying God's assimilative aims by personifying matter. My estimates of what it would take for universal Stage-III horror-defeat requires life after death and hence either temporary disembodied survival or temporally interrupted existence followed by resurrection (see chapter 8). These desiderata might be accommodated by a dualism that posited a sufficiently intense degree of psycho-physical causal interaction and vulnerability of mind to body. But my analysis of horrors and my experience of life leaves me convinced that embodied persons is what we *are essentially*, and to suspect that something in the neighborhood of medieval hylomorphic theories of human nature might be more apt.

If I incline to a metaphysically tighter connection between the human mind and the human body, I feel more comfortable with the medieval way of dividing Christ's minds (i.e., by making them really distinct things). For Swinburne, the independence of Christ's human from Christ's Divine way of thinking and acting is a function of how the Divine way of thinking and acting chooses to split off the human range. Swinburne's vision of Divine manipulation of the "human" affections to secure the right moral profile not only threatens the human *freedom* of Christ (this would happen as well on medieval Aristotelian theories); on his account, it also jeopardizes the *humanness* of Christ by blurring the boundaries between His human and His comprehensive Divine ranges of consciousness. Swinburne may protest that his accounts have taken care to keep them distinct enough. But I find it preferable to keep the Divine and human minds and wills of Christ distinct by identifying them with really distinct things.

6 | Learning the meanings: Christ in the hearts of all people

1. Christ in the hearts of all people

In his monumental *Atonement and Personality* (1901), R. C. Moberly insists not only that

> "[t]he meaning of Incarnation was not exhausted . . . when Jesus Christ passed away from this visible scene of mortal life," but also that it is "not more directly" "to be recognized" "in the contemplation of the Presence of the Son of Man in Heaven . . . than in the recognition of the Presence working here on earth, of the Spirit of the Incarnation and of the Incarnate" in the hearts of all His people.[1]

Moberly and others of his Anglican contemporaries (e.g., Weston, Forsyth, and Temple) were brought to this conviction by a kind of triangulation, this time among systematic desiderata on the one hand, and the testimonies of Scripture and Christian experience on the other.

(1) *Systematically*, Moberly contends against mere retributivists that "external" transactions will not win Divine–human at-one-ment apart from the "internal" transformation of alienated human beings.[2] He declares that nothing less is necessary than a change in the very meaning and significance of the word "I," in which we are "translated into the Spirit of the Crucified" in such a way that "[t]he Spirit of the Crucified, the Spirit of Him who died and is alive,"

---

[1] Moberly, *Atonement and Personality*, ch. VIII, 194–195.
[2] Moberly, *Atonement and Personality*, ch. III, 71–72, ch. VII, 138, 140, 152–153.

is "the very constituting reality of ourselves."[3] Like many turn-of-the-twentieth-century British Christologians, Moberly conceives of human non-optimality problems moralistically, beginning with a Kantian paradox about how a righteous God, Whose systematic role is to render to each his/her just deserts, can forgive sinners who don't merit pardon. Moberly slices through this puzzle by appealing to the notion of *personal identification*. Focussing first on self-identification with *principles*, Moberly insists that sin affects the whole structure of personality, insofar as the sinner identifies him/herself with sin, and so "perverts the central subject," "the essential self," and "its very character."[4] The purpose of punishment is penitence – i.e., to bring it about that the sinner renounces his/her old allegiance to sin and identifies him/herself with righteousness instead, thereby making righteousness the organizing principle of his/her personality. S/he does this to the extent that s/he accepts the pain of the punishment as meet and right in view of his/her sin.[5] Moberly can even speak of perfect penitence as involving "*a real killing out* and eliminating of the past from the present 'me'" so that the past would be *dead*.[6]

We human persons also identify ourselves with other *persons* to whom we are related by nature and love in such a way that one may be appropriately taken to speak or act or even suffer on behalf of the other. Rejecting the scholastic philosophical tradition that defined personality primarily in terms of separation or distinctness from others,[7] Moberly denies that human persons are islands or monads with no windows. Rather personality is ideally inclusive. Who we are is a function of our relations to others,[8] in interaction with whom we become more fully ourselves.[9] Moberly recognizes that

[3] Moberly, *Atonement and Personality*, ch. VII, 150–151.

[4] Moberly, *Atonement and Personality*, ch. II, 31–35.

[5] Moberly, *Atonement and Personality*, ch. I, 7–10, 22–24, ch. II, 40–41, 43, 45–46.

[6] Moberly, *Atonement and Personality*, ch. II, 35–39, 41.

[7] Moberly, *Atonement and Personality*, ch. VIII, 157.

[8] Moberly, *Atonement and Personality*, ch. IV, 87–88.

[9] Moberly, *Atonement and Personality*, ch. VIII, 176.

the identification of parents with their children may be so strong that there is a sense in which they may – by simultaneously identifying with the law of righteousness – be in a position to do penitence for their wayward children's sins. The sins of the children ascending![10]

Perfect penitence is impossible for merely human sinners: we are never able unequivocally to admit the justice of the punishments that we suffer.[11] Hence, we all need Christ, a Mediator Who is capable of simultaneous double identification: utter identification with righteousness that admits the full justice of the suffering consequent upon sin; and unflinching identification with us, a sharing of our nature out of love for us.[12] This puts Christ in a position to render perfect penitence on our behalf.[13] We appropriate the benefits of Christ's saving work the more we identify with Christ, not so that we cease to be ourselves, but so that "the Spirit of the crucified *constitutes our capacity* for responsive holiness." Indeed, Moberly claims, it is only insofar as we are "in Christ" that merely human beings can be perfected as persons. Only insofar as we are reconstituted in Christ do we have *freedom of the will* – i.e., the capacity for a perfect response of personal will and character to God. Only insofar as we are reconstituted in Christ does human reason move beyond the capacity for dialectical maneuvering towards *integrating wisdom* – wisdom which gains insight into the universal law of perfection through sacrifice, which recognizes God in Christ crucified, and which peers into the depths of the ultimate meaning of life.[14] Only insofar as we are reconstituted in Christ can our capacity for *love* be refined and purified by a progressive surrender to the Spirit of the Incarnate One.[15] Thus, for Moberly, at-one-ment is not identification through mere

[10] Moberly, *Atonement and Personality*, ch. VI, 126–128.
[11] Moberly, *Atonement and Personality*, ch. II, 31–32, 40–46.
[12] Moberly, *Atonement and Personality*, ch. V, 95, ch. VI, 126–128.
[13] Moberly, *Atonement and Personality*, ch. VI, 129–130; see also ch. IV, 80, ch. VI, 118–122.
[14] Moberly, *Atonement and Personality*, ch. IX, 236–239.
[15] Moberly, *Atonement and Personality*, ch. II, 47, ch. IX, 245–246.

admiration or imitation, but rather the reconstitution of our very persons – "Christ in us; ourselves realized in Christ."[16]

(2) Moberly finds his soteriological plot, his account of the personal dynamics of atonement, amply confirmed – indeed, in the first instance, suggested – by *Scripture*. John 14–17 construes Christ's lifelong identification with righteousness in terms of His unqualified obedience to the Father, so much so that Christ is a perfect expression of the will and character of God.[17] Thus, the center of Christ's human life was never in Himself but in His Father, without nursing any separateness of self.[18] Christ as human was the willing exposition, reflection, of His Father.[19] The thrust of so many of Jesus' Johannine discourses is "I do only what the Father tells me to do, say only what the Father tells me to say." "I-not-I-but-the-Father" is the essential inclusive structure of Christ's own self.[20] Moreover, this submission of will is nurtured by personal communion through continual prayerfulness.[21] Likewise, Moberly insists, both the Johannine corpus and the other New Testament letters speak of Christ or His Spirit abiding with or indwelling us disciples who pray without ceasing and obey His commandments, so that the meaning of the word "I" is transformed into "I-not-I-but-Christ."[22]

(3) *Christian experience* also bears witness. Thus, P. T. Forsyth identifies the "evangelical experience" as that of the "*recreation* of one's inmost self by Christ," in which "my contact with Christ is not merely visionary" but "moral, personal, and mutual." So far from a temporary and transient connection, or a momentary, once-for-all "zap," "Christ *becomes* my moral life; He has *possessed* me as His absolute property." Because the very Christ Who died in Jerusalem

---

[16] Moberly, *Atonement and Personality*, ch. XI, 286.

[17] Moberly, *Atonement and Personality*, ch. V, 99–102, ch. VI, 111–112.

[18] Moberly, *Atonement and Personality*, ch. V, 99.

[19] Moberly, *Atonement and Personality*, ch. V, 107.

[20] Moberly, *Atonement and Personality*, ch. VI, 99–101, 107.

[21] Moberly, *Atonement and Personality*, ch. V, 101.

[22] Moberly, *Atonement and Personality*, ch. VIII, 169, 173, 204–205.

becomes the (hopefully) permanent director of the functioning of my personal being, "[t]hat *centre* from which I act (and therefore am real), meets, in a way decisive for all life, with Christ in His act on the cross." "In this experience of transformation I experience Christ as my *creator*, as the author as well as the object of my faith."[23]

I believe that Moberly, Forsyth, Weston, and Temple were substantially correct in concluding that personality is inclusive, and that Christian conversion makes Christ the center of the believer's personality. But – because I find Moberly's moral categories lame when it comes to understanding horrendous evils and their consequences – I need to recontextualize this idea of at-one-ment in Christ within my own soteriology. Moreover, central to their vision is their swelling conviction that – ideally – personality is not exclusive, dividing one from another, but inclusive. Trying to understand this will force further consideration of the psychology and the metaphysics of personality (see chapters 4 and 5).

2. Reassessing the damage

Viewing human non-optimality problems through the lens of horrendous evil – as much as from the angle of Kant's paradox of forgiveness – drives the conclusion that their remedy involves changes both outside and within. Horror-defeat demands alterations on the outside. Stage-I defeat is accomplished by God-with-us, taking to Godself a human nature, identifying with our participation in horrors throughout His human career, culminating in His death on the cross. Stage-III defeat is won by God the Re-creator, transforming, replacing us in a new environment, a new heaven and a new earth, a utopia better than Eden, where the consequences of mistaken choices

---

[23] Forsyth, *The Person and Place of Jesus Christ*, ch. VII, 197–198, 201.

would not be amplified in horrendous proportions (see chapter 8). But everyone agrees that human non-optimality problems – that both the human condition and Divine–human relations are non-optimal – will not be solved without *changes on the inside*: in the language of Ezekiel 18:31, new hearts for each and every human being (on my scheme, crucial for Stages II and III).

2.1. Desperate emergency or chronic condition?

Prima facie life-ruinous as it is, actual horror-participation creates the meaning-making emergency, which stuns and often damages our meaning-making capacities beyond our natural capacities to repair. But this is symptomatic of the general underlying vulnerability of personal animality. Tying personality to an animal life cycle means that the task of organizing our subjective worlds in relation to the outside world is repeatedly thrust upon immature powers, which are unequal to the task. At first, the organism probes blindly and instinctively; when it reaches a level of consciousness, its successive hypotheses ever oversimplify the data (from inside and outside its own organism) within its psychic field. The mind makes its task more nearly manageable by enforcing a conscious/unconscious divide. Our affective responses are both "informed" by our oversimplified and caricaturing pictures of the world and/or issue from the unconscious, so that in multiple senses we "know not what we do." Moreover, despite our evolution through various developmental stages, earlier and cruder pictures along with their distorted responses become entrenched, are ready and waiting to "kick in" when our situation seems dire. With what reserve, then, does Augustine remark that ignorance and difficulty beset every sinful soul! *The consequence is that we humans need not only emergency assistance to recover from the crisis of actual horror-participation, but a helper, a companion, and a teacher to enable, guide, and work with us all along.*

2.2. *Design flaw or Divine deliberation?*

My cosmological hypothesis allows me to give such necessity a positive spin, to view it not as a design flaw, but as an integration of God's unitive and assimilative aims. A God Who wanted matter to be as Godlike as possible while still being itself might prioritize *independence* as a dimension of imitation. We might expect such a God to make an Aristotelian universe in which created natures consist of packages of powers that operate always-or-for-the-most-part to reach their resultant end. No special Divine intervention – over and above creation, conservation, and general concurrence – would be required for earth to seek its center or fire to heat nearby combustibles. Nor would further Divine assistance be needed for normal human functioning – for us to formulate and apply general principles and exercise our capacities for free choice. Our current predicament, which is much further from optimal, would have to be and traditionally was accounted for in terms of some cosmic disaster – viz., Adam's fall.

Yet there are plenty of reasons for thinking that God might not prioritize independence. Certainly, medieval philosophical theology offers us a God Whose Divine functions are exercised independently of any causal influence or assistance from creatures. But that does not make Divine functioning utterly independent, insofar as the Divine persons necessarily function in consort with one another. Western Trinitarian theology understands the Divine persons so to co-inhere that there is one action, one will *ad extra*. More than independence, God might want personal creatures to imitate Trinitarian co-inherence, and so deliberately design us for *functional* collaboration with Godself. Such assimilation would serve God's unitive aim. Not only would God join Godself to creation via hypostatic union with an individual human nature. Not only would God act together with every secondary cause in the production of its effect. God would insinuate Godself into the intimate personal functioning of every human being. Whether or not noticed and consciously engaged, God would be a senior partner in our efforts to harmonize the material and spiritual dimensions of ourselves and to make positive sense out of our lives.

This idea is not novel. Augustine asserts that human nature is "designed" to require an "Inner Teacher" to grasp the immutable truths of ethics and mathematics, and – by extension – the essences of created natural kinds. Bonaventure agrees that God must illumine our intellects to disclose such *a priori* truths and to furnish the standards for our value judgments. Human thought and evaluation are so God-infested that in the *Itinerarium* Bonaventure wonders aloud how any human being can fail to be aware of it. In between, Anselm seems to make Divine inputs the trigger of *intellectual imagination*. In the *Monologion*, and yet more explicitly in the *Proslogion*, Anselm questions God from many and various angles; there follows Divine disclosure which he must struggle to articulate and which clarifies by reframing the puzzling material. Anselm then questions and disputes these results, then waits for another Divine disclosure which reconfigures, complexifies, and integrates the conceptual field.[24] For these thinkers, Divine illumination does not interfere or interrupt; neither does it miraculously furnish what natural but malfunctioning powers were supposed to supply. Rather, Divine illumination is a piece of the natural process, and the highest human functioning involves the active collaboration of God. They speak of the Divine partner as "within" because these inputs are intellect-to-intellect, unmediated by the senses, and over and above anything that could be derived from what the senses supply.

My proposal generalizes Anselm's picture – of the Divine gadfly collaborating with humans to conceive and give birth to imaginative reconfiguration – to the more comprehensive human function of

---

[24] For a fuller discussion of Anselm's method, see my articles "*Fides Quaerens Intellectum*: St. Anselm's Method in Philosophical Theology," *Faith and Philosophy* (October 1992), 409–435, and "Praying the *Proslogion*," in *The Rationality of Belief and the Plurality of Faith*, ed. Thomas Senor (Ithaca, NY: Cornell University Press, 1995), 13–39.

meaning-making, to the construction of the human agent's subjective world, and hence to the structure of his/herself.

3. *Functionally* inclusive personality

When Moberly and Weston, Forsyth and Temple, speak of *inclusive* personality, they are conscious of moving away from remote and recent historical understandings of the term. I have noted (in chapter 5) how – on the medieval metaphysical front – Boethius, in his theological treatises on Trinity and Christology, makes a stab at philosophical precision by appealing to Aristotle's distinction between second substances (substance-kinds) and first substances (or individuals) to define "person" as "an individual substance of a rational nature." Later school theologians saw a need to distinguish between individual substance natures (e.g., this humanity or that bovinity) and substance individuals (e.g., Socrates or Beulah), so as to allow that the Divine Word assumed an individual human nature, but not an individual human being. Richard of St. Victor responded to the further worry that "individual" might be ambiguous between "numerically unmultipliable" and "unsharable." Socrates and Beulah are both. But both the Divine essence and Christ's individual human nature are numerically unmultipliable, yet sharable (among the three persons of the Trinity on the one hand, and with an external supposit on another). For Richard, precision requires us to say that persons are not only numerically unmultipliable but also altogether unsharable.[25] Metaphysically speaking, you can't – and this was Richard's intention – get any more exclusive than that!

Likewise on the psychological front, I have reviewed how turn-of-the-twentieth-century British Christologians were inclined to conceive of the unity of Christ's person in terms of a single center of consciousness, of some ego to serve as the underlying subject of His

[25] Richard of St. Victor, *La Trinité/De Trinitate* IV, chs. XVI–XIX, 262–272.

thoughts and choices throughout His Gospel career (see chapter 4). In pressing their contrary case – that the essence of personality is not to divide, cut off, or separate, but to relate and include – Moberly and Forsyth allow their language to shift from images of *how something works*, over into *what it is*. Thus, once again, P. T. Forsyth speaks of the "evangelical experience" as that of the "*recreation* of one's inmost self by Christ," in which "Christ *becomes* my moral life; He has *possessed* me as His absolute property." Christ becomes "[t]hat *centre* from which I act *(and therefore am real)*" so that "I experience Christ as my *creator*, as the author as well as the object of my faith."[26] Likewise, Moberly talks about identification with principle as shaping the "very character" of "the essential self," and of penitence as "a real killing out of the past from the present 'me.'"[27] Again, Moberly explains that "the Spirit of the crucified becomes *the very constituting reality* of ourselves."[28]

At one level, this blurring of the line between psychology and metaphysics is appropriate, since it can belong to *the nature* of the personal – just as much as to that of Aristotelian fire or sheep – that it normally functions and/or develops in a certain way. Moreover, claims about *natural* functioning are logically independent of other metaphysical issues – e.g., about how to distinguish individual natures or supposits that share a nature, or whether the persons involve a substrate ego or are instead reducible to bundles, streams, or aggregates of experiences and interactions. I will save the latter for the last two sections of this chapter, in order to focus now on the proposal that personality is *functionally* inclusive, at levels both human and Divine.

Human experience and aspirations motivate the idea – that one cannot be a psychological-sense person in isolation – from a variety of angles.

[26] Forsyth, *The Person and Place of Jesus Christ*, ch. VII, 197–198, 201.
[27] Moberly, *Atonement and Personality*, ch. II, 31–39.
[28] Moberly, *Atonement and Personality*, ch. VII, 150–151.

3.1. Child development

Developmental psychologists make clear that these claims are true of human personality in its beginnings. Human beings are born with a capacity to be personal (by contrast with rocks, oak trees, and mice), but this capacity has to be evoked by a personal context, usually that of the adult caretaker who draws that potency into act. In many and various ways, the adult caretaker enfolds the infant with tender-loving-care. In the beginning, the infant's psychic field is a booming, buzzing confusion, which sets the organism to groping instinctively for some organizing principle. At the age of three months, the infant "imprints" on the human face, usually that of the adult caretaker, and uses it as the focus around which to organize its psychic field. This stage can be referred to as the stage of *"semi-differentiation."* The child differentiates the face out of the psychic field which is its subjective self, and so is able to make the face the organizing principle. But the face can serve this function only because it is an item within that psychic field which is thus organized. So it is clear that the child's emerging consciousness is "inclusive" of another who orders its world. The adult caretaker talks to the child, treats its gurgles as communication, positively reinforces some sounds rather than others, eventually teaches it to speak. With smiles and frowns, praise and "nos," s/he teaches the toddler how to behave in a "civilized" manner. These personality-forming influences begin before the child has any self-consciousness at all. Although they *enable* the child to become self-conscious, they themselves remain permanently, partially unconscious from the child's point of view. Feral children who survive in the wilderness and "imprint" on animals (or in locked closets where they fail to "imprint" on anyone) do not actualize this capacity to be personal. If personality is inclusive at the beginning, it is normally and naturally relational throughout. Because no mere human can be everything to anyone, many different types of relationships will be required over a lifetime to bring out the full dimensions of an individual's personality. Once personality is evoked, individuals can remain personal in isolation for extended periods. But if this continues too long, they become "peculiar" and in some cases (e.g., solitary-confinement torture chambers) may "lose it" so that their ability to function as persons is seriously impaired.

3.2. Ideals of friendship

Likewise, for adulthood and maturity, ancient ideals advertise friendship as another way in which one psychological-sense person may include others. Giving elegant expression to ideas that were "in the air," Cicero argues in *De amicitia* that, insofar as human beings are political animals, they/we have a natural tendency towards connection, towards intimacy and affection, with others. Likewise, they/we have an inclination to generosity, to benevolence and charity, towards our fellow human beings.[29] Nature may set up a preference for blood relatives and fellow citizens as opposed to strangers and foreigners, but good men are attracted to nothing so much as the virtues of others.[30] Ideally, friendship is between persons already advanced in virtue, between whom there can be such harmony of outlook and values[31] that we could say there was "one soul in two bodies."[32] Insofar as ancient ethics tends to subsume virtue under the general rubric of self-sufficiency, this can sound as if there are two "atomic" virtuous individuals that reach out in friendship after the fact. The more usual case is of two persons stabilized in a certain bent, wanting to grow in a certain direction; persons who are so agreed that each can be alter ego to the other, to act on behalf of the other, to give the other constructive criticism and advice to growth towards their common goal.[33] Such intensity of shared purpose and affection trusts without reservation, supports without hesitation,[34] loves the other more

[29] Cicero, *De amicitia*, ch. V, 19–20, ch. XXIII, 88.
[30] Cicero, *De amicitia*, ch. VIII, 27–28, ch. XIV, 50, ch. XXI, 81.
[31] Cicero, *De amicitia*, ch. IV, 15, ch. VI, 20.   [32] Cicero, *De amicitia*, ch. XVII, 61.
[33] Cicero, *De amicitia*, ch. XVI, 56–57, 59, ch. XXII, 83.
[34] Cicero, *De amicitia*, ch. XVIII, 65–66.

than self,[35] creates such a depth of understanding as to put the one in a position to act and speak on behalf of the other. Collaborative relationships of this sort are ideally permanent, to be ended only if one partner turns to vice, and then to be unraveled rather than broken, to be burned out (like a candle) rather than stamped out.[36] Friendship is thus an end itself, one of the great joys of life.[37] And if paradigm friendship is between peers, *mutatis mutandis*, analogical relations can occur between ruler and subject (e.g., God and creatures),[38] teacher and student (e.g., Jesus and the disciples), parent and child.[39]

4. Projecting the analogies

At the functional level, these models furnish fruitful analogies for conceptualizing Godhead, Divine–human relations, and Christ's mediating role.

4.1. *Cosmic friendship*

With Cicero's model multiply applied, the whole universe is envisioned as a society of friends, with Christ as center. The Holy Trinity is a paradigm of mutually inclusive personality. Richard of St. Victor argues that Godhead must be a triune because Divine perfection demands friendship and friendship requires it, for tradition insists that God is all-powerful, of immeasurable wisdom and goodness. Yet – Cicero articulates it – the heart of goodness is charity and benevolence, happiness and joy. Charity is always other-directed and

---

[35] Cicero, *De amicitia*, ch. XVI, 56–59, ch. XXII, 82.

[36] Cicero, *De amicitia*, ch. XXI, 76–78.

[37] Cicero, *De amicitia*, ch. VI, 22, ch. IX, 29, 31–32, ch. XIV, 49, ch. XXVII, 102.

[38] Julian of Norwich comments on God's friendly welcome to us in heaven, in her *Revelations of Divine Love*, ch. 14, 85, ch. 39, 120–121, ch. 40, 121.

[39] Cicero, *De amicitia*, ch. XIX, 69–70, 71–73, ch. XX, 73.

so involves the will to love another and the will that the other be loved as oneself.[40] Benevolence acts to share benefits; perfect benevolence shows itself in such largeness of spirit that would hold nothing back.[41] Since omnipotence is able to share infinite abundance,[42] it would be shameful for God to keep it to Godself; God's greatest glory would be to share it.[43] Outward-bound charity is needed for highest happiness; the mutuality of shared love for highest joy.[44] But God would not give the full measure of Divine riches to anyone unworthy of them; neither would Divine benevolence bestow them on anyone unable to contain them. Only another Divine person would be an appropriate recipient.[45] Because there cannot be more than one Divine essence, their equality involves literal sharing of essence.[46] And the relationship involves paradigmatic permanence. Thus Divine Goodness "twins" itself[47] to share the riches of its greatness in a community of majesty.[48] Nevertheless, Divine Goodness consummates charity only when the two produce a third, a common love-object, so that they can share in loving the very same thing – so that their sharing may be unrestrained.[49]

Borrowing from Richard, Bonaventure goes on to emphasize that God the Son is the center, both fruit and fruit-bearer, in this fertile Trinitarian friendship. But earlier, Johannine writings (both the Gospel and epistles) made Christ the locus where Trinitarian friendship paradigmatically reaches down to humankind. Jesus and the

---

[40] Richard of St. Victor, *De Trinitate* III, ch. II, 168, ch. XI, 90.

[41] Richard of St. Victor, *De Trinitate* III, ch. IV, 174, 176, ch. VI, 178, ch. XIV, 198.

[42] Richard of St. Victor, *De Trinitate* III, ch. VIII, 182.

[43] Richard of St. Victor, *De Trinitate* III, ch. IV, 176, ch. VI, 178, ch. XIV, 198.

[44] Richard of St. Victor, *De Trinitate* III, ch. III, 172.

[45] Richard of St. Victor, *De Trinitate* III, ch. IV, 176.

[46] Richard of St. Victor, *De Trinitate* III, ch. VIII, 182, 184, ch. XIX, 186, 188, ch. XXIII, 216, ch. XXIV, 218, VI, ch. IX, 394.

[47] Richard of St. Victor, *De Trinitate* III, ch. XVII, 206.

[48] Richard of St. Victor, *De Trinitate* VI, ch. VI, 388.

[49] Richard of St. Victor, *De Trinitate* III, ch. XI, 190, 192, ch. XII, 194, ch. XIV, 200, ch. XVIII, 208, ch. XIX, 208, 210, VI, ch. VI, 388.

Father abide with, mutually indwell, one another, insofar as His perfect obedience through the mediation of His human nature constitutes the non-peer analogue of *idem velle, idem nolle*: Jesus does only what the Father gives Him to do, says only what the Father tells Him to say. This sort of friendship is transitive. Reaching down, at the end of His ministry, Jesus calls His disciples "friends," because He has initiated them into His wider outlook and program. The Paraclete will come and teach them all things, so that they will understand it (John 14:15–21; 16:12–14). Disciples who obey His/the Father's/the Paraclete's commandments will abide in His love, not only in the sense that they will enjoy Divine presence, but also in that their actions will be governed by what Divine Love purposes, so that they will have become collaborators with God (John 15:12–17; 17:11). Primary among these is the commandment that disciples love one another, to imitate Jesus in readiness to lay down life for friends (John 15:12–13; I John 2:9–11; 4:7–21).

Writing perhaps in the same year as Richard of St. Victor, Aelred of Rievaulx adapts Cicero's idealization into a portrait of spiritual friendship, and uses it to expand upon relations between Christ and the Church. Divine liberality leads God to create; Divine providence works towards the unity of the universe by endowing all creatures with a natural connection to one another. Angels were created for society among pleasant and harmonious companions, whose wills and desires agree. Humans were made for society among equals; Aelred presents Adam and Eve as the original human friends.[50] For humans a solitary life without the giving and receiving of love in friendship would be bestial[51] and devoid of happiness.[52] But Adam's fall corrupts human social inclinations. There is a cooling of charity, a rise of concupiscence, self-centeredness, and a preference for private

---

[50] Aelred of Rievaulx, *Spiritual Friendship*, Book I, 61–63.
[51] Aelred of Rievaulx, *Spiritual Friendship*, Book II, 71, 82.
[52] Aelred of Rievaulx, *Spiritual Friendship*, Book III, 110.

advantage over the common good.[53] Psycho-spiritual disorganization explains why we find ourselves in situations with conflicting loyalties, and enmeshed in puerile friendships based on inordinate attachments to sensory beauty and pleasure as unstable as passing fancies,[54] and worldly friendships born of desire for temporal advantage or possessions and fickle as the changing winds of fortune.[55] Spiritual friendships provide a shelter in which the consequences of Adam's fall can be reversed. Spiritual friendships are possible between persons committed to grow in the knowledge and love of Christ, and ascend by degrees until the friends are made one in heart and soul with Christ – *idem velle, idem nolle*.[56] Christ is friendship's pattern, laying down His life for friends.[57] Spiritual friendship is bought by love and won by competition in generosity.[58] Its currency of exchange is counsel in perplexity, consolation in adversity, prayer without ceasing, empathetic identification in grief and shame as much as in honor and joy.[59] Spiritual friendship is grounded in trustworthiness, which allows candor in confession and criticism, and opens a safe place for secrets to be aired.[60] It begins with the good, progresses among the better, is consummated among the perfect.[61] In advanced stages, it crosses over from mere virtue to spiritual zeal, to a resurrection of the spiritual senses, to shared intimacy with God.[62] In the world to come, all friends of Christ will be friends of one another, so that God will be all in all.[63] The communion with saints is love stronger than

---

[53] Aelred of Rievaulx, *Spiritual Friendship*, Book I, 63.

[54] Aelred of Rievaulx, *Spiritual Friendship*, Book II, 83.

[55] Aelred of Rievaulx, *Spiritual Friendship*, Book I, 60.

[56] Aelred of Rievaulx, *Spiritual Friendship*, Book II, 73.

[57] Aelred of Rievaulx, *Spiritual Friendship*, Book I, 58, Book II, 72–73.

[58] Aelred of Rievaulx, *Spiritual Friendship*, Book I, 60, Book II, 84–85.

[59] Aelred of Rievaulx, *Spiritual Friendship*, Book II, 84, Book III, 119, 131.

[60] Aelred of Rievaulx, *Spiritual Friendship*, Book II, 72, Book III, 111.

[61] Aelred of Rievaulx, *Spiritual Friendship*, Book II, 79.

[62] Aelred of Rievaulx, *Spiritual Friendship*, Book III, 114, 131.

[63] Aelred of Rievaulx, *Spiritual Friendship*, Book III, 132.

death,[64] and is consummated with a spiritual kiss, with such contact of the hearts' affections, such a mingling of spirits with one another and with the spirit of God, that there may be said to be one Spirit in many bodies.[65]

4.2. Universal nursery

In her *Revelations of Divine Love*, Julian of Norwich portrays Jesus/the Blessed Trinity as mother to us spiritual infants and toddlers. There is *metaphysical* mothering in that God is the ground of our being,[66] and in that we are so deeply set in God (through our utter dependence upon God for our being and well-being) that we cannot know ourselves at the core without knowing God.[67] There is also *functional* mothering. The Trinity/Jesus provides the loving personal environment in which we are always enfolded, before and whether we are actually aware of it or not. The Trinity/Jesus indwell us, make their home within us at the core of who we are.[68] The Trinity/Jesus exercise that omnipresent influence, below as well as above the level of our conscious awareness, without which our capacity to be spiritual persons could not be awakened and evolved. But the goal of spiritual life is for us to become ever more aware of and cooperative with such enfolding presence that we are best seen functionally, consciously as well as unconsciously, as only semi-differentiated.[69]

Here Julian echoes St. Paul, who speaks of the Spirit searching and groaning in us with sighs too deep for words (Romans 8:26–27; Galatians 4:6), presumably influencing us at unconscious levels of our personality; of Christ, our only true Teacher, dwelling within

---

[64] Aelred of Rievaulx, *Spiritual Friendship*, Book II, 70, Book III, 111.

[65] Aelred of Rievaulx, *Spiritual Friendship*, Book II, 75–76.

[66] Julian of Norwich, *Revelations of Divine Love*, ch. 53, 157, ch. 78, 201.

[67] Julian of Norwich, *Revelations of Divine Love*, ch. 54, 157, ch. 56, 160–161.

[68] Julian of Norwich, *Revelations of Divine Love*, ch. 1, 63, ch. 51, 149, ch. 54, 157, ch. 67, 183, ch. 81, 206.

[69] Julian of Norwich, *Revelations of Divine Love*, ch. 57, 164.

the inner human being; of our growing up into such functional collaboration that our agency is best described dialectically – I-not-I-but-Christ (Galatians 2:18–20).

5. Horrors, defeated by inclusive personality?

Such functional analogies drive home the point that personal relationships are – for better and worse – both the context and the stuff out of which personal meaning is made. They also make plausible the suggestion that God-with-us furnishing the ingredients of meaning-making and Divine assistance in reconfiguring ourselves by appropriating the meanings are not just emergency measures but the natural and normal state of affairs.

In chapter 2, I ventured the diagnosis that the radical vulnerability of personal animality to horrors arises from the fact that spirit and matter form an "odd couple" that by their natures "run interference" with each other. I agree with Julian of Norwich that the emergent capacities of human spirit are at every stage too meager to harmonize them,[70] and that this power deficit would be a design defect if human being were intended – given Divine creation and conservation – to be always-or-for-the-most-part left to its own devices. My understanding of God's purpose in creation – focussed by Divine desire to sanctify the material – motivates the hypothesis that God's design for human agency essentially involves functional collaboration with Divine agency, which has not only the wisdom, power, and resourcefulness to harmonize matter and spirit, but also the pedagogical imagination to rear us up into conscious and willing participation.

The infant/early childhood analogy reminds and helps us to understand the implications of the metaphysical size-gap, the radical incommensuration between Divine and human agency. Coercion requires approximate peerage among agents – one child with another

---

[70] Julian of Norwich, *Revelations of Divine Love*, ch. 51, 141–151, ch. 61, 172–173.

on the playground, one adult with another in the workplace. The mother's influences on her infant child cannot count as coercion, because – so far from equal – the child's personal agency isn't even formed yet. Rather, the mother's influences are needed to call the child's personal agency into being. *Mutatis mutandis* and *a fortiori*, Divine influences are not coercive but agency-enabling in relation to human beings. Moreover, this analogy calls attention to the fact that multiform Divine influence always occurs, willy-nilly, below the level of our consciousness. Willing cooperation is grown into and evoked. But – as noted contra William Temple – it can never be a matter of literal *idem velle, idem nolle*: rather it is a matter of willing/nilling what God wants us to will/nill, seeing and understanding as God wants us to see at the time.

The friendship analogy is complementary, and allows us to do a "developmental double-take" on who we are in relation to God. It reminds us that God calls us to bring our full adult capacities into the partnership; indeed that Divine-indwelling is the very environment that enables us to "stand up to our full stature in Christ." It takes seriously how Jesus counts stumble-bumbling disciples as friends, entrusts them to carry out the Kingdom platform, with the help of the indwelling Paraclete/Father, Son, and Spirit Threesome Who continue(s) to teach us all things. It reminds us that – even within His psychological-sense human personality – Jesus was a friend and teacher to His disciples, One Who out of love identified with us by sharing our nature and our radical vulnerability to horrors. It reasserts that Jesus' mature friendship with His Father is paradigmatic for ours. Once again, this means that we are called into an ever more explicit, conscious, voluntary collaboration with God, through prayer and meditation that draw us into His purpose by an unending succession of approximations.

Thus, once again, Divine assistance with making positive sense of horrors is a dramatic and emergency version of what goes on all of the time. Everywhere and always, indwelling Divine presence operates below the level of our consciousness, helping us to coordinate spirit and matter, and influencing our meaning-making processes. Superficially, experience suggests that such Divine influence is quite permissive, allowing us to attempt to organize our lives around individually and collectively destructive and self-defeating goals and principles. P. T. Forsyth identifies the "evangelical" or conversion experience with occasions in which we are conscious of being "possessed" by Christ Who establishes a thoroughgoing functional reorganization within us, placing Himself at the center.[71] Making positive sense of our actual participation in horrors will involve a series of conversions, both dramatic – subjective world upheavals of truly apocalyptic proportions, of the sort triggered by participation in horrors in the first place – and gradual.

Divine indwelling of each and every created person also bears social fruits on the outside. Divine indwelling works in each and every created person in such a way that the coordinated and harmonizing transformation of each moves towards wholesome community (I will return to this topic in the next chapter). In the manner envisaged by Aelred of Rievaulx, pairs and groups of individuals committed to growing in the knowledge and love of Christ can grow together into functional organs of Christ's Body in the world.

6. The metaphysics of psychology – logically independent issues

So far, our survey illustrates how inclusive personality as a *functional* notion is taken for granted in many traditional sources. Whether or not they use the *term* "inclusive personality," they nevertheless recognize that the functional organization of one human being's personality is more and less affected, for good and ill, by his/her interaction with other persons, human and Divine. The point I would now like to emphasize is this: the hypothesis that human personality is

[71] Forsyth, *The Person and Place of Jesus Christ*, ch. VII, 197–198, 201.

functionally inclusive is logically independent of theories to the effect that human personality is *metaphysically* inclusive; indeed the hypothesis of *functionally* inclusive personality is consistent with many different accounts of the *metaphysics* of Christology.

J. S. Lawton thinks that Moberly, Weston, Forsyth, and Temple combine functional inclusion with an "idealist" understanding of the metaphysics of personality: they have made a point of discarding Greek metaphysics and have substituted the psychological-sense person for the metaphysical-sense person in their construals of the Chalcedonian definition (see chapter 4). Their frequent slide from functional language to talk of "constituting realities" convinces Lawton that they understood persons to be metaphysically constituted by bundles of perceptions (in Humean fashion) or by streams of consciousness (à la William James) or by systems of "personal" relations, and to involve no substrate "ego" that underlies as the subject of that bundle or stream, or that serves as one term that unifies that system of relations to many others. Such an "idealist" metaphysics allows personality to be literally inclusive, insofar as there is no sufficient reason why bundles or streams or systems of relations might not overlap and include some components that are literally the same.[72]

Be that as it may, functionally inclusive personality does not require bundle- or stream-theories of the metaphysics of personality. It also fits with more Aristotelian theories (both Swinburnean and medieval; see chapter 5) which posit substances or things which are the subjects of powers to act and/or interact in various ways. Transplanted into this metaphysical context, functional inclusion becomes a hypothesis about the *content* of human nature, about what sort of powers constitute and/or flow from it. The claim would be that the human capacity for personal function is merely potential until it gets

---

[72] Lawton criticizes Weston for equivocating about the metaphysics of personhood, insofar as Weston's book is devoted to the search for the substrate ego that underlies Christ's human career, while – on Lawton's reading – defining personality in terms of a system of relations. Actually, however, Weston defines not "person" but "sphere" in terms of a system of relations.

evoked by a personal context, and so human personhood would move from potentiality to actuality in the context of many and diverse personal interactions. Actualized personality would be interactive and inclusive because partly constituted by relations, although there are relata to whom the capacity for such relations belong, whether or not the capacities are actualized, and to whom they would belong even if the capacities got actualized in different ways.

Put otherwise, metaphysical and psychological are not competing but complementary levels of analysis. If the "one-soul-in-two-bodies" ideal of ancient friendship was surely a metaphysical metaphor for a functional interaction, that paradigm *dynamic union* of the western Trinity takes the image more straightforwardly, insofar as three supposits are united in numerically one essence, and so in *metaphysically* one thought and one will (one action, one will *ad extra*). Paradigm Divine/human *dynamic union* is found between Jesus' human soul and the Father, but this dynamic union is not what Incarnation consists in. Rather, I have argued (see chapters 4–5) that it is *metaphysically grounded* in hypostatic union between the Divine Word and the individual human nature of Christ. The I-not-I-but-Christ *dynamic* union of all Christians with the Spirit of Christ is *functional*. Yet, it is a metaphysical fact, pertaining to the *nature* of human being (perhaps of created persons in general), that its smooth functioning should involve not only mind and body but the Holy Spirit of God, collaborating together to get organized, and so involve a *dynamic* union with the Spirit of God. The nature doesn't change as personal capacities pass from potency to act. Rather, the more harmoniously the dynamic union is entered into, the more *explicit* what is *implicit* in the nature becomes. When – e.g., in midlife crisis or in conversion to Christ – one dynamic organization is exchanged for another, the content of personality is so transformed that the biblical language of death and resurrection (invoked by Moberly) is still an appropriate metaphysical metaphor for a functional alteration. If so-called idealist bundle, stream, or relational theories of personhood make Moberly's talk of death and Forsyth's language of (re-)creation literally true (as segments are removed or drastically rearranged), even an Aristotelian substance theorist can recognize the *metaphysical* fact that human being cannot function smoothly apart from collaboration with a Divine agent, and can agree that changes in functional organization do constitute *real* changes in the transformed human being.[73] Moreover, an Aristotelian substance theorist can admit that dynamic union is different from and additional to both the real relation of dependence for existence in creation, and the real relation of activation (by which the unmoved mover "turns" created powers "on").

7. Appropriate economy?

My thesis is the coherence of Christology. Elegant theories achieve economy by making a single explanatory entity fill a variety of roles. Inclusive personality seems relevant Christologically, only insofar as it offers Christ another explanatory job. Certainly, Stage-II horror-defeat requires *Divine* initiative. And I have argued that Stage-II horror-defeating activities fit with an understanding of human nature that makes functional collaboration with the Divine not a rare intrusion, but a further expression of our normative design. Moreover, Moberly is right: Scripture and tradition *do* speak not only of Christ walking the roads between Galilee and Jerusalem, not only of Christ on His glorious throne in heaven, at God's right hand, but also of Christ in the hearts of all His people.[74]

Nevertheless, I have argued that no merely human powers will suffice to restore personal integrity after participation in horrors; *Divine* competencies are required for Stage-II horror-defeat. Likewise, as noted above, Scripture speaks of this Divine assistance in many ways – very often in terms of the Paraclete or Spirit, sometimes of Father, Son, and Spirit together. If the Christian God is triune,

[73] Eric Mascall stresses this point in *Christ, the Christian, and the Church*, ch. V, sec. II, 82.
[74] Moberly, *Atonement and Personality*, ch. VIII, 194–195.

why suppose it is Christ – rather than the Father, the Spirit, or the Trinity together – that dwells within the inner human being?

Moberly is sensitive to this question, and to ambiguities in the biblical term "the Spirit of Christ." Explicitly, Moberly insists that the Johannine corpus[75] does not speak of our having the Spirit *instead of* the Son; rather to have the Spirit *is* to have the Son.[76] Likewise, I John 3:24 (Christ abides in us by His Spirit) and I John *passim* speak of the abiding and indwelling of Christ.[77] Other New Testament texts also identify the Spirit of God with the Spirit of Christ – Acts 16:7 (the Spirit of Jesus); II Corinthians 3:17–18 (the Lord is the Spirit, and the Lord is the transfigured One); Galatians 4:6 (the Spirit of his Son cries "Abba, Father"); Philemon 1:19 (the Spirit of Jesus Christ), I Peter 1:10–11 (the Spirit of Christ). In any event, Moberly seems to hold to the Augustinian "one action, one will *ad extra*." He says it is not as if there are three distinct spheres of operation for the three persons. To let one's personality be organized by the One is equivalent to letting it be organized by the other.[78]

I, too, want to say that – strictly speaking – it is not one person of the Trinity *rather than* the other that indwells the hearts of all God's people. Still, even within this Augustinian tradition, some functions of the Trinity are "appropriated" to one person rather than the other. My claim is that the function of Inner Teacher should be appropriated to Christ, because Christ is the One in Whom all three stages of horror-defeat hold together. Christ effects Stage-I horror-defeat primarily through what He does and suffers in His human nature. Christ *effects* Stage-II and Stage-III horror-defeat primarily through His Divine nature but *manifests* them in His human nature. The Divine Word is the Divine person Who is operative in all three.

Christ is the One in Whom God's friendliness towards the human race is integrated. Christ is the One Who shares our human nature,

[75] John 10:30; 14:9, 16–20, 23; 16:16, 19, 22; I John 4:3; II John 9.
[76] Moberly, *Atonement and Personality*, ch. VIII, 169.
[77] Moberly, *Atonement and Personality*, ch. VIII, 204.
[78] Moberly, *Atonement and Personality*, ch. VIII, 173.

and His friendship with His disciples during His earthly career was mediated by His human personality. It is within the framework of His human personality that God especially befriends the whole human race, not least by sharing both our vulnerability to and our actual participation in horrors. Christ befriends us in a more intimate way through His Divine nature, through psychological-sense personal omnipresence and functional collaboration: I-not-I-but-Christ. "What a friend we have in Jesus!" Someone powerful and resourceful enough to trample the chaos, calm the storm of our inward dysfunction; and yet with Someone to Whom the human experience is not alien, Someone to Whom the worst has happened, Someone to Whom a human nature still belongs.

Likewise, Christ is the One in Whom God's mothering functions are united. Although Julian of Norwich can sometimes speak of Trinitarian mothering, she nevertheless declares:

> A mother's is the most intimate, willing, and dependable of all services, because it is the truest of all. None has been able properly to fulfil it but Christ.[79]

Mother Jesus creates us and joins us inseparably to Godhead forever; God the Son is Mother of our sensual nature, by taking it on Himself in the Incarnation.[80] Mother Jesus "carries us within himself in love."[81] Julian was allowed mystically to enter the wound in His side into a place "large enough for all saved mankind to rest in peace and love,"[82] like baby kangaroos in their mother's pouch. Mother Jesus bears us with the labor pangs of His suffering and death on the cross.[83] But we are never more than semi-differentiated from Mother Jesus: "our Saviour himself is our Mother for we are ever being born of him, and shall never be delivered!"[84] Where earthly mothers feed

---

[79] Julian of Norwich, *Revelations of Divine Love*, ch. 60, 169, 170.

[80] Julian of Norwich, *Revelations of Divine Love*, ch. 58, 165.

[81] Julian of Norwich, *Revelations of Divine Love*, ch. 60, 169; see also ch. 57, 163.

[82] Julian of Norwich, *Revelations of Divine Love*, ch. 24, 100.

[83] Julian of Norwich, *Revelations of Divine Love*, ch. 60, 169–170.

[84] Julian of Norwich, *Revelations of Divine Love*, ch. 57, 164.

with their own milk, Mother Jesus feeds us with Himself, and leads us to His breast through His open side.[85] Through His Divine nature, Mother Jesus "functions as a kindly nurse who has no other business than to care for the well-being of her charge,"[86] to rear us up in those virtues which will enable us to enjoy Him forever.[87] Mother Jesus guides us by His laws,[88] and sometimes punishes to correct faults.[89] Like any mother, Jesus sometimes allows His children to learn the hard way, but never allows the situation to become dangerous or life-threatening for them.[90] When we fall, it is the gracious touch of Mother Jesus that enables us to get up and try again.[91] Whenever we are frightened, whether by suffering or our own disobedience and failures, Mother Jesus wants us to run to Him at once and cling to Him forever.[92] Summing up, Julian exclaims,

> Jesus Christ who sets good against evil is our real Mother. We owe our being to Him – and this is the essence of motherhood! – and all the delightful, loving protection which ever follows.
>
> Jesus is the true Mother of our nature, for he made us. He is our Mother, too, by grace, because he took our created nature upon himself.[93]

And she invites us to find blessed assurance in those Divine–human bonds of motherly love which sin and death cannot break.[94]

---

[85] Julian of Norwich, *Revelations of Divine Love*, ch. 60, 170.

[86] Julian of Norwich, *Revelations of Divine Love*, ch. 61, 173.

[87] Julian of Norwich, *Revelations of Divine Love*, ch. 58, 166–167.

[88] Julian of Norwich, *Revelations of Divine Love*, ch. 55, 158.

[89] Julian of Norwich, *Revelations of Divine Love*, ch. 61, 171–172.

[90] Julian of Norwich, *Revelations of Divine Love*, ch. 61, 172.

[91] Julian of Norwich, *Revelations of Divine Love*, ch. 52, 153.

[92] Julian of Norwich, *Revelations of Divine Love*, ch. 61, 172.

[93] Julian of Norwich, *Revelations of Divine Love*, ch. 59, 168.

[94] Julian of Norwich, *Revelations of Divine Love*, ch. 78, 201.

7 | Cosmic coherence and the primacy of Christ: Christ, the One in Whom all things hold together

1. Christ, the One in Whom all things hold together

The letter to the Colossians celebrates the preeminence (later dubbed the "primacy") of Christ as a surprising fact of startling scope. Christ is the image of the invisible God. Christ is the first-born of all creation. Christ is before the One in Whom and through Whom and for Whom all things were created – things in heaven and things on earth, things visible and invisible. Christ is before all things, and Christ is the One in Whom all things hold together. Moreover, Christ is the One in Whom the whole fullness of God dwells bodily. Christ is the One in Whom God triumphs over the principalities and powers and makes a public example of them. Christ is the first-born from the dead. Christ is the One through Whom God reconciles all things to Himself, whether on earth or in heaven, making peace by the blood of His cross. Consequently, Christ is the head of the body, the Church, the One through Whom the whole body is nourished and knit together through its joints and ligaments, and grows with a growth that is from God. Christ is the One in Whom we have redemption, the forgiveness of sins. Christ is the One in Whom all the treasures of wisdom and knowledge are hidden. We have died, been buried with Christ in baptism; Christ is the One with Whom we have been raised, so that our life is a mystery hid with Christ in God. But when Christ Who is our life appears, we will appear with Him in glory (Colossians 1:15–20; 2:3, 9, 12, 15, 19; 3:1–4).

For the letter to the Colossians, Christ is of both cosmic and soteriological significance. Holding together in Christ has both a *metaphysical dimension* – Christ, not some merely spiritual being, is forwarded as the One Who gives the universe its metaphysical coherence – and *a psychological-sense personal or purposive dimension* – Christ is the focal center of God's cosmic purposes. The declaration – that Christ is the One in Whom all things hold together – is suggestive of *cosmic unity*, that what there is is a *uni*verse. That it is *Christ* Who is unifier and integrator also sounds the theme of *Divine immanence* in the universe, not only in the sense of God's having purposes for it (unlike Epicurean gods), but also in the sense of being metaphysically united to it.

Latin medievals followed patristic authors in taking these ideas in both familiar and unexpected ways. I will borrow from many of them in forwarding the preeminence or primacy of Christ.

2. God as One-over-many

Medieval Latin school theologians took it for granted that many things exist here below: Socrates and Plato, Brownie the donkey and Beulah the cow, Abelard's oak in the gardens at Cluny, the rock in the river that provides a stepping stone. Mostly, they gave such data of experience an Aristotelian philosophical interpretation. What there is here below is a plurality of individual substances that come in different natural kinds and get characterized by a variety of accidents. Such thinkers also made theological assumptions with philosophical ramifications: that God is really distinct from creatures, that everything other than God exists by God's free and contingent volition – among other things, that God could have refrained from creating and could at any time annihilate some or all of what God has made. These latter claims set them at odds with noted Muslim and Jewish predecessors who were persuaded by neo-Platonic schemes according to which God necessarily emanates the first, the first the second, etc., of a series of effects. Moreover, most medieval Latin Christians insisted that created personal agency is sufficiently self-determined and distinct from Divine (psychological-sense) personal agency for rational creatures to have obligations to and to be held accountable by God on Judgment Day.

Clear as they were that God had created a plurality of things really distinct from Godself and one another, medieval Latin theologians were equally unanimous that under no circumstances would God create, no way could a *universe* be constituted by, a mere heap of things. Their philosophies taught them well: a merely chaotic congeries of things is metaphysically impossible; what there is would have to be structured by causal and excellence hierarchies. Thus, Anselm, Christian Platonist that he was, believed creation to be unified by "One over Many": the Supreme Nature is the source of the being and well-being of everything;[1] a being a greater than which cannot be conceived is the metaphysical norm relative to which the Great Chain of Goodness and Being is arranged.[2] For Anselm and Aquinas, what creatable natures are, at metaphysical bottom, are ways of imperfectly imitating Divine Being and Goodness. Henry of Ghent would say that the Divine essence is the exemplar cause of any and all creatable natures. Moreover, for Aquinas, there is no best batch of creatable things, but it takes a tolerably rich diversity of creatures to make a good collective Godlikeness, and God will always impose on all God makes the best collective order of which they are capable.[3] God unifies the universe by being first mover, first efficient cause, first final cause, and the One that is all perfections through itself.[4] Likewise, Scotus argues for an infinite being that is at once

---

[1] Anselm, *Monologion*, chs. 1–4; Schmitt I.13–18.

[2] Anselm, *Proslogion*, ch. 2; Schmitt I.101–102; cf. *Monologion*, chs. 4 and 31; Schmitt I.16–18, 49–50.

[3] Aquinas, *De Potentia* q. 3, a. 16 ad 1um, 2um, and 10um.

[4] Aquinas, *Summa Theologica* I, q. 2, a. 3.

first in the essential orders of dependence (first efficient and first final cause) and first in the essential order of excellence (the most eminent being).[5] Certainly, they agreed, no matter what metaphysically possible world existed, all things would hold together in *God*!

Yet this strategy, of securing the unity of the universe by making God the unitary ultimate explainer of being and goodness and change, threatens to make God metaphysically aloof. This is because the explanatory models they deployed insisted that the ultimate explainer had to be self-explanatory with respect to being and goodness and action, from which they inferred that God was eternal, simple, immutable, and impassible. Like Platonic forms, the unitary ultimate explainer is in such a different ontological category from things here below that Anselm can declare that – by comparison – creatures are "almost nothing," "scarcely exist at all."[6] Nevertheless, Anselm balances this vertical-hierarchy picture of Divine transcendence and independence with an insistence on Divine immanence, with claims that God is omnipresent, even contains all things. Non-controversial among thirteenth- and fourteenth-century Latin Christian thinkers was the notion that God is present to all things by Divine knowledge and power. God knows any and all creatures; whenever and wherever they may be, they are present to Divine awareness. Moreover, Divine power creates, sustains, and enables the functioning of every actual creature. Divine concurrence is necessary for any created action. Nothing else can exist or be good, nothing else can do or suffer anything, apart from Divine informed consent. Nevertheless, metaphysically, no *inter*action is possible; it is not possible for creatures to affect Godhead in any way.

[5] Scotus, *Ordinatio* I, d. 2, p. 1, qq. 2–3; Vaticana II.128–243 (=Vatican edition, vol. II, pages 128–243).
[6] Anselm, *Monologion*, ch. 28; Schmitt I.45–46.

3. Incarnation anyway!

Robert Grosseteste[7] and Bonaventure[8] report that certain twelfth-century theologians (probably including Honorius of Autun and Rupert of Deutz[9]) saw God as further integrating the universe by hypostatically uniting Godself to it in Incarnation and relating to us through a changeable, passible, and hence causally interactive and vulnerable human nature. Their predecessors agreed: soteriology is sufficient to motivate an Incarnation. But these twelfth-century thinkers reckoned that the desirability to God of being *immanent* in the universe was so great from the point of view of God's creative purpose that God would have become Incarnate anyway, whether or not and hence even if humankind had never sinned.

3.1. Self-diffusing Goodness

First, they discovered *philosophical* reasons for thinking God would want to unite heaven to earth and earth to heaven *metaphysically*: Pseudo-Dionysius' conception of Goodness as self-diffusing, as having – or rather being – a positive tendency to share itself out. From this notion, they derived two principles: one general,

(P1) that God would have wanted to confer on creation as much goodness as God could, whether or not rational creatures sinned;

and one particular,

---

[7] Robert Grosseteste, *De cessatione legalium,* ed. Richard C. Dales and Edward B. King (London: Oxford University Press for the British Academy, 1986), Part III, sec. I.1– sec. II.4, 119–135.

[8] Bonaventure, *Sent.* III, d. 1, a. 2, q. 2; Quaracchi III.20–26.

[9] See James McEvoy, "The Absolute Predestination of Christ in the Theology of Robert Grosseteste," in McEvoy, *Robert Grosseteste, Exegete and Philosopher* (Aldershot: Variorum, 1994), 212–230.

(P2) that God would want to actualize creation's noblest capacity for hypostatic union, no matter what.

From each they reasoned to their conclusion: that God would have become Incarnate anyway, would have united a Divine person to creation in hypostatic union, whether or not rational creatures sinned.[10]

Both principles (P1) and (P2) were controversial. Bonaventure agrees that Divine Goodness is bound to share Itself out as much as it can, and insists that It does so when the Father begets the Son. Given such maximal sharing within Godhead, Bonaventure insists, there is no presumption (P1) that God will maximize in creation by pouring out on creatures as much goodness as they can hold.[11] Aquinas agrees that generosity is God's motive in creation, and that the nature of Goodness as self-diffusing rebuts Anselm's presumption against Incarnation.[12] Both Bonaventure and Aquinas assume – with Anselm – that a good cosmos would involve a plurality of created natures imperfectly imitating God in a variety of different ways.[13] But they do not agree with advocates of (P1) that God would create a plenum by actualizing every creatable species.[14] Contrary to (P1), experience proves that God does not make every creature a perfect specimen. (Aquinas does not say, but I would urge, maximally self-diffused Goodness would not give us a universe strewn with horrors!) Bonaventure and Aquinas forward the weaker thesis that Divine consistency of purpose in making things of a given species will confer on at least some members the ability and opportunity to engage in their natural functions. Aquinas goes further to claim that Divine Goodness would so order any collection of creatures into the

---

[10] Grosseteste, *De cessatione legalium*, Part III, sec. I.3–4, 120, Part III, sec. I.9, 122.

[11] Bonaventure, *Itinerarium Mentis in Deum*, ch. 6.2; Quaracchi V.310–311; Bonaventure, *De mysterio Trinitatis*, q. 2, a. 1 ad 7um; q. 2, a. 2, c; Quaracchi V. 59–68. Cf q. 4, a. 2 ad 7um; Quaracchi V. 85–86; q. 7, a. 2; Quaracchi V.110–111; q. 8, pro arguments 1, 2, 3, 4, 5; Quaracchi V.112–113.

[12] Aquinas, *Summa Theologica* III, q. 1, a. 1, c.

[13] Aquinas, *Summa Theologica* I, q. 22, a. 4, c.

[14] Grosseteste, *De cessatione legalium*, Part III, sec. I.9, 122.

best *collective* Godlikeness they could be.[15] While Bonaventure and Aquinas hold that it is metaphysically possible for created substance natures to be assumed by a Divine person (*ab esse ad posse valet consequentia*), both deny that Divine Goodness sets up any *necessary* tendency to hypostatic union. Since hypostatic union goes beyond what belongs to the natural perfection of creatures – i.e., since it is supranatural – we can't infer from a policy of Divine follow-through (P2) that God would become Incarnate to make the universe a better place.[16]

Twelfth-century Incarnation-anyway advocates do not infer (P2) from Divine follow-through, however. They advance (P2) as independently plausible. How unreasonable, they think, if the God Who created worms and flies and reptiles should miss out on actualizing the most startling characteristic of creatables – viz., the capacity creatable substance natures have for hypostatic union with a Divine person![17] How metaphysically preposterous to suppose that creatable substance natures acquire their most dignifying capacity for union with God as a consequence of Adam's fall![18]

3.2. Church and household

If the first set of arguments interprets and applies a neo-Platonic *philosophical* notion, the other two groups take their cue from *biblical* ways of talking to infer that God aims to unite Creator to creature and creatures to one another through a commonality of shared natures. The second set of arguments assumes that *whether or not humans and angels had sinned, and hence even if we hadn't, Divine cosmic purposes would include adopting us as God's children, making us not to be isolated*

---

[15] Aquinas, *Summa Theologica* I, q. 25, a. 5, c and ad 3um.

[16] Bonaventure, *Sent.* III, d. 1, a. 2, q. 2; Quaracchi III.25–26; d. 2, q. 1; Quaracchi III.37–38; Aquinas, *Sent.* III, d. 1, q. 1, a. 3 ad 4um; Aquinas, *Summa Theologica* III, q. 1, a. 3 ad 3um.

[17] Grosseteste, *De cessatione legalium*, Part III, sec. I.9, 122.

[18] Grosseteste, *De cessatione legalium*, Part III, sec. I.5–7, 120–121.

atoms but members of the Church, that mystical body of which Christ is the head. To be fit for either, we would have to be *justified.* Incarnation-anyway advocates understand St. Paul to mean that – quite apart from sin – no human being could be justified of him/herself.[19] Perhaps they have in mind Anselm's doctrine that the will's orientation to justice (both the affection for justice and the initial will-use) is not a natural endowment but a superadded gift of grace.[20] Perhaps they anticipate Scotus' point that given the metaphysical size-gap, even personal "almost nothings" have no entitlements to be included in the household of God![21]

Moreover, the way Incarnation-anyway advocates read, the epistles proclaim that human being is destined to be joined to God, not merely in a conformity of wills, but through a union of natures, not just by spiritual harmony but by a union of flesh.[22] Willing what God wills us to will, nilling what God wills us to nill, might make us friends of God or obedient servants. But to be God's *adopted* children and Christ's siblings, we have to share a nature with Christ, the natural Son. Since we cannot take on the Divine nature, God the Son would have assumed our human nature, even if Adam had never sinned.[23] The idea of *headship* pulls in the same direction: the head of a body shares the nature of its members. Thus, Christ our head would have taken up human nature quite apart from Adam's fall.[24]

Putting Genesis 2:24 ("Therefore a man leaves his father and his mother and clings to his wife, and they become one flesh") together with Ephesians 5:31–32 (quote of Genesis 2:24), Incarnation-anyway advocates understand *marriage* to be a sacrament of the indissoluble *one-flesh union* between Christ and the Church and of the indivisible

---

[19] Grosseteste, *De cessatione legalium*, Part III, sec. I.11, 123, Part III, sec. I.15, 125.

[20] Anselm, *De Concordia Praescientiae et Praedestinationis et Gratiae Dei cum Libero Arbitrio* III.2–3; Schmitt II.264–267.

[21] Scotus, *Op.Ox.* III, d. 19, q. u, nn. 6–7; Wadding VII.1.415, 417–418.

[22] Grosseteste, *De cessatione legalium*, Part III, sec. I.16, 125–I.17, 126, sec. I.30, 132–133.

[23] Grosseteste, *De cessatione legalium*, Part III, sec. I.16–17, 125–126.

[24] Grosseteste, *De cessatione legalium*, Part III, sec. I.10, 123, Part III, sec. I. 18–19, 126–127.

hypostatic union of Christ's humanity and Christ's Divinity. Identifying Adam as the speaker, they take Genesis 2:24 to be a prophecy. They assume that, because Adam did not foresee his own fall, the content of his prophecy – Christ's marriage to, His one-flesh union with the Church – was not conditioned upon it and so would have come true even if humankind had never sinned.[25] Not only does God the Son take our flesh up into hypostatic union, so that we share the same natural kind. Our one-flesh union with Him is more concrete than that, because in *the eucharist* we share the very flesh that He assumed (see chapter 10).[26]

Expounding John 17:22 (one even as we are one), Incarnation-anyway advocates reflect on the Great Chain of Unity: just as Father, Son, and Holy Spirit are one not only in will, but also in nature; so also members of the Church are one in Christ not only through harmony of will but also through human nature, doubly shared (via hypostatic union and eucharistic participation). With Christ as Mediator, we are also one in the Trinity, because the Father is in Christ and Christ is in us. This is the way things are now. Surely such unity would have been too good to pass up, even if there had been no human fall.[27]

3.3. Cosmic household, universal Church

The third set of arguments assume that *whether or not, even if we hadn't sinned, God would want to make Christ the One in Whom the cosmos holds together.* Twelfth-century Incarnation-anyway advocates understand the Bible's God to embrace the comprehensive organizational aim of uniting not just rational creatures, but all parts of the universe under *one head*. As above, headship requires the head

[25] Grosseteste, *De cessatione legalium*, Part III, sec. I.20–21, 127.
[26] Grosseteste, *De cessatione legalium*, Part III, sec. I.30, 132–133.
[27] Grosseteste, *De cessatione legalium*, Part III, sec. I.30, 132–133.

to share in the nature of the other parts but still to be somehow chief among them. Incarnation-anyway advocates insist that merely Divine persons cannot be head of the universe, because no creature shares a genus or species with them. Neither can any mere angel or mere human, because they are metaphysical equals and so disqualified from lording it over each other. A God-angel would not do either, because it would not share in the nature of material things, any more than material things share in the nature of spirits. Human nature does share in the nature of angels (through the rational soul) and in the nature of all bodies (insofar as the human body includes each and all of the four elements). Thus, unifying any universe containing material and spiritual creatures under a single head calls for a God-man in Whom Divinity and humanity are joined in unity of person.[28]

3.4. The primacy of Christ!

What lies behind these last two sets of arguments is a distinctive, bold, and biblical estimate of God's cosmic purposes. *In creating a diversity of things, God is aiming for organic bodies – the Church and the universe as a whole – united under a single head.* Twelfth-century Incarnation-anyway advocates take the language – of the Church as Christ's Body with individuals as body-parts and Christ as head – not merely metaphorically but at least analogically, when they insist that the head must share in the nature(s) of the body-parts and be somehow chief among them. Turning the point upside down, *Church and cosmos are unified, not merely by causal orders and natural excellence hierarchies, but by a sharing in the creatable and created nature(s) of Christ their head!*

Aquinas and Bonaventure worried that if God becomes Incarnate to perfect the universe, then Christ would be seen as a means to

---

[28] Grosseteste, *De cessatione legalium*, Part III, sec. I.25, 129, Part III, sec. I.28, 131.

that end. Likewise, in general, even where parts are naturally prior to a whole – in the sense that the whole depends for its existence on its component parts, but it is *metaphysically* possible for the parts to exist apart from the whole – it might seem that parts actually exist for the sake of the whole of which they are a part. Once again, Christ as head would exist for the sake of the whole body. Thus, not Christ but the cosmic whole would be forwarded as preeminent among Divine aims!

Grosseteste remains agnostic as to whether God would have become Incarnate anyway apart from human sin.[29] But this does not keep him from arguing that Incarnation-anyway advocates mean to be committed to the primacy of Christ. Grosseteste applies a different and perhaps contrary principle – that wholes are for the sake of their nobler/noblest parts – when he identifies a hierarchy of ends: the cosmos is made *for the sake of* human beings, in particular the best state of human beings, the Church triumphant; and the body is *for the sake of* the head. For example, stomach- and lung-functioning are for the sake of head-functioning, digestion and respiration for the sake of doing philosophy and loving God above all and for God's own sake. Thus, all creatures are made for the sake of the Church triumphant, but for the sake of the God-man as their ultimate end and God's principal aim. Because the end is prior in intention to those things that are for the sake of the end, Christ *qua human and Divine* is the "first born of all creation" (Colossians 1:15).[30] If Bonaventure[31] and Aquinas read the first and philosophical set of arguments as implying that Christ would exist for the sake of the perfection or completion of the universe, Grosseteste takes the thrust of the second and third sets of biblical arguments to be the opposite: that cosmos and Church,

---

[29] Grosseteste, *De cessatione legalium*, Part III, sec. II.1, 133.

[30] Grosseteste, *De cessatione legalium*, Part III, sec. II.1, 134.

[31] Bonaventure, *Sent.* III, d. 1, a. 2, q. 2; Quaracchi III.25; see also d. 2, q. 1; Quaracchi III.37–38.

each and every creature, humans included, exist for the sake of Christ!

4. Maximally well-organized lover!

Scotus brings the structure of means and ends among the objects of Divine choice into even sharper focus. Although God thinks whatever God thinks and wills whatever God wills by one simple, eternal act, Scotus thinks it is possible to distinguish natural or explanatory priorities and posteriorities among the objects of that act within a single instant of time or within the "now" of eternity, so that he speaks of God's thinking or purposing one object at an earlier or later "instant of nature" than another. Since the All-Wise God is a maximally well-organized lover, God wills first the end, then the proximate, and then the remote means to it. (i) God first loves God-self above all with friendship love *(amor amicitiae)* that values the love-object for its own sake and not merely as a means to something else.[32] (ii) Since friendship love is non-possessive, it partly expresses itself in the will that others should value the love-object the same way. The persons of the Trinity love one another with such friendship love. (iii) That this love should be shared by others, the soul of Christ preeminent among them, is, for Scotus, God's *principal end in creation*. Scotus says that God so loved the rational soul of Christ that God wanted to create and be loved by it whether or not any other creatures existed.[33] In fact, God has willed that Christ should be the head of many co-lovers, including both angels and other human souls.[34]

---

[32] Scotus, *Op.Ox.* III, d. 7, q. 4; in Scotus, *Theologiae Marianae Elementa*, ed. Carolus Balić, OFM (Kačić: Šibenik in Yugoslavia, 1933), 12 (afterwards =CB).

[33] Scotus, *Op.Ox.* III, d. 7, q. 4; CB 14; cf. 14–15.

[34] Scotus, *Op.Ox.* III, d. 13, q. 4, n. 8; Wadding VII.1.267.

(iv) Next, God wills the *proximate means* to that end. Since sharing in the Trinitarian friendship circle is a destiny that exceeds the natural powers or requirements of human souls and angels, something must be done to *fit* them for this intimacy. The human soul of Christ is hypostatically united to the Divine Word,[35] so that it may be fittingly infused with fullness of grace, maximal human knowledge, and impeccability of will.[36] Other human and angelic co-lovers are supplied with graces in lesser degree. Moreover, God freely and contingently legislates a system of merit which creates *conventional and statutory* connections between the finite and temporal acts and states of created persons, on the one hand, and Divine acceptance, infused grace, and eternal glory, on the other, thereby giving finite and temporal created acts and states eternal significance.[37]

(v) Next, God wills the *remote means* to His end by creating other things naturally suited to human souls.[38] Thus, God wills to create the material world, so that human souls may be united to human bodies and function accordingly.

Scotus' account begins with glory, the glory of Divine self-love and of the Trinitarian friendship circle. It continues with God's predestining rational creatures to glory – first and foremost, the soul of Christ, and secondarily other human souls and angels of which Christ is the head. It proceeds to the provision of those things which are for the sake of their glory – hypostatic union, graces and spiritual endowments – and then on to other suitables that will make it all possible. Thus, Scotus' analysis clearly asserts that the soul of Christ is made for God's sake, for the sake of widening the Trinitarian friendship circle; that the soul of Christ is God's first end in creation; and that other created co-lovers and the whole material cosmos are made for Christ's sake. There is thus no question of God's first purposing

[35] Scotus, *Op.Ox.* III, d. 7, qq. 3–4; CB 8, 12, 14.
[36] Scotus, *Op.Ox.* III, d. 12, q. u, n. 3; Wadding VII.1.255.
[37] Scotus, *Op.Ox.* III, d. 19, q. u, nn. 6–7; Wadding VII.1.415, 417–418.
[38] Scotus, *Op.Ox.* IV, d. 46, q. 1, n. 7; Wadding X.252.

a certain sort of world and then opting for Incarnation as a means to the end of cosmic perfection. On Scotus' representation, the material world does not interest God except insofar as it is what is naturally suitable for Christ and the other human co-lovers of which Christ is the head.

Moreover, in forwarding this analysis, Scotus intends to make clear that Divine predestination of created co-lovers to, and their equipment for, glory is prior in the order of explanation to any Divine consideration of sin – its permission, its future actuality, or its consequences. This means that – on Scotus' account – God does not will a God-man for the sake of solving the sin-problem. It means that God intended to become Incarnate anyway, whether or not, even if humans never sinned.

Not only is sin not a *sine qua non* of Incarnation; for Scotus, Incarnation is not a *sine qua non* for solving the sin-problem either. Against Anselm, Scotus contends that not even a God-man can render satisfaction that is metaphysically commensurate with human guilt, because the obedience, passion, and death that Christ offers take place within His human nature and so are metaphysically finite.[39] Scotus infers that whether or not to require satisfaction for sin (and if required what the satisfaction is to be) is entirely a matter of God's free and contingent volition.[40] Even if satisfaction were required, the passion of Christ would not be the only way. Neither God nor any human being would have to be the satisfaction-maker; God could accept something from an angel.[41] Likewise, God could allow a sinner to make satisfaction for him/herself through an act of loving God more intense than the sinful act.[42] As things stand, we owe God obedience in everything. But God could have considered our fragility and lowered the requirements to keeping the Ten Commandments,

---

[39] Scotus, *Op.Ox.* III, d. 20, q. u, n. 8; Wadding VII.1.429; III, d. 19, q. u, nn. 5, 7; Wadding VII.1.413, 418.

[40] Scotus, *Op.Ox.* III, d. 20, q. u, n. 9; Wadding VII.1.429.

[41] Scotus, *Op.Ox.* III, d. 20, q. u, n. 8; Wadding VII.1.428–429.

[42] Scotus, *Op.Ox.* III, d. 20, q. u, nn. 8–9; Wadding VII.1.428–429.

thereby putting us in a position to perform supererogatory acts.[43] If Christ were the satisfaction-maker, God might have deemed an act of good will sufficient.[44] By pointing out these other options, Scotus is emphasizing that *Incarnation and redemption are logically independent projects.*

Relative to the Incarnation, the free and contingent election of Christ as the Redeemer comes much later in the structure of Divine intentions. Only after predestining the soul of Christ and other co-lovers to glory, and willing to furnish the proximate and remote means to that end, does God will to permit rational creatures to exercise free choice. Only after that does God see human and angelic sin;[45] and only after that does God see the human soul of Christ volunteering to solve the sin-problem by His passion and death; and only after that does God will to furnish Christ with a passible body as a means to that end.[46]

Yet, for Scotus, it was not unfitting that Christ the best-beloved, the first-born in bringing many sons to glory, should be accepted for the Redeemer's role. In Christ, God the Son gets into the act Himself, the higher serves the lower, so that human sinners may be more bound in gratitude to their Maker and more attracted to His love.[47]

5. Christ as center

In his *Sentence*-commentary, Bonaventure could not bring himself to agree that God would have become Incarnate anyway, even if humans had never sinned. He felt the persuasive power of the arguments he

---

[43] Scotus, *Op. Ox.* IV, d. 15, q. 1, n. 7; Wadding IX.107.

[44] Scotus, *Op. Ox.* III, d. 20, q. u, n. 11; Wadding VII.1.430.

[45] Scotus, *Op. Ox.* III, d. 41, q. u, n. 45; Vaticana VI.334.

[46] Scotus, *Op. Ox.* III, d. 20, q. u, n. 10; Wadding VII.1.430. Cf. *Op. Ox.* III, d. 19, q. u, n. 6; Wadding VII.1.415.

[47] Scotus, *Op. Ox.* III, d. 20, q. u, n. 10; Wadding VII.1.415.

rehearsed. He conceded that the position stirs piety and devotion. In the end, however, he gave greater weight to Scriptures and cites from Augustine and Pope Leo that explicitly link Incarnation with the remedy for sin. He also thought the faithful would be more inflamed by Christ's coming to die for our sins than by an abstract consideration of how a God-man perfects the universe.[48]

Nevertheless, when Bonaventure turns from what might have been to the universe as we now have it, his focus is not narrowly soteriological. His eye is on the cosmos, his passion fired to celebrate in how many ways Christ is its center (*medium*). Where Anselm and Incarnation-anyway advocates concentrate on what good might come of God the Son's taking a human nature into hypostatic union (*cur Deus homo?*), Bonaventure looks to the whole Christ, to show how each nature and both united in a single person make Him the One in Whom all things hold together (Colossians 1:17).

Beginning at the top, Bonaventure explains how *Christ qua Divine* is the center (*medium*) of the Trinity. To do this, Bonaventure has to put a number of philosophical ideas in play. First, he assumes that omnipotence is perfect productive power, that perfect productive power would necessarily express itself in a perfect product, and that a perfect product would be of the same nature as the producer. Second, he maintains that natures (bovinity, humanity) cannot produce but rather individuals of those natures (Beulah the cow, Socrates; in general, supposits or persons), and that – even where product and producer are of the same nature – no product can be the same individual as its producer. From these, Bonaventure infers, there must be more than one person in Godhead.[49]

Bonaventure recognizes two types of productive power in the Divine essence – intellectual power that naturally produces thoughts, and will that acts voluntarily – and reckons that each would

[48] Bonaventure, *Sent.* III, d. 1, a. 2, q. 2; Quaracchi III.24–25.
[49] Bonaventure, *De mysterio Trinitatis*, q. 1, a. 1, c; q. 2, a. 1, c and ad 5um–7um; Quaracchi V.49–50, 60–62.

necessarily express itself in a perfect product. Moreover, intellectual and will power are ordered to one another – an agent can will only what it thinks of – so that the intellectual product is something through which will power produces its own product. Bonaventure concludes that there are three Divine persons: the Father as unproduced producer, Christ the Son as perfect product and (with the Father) co-producer of the Spirit Who is unproducing but produced. Christ is thus the center (*medium*) of the Trinity, like the Father in producing but like the Spirit in being produced![50]

Christ qua Divine is also the *medium* through which all things are made (see John 1:1–2). The Son is the perfect product of intellectual Divine power; He is the Father's perfect self-expression, the Divine Word Who is the perfect image and likeness of the Father. Christ the Divine Word is also the exemplar of all creatable natures, since they are – for Bonaventure – just ways of imperfectly imitating Godhead. Thus, all creatures are Godlike by being like the Son to Whom they owe their form and structure; and humans are an image of the Image!

Christ qua God and man centers, is the *medium* of, creation in another way. Bonaventure did not find considerations of cosmic excellence sufficient to secure the conclusion that God would have become Incarnate anyway, apart from human sin. But Bonaventure did understand human nature to be composed of two substances, soul and body, and so to straddle the divide between spiritual and material creation. And he did agree that Christ unifies the cosmos by entering at its center (*medium*), when God the Son hypostatically unites Himself to humankind.

Christ qua God and man is the soteriological center, the *medium* of our salvation. Christ is the Mediator Divine mercy provides to make the satisfaction for sin that Divine justice requires.[51] If Adam's fall

---

[50] Bonaventure, *De mysterio Trinitatis*, q. 4, a. 2, c and ad 1um, 3um, 4um, 7um; Quaracchi V.85–86. Cf. q. 8, c and pro arguments 6–7; Quaracchi V.113–114.

[51] Bonaventure, *Sent.* III, d. 20, a. u, q. 2; Quaracchi III.419–422.

distorts God's image in us, Christ's human career takes its shape (humility, poverty, obedience, and brotherly love) from what is needed for our reform.[52] Christ crucified is an outward and visible sign of the caricature into which sin has twisted us, as well as a symbol of the soul's transformation through Christ-like disciplines. Spiritually, the soul begins its journey with a burning love for the crucified, ends its journey by dying in the arms of the crucified, and in the middle practices spiritual disciplines to "crucify the flesh and all of its desires."[53]

Thus, for Bonaventure, whatever might have been the case if humans hadn't sinned, Christ is *de facto* not marginal but central. Christ is the *medium* of Godhead. Christ is the cosmic *medium*, the One through Whom all things go out from God, the One through Whom all things hold together. And Christ is the redemptive *medium*, the One in Whom and through Whom all things are led back and restored.[54]

6. Incarnation, conditionally inevitable!

The disputed question – whether God would have become Incarnate anyway, even if human beings had never sinned – forced Latin medievals to examine whether God's decision to become Incarnate issues out of Divine purposes for *creation*, or whether it arises out of the human need for *redemption*, or both. Middle-third-of-the-thirteenth-century "Incarnation-anyway" authors answer "both/and": God's creative aim at universal excellence would have been enough, and the human need for redemption would have been

---

[52] Bonaventure, *Opusculum XXII: Epistola de Imitatione Christi*; Quaracchi VIII.499–503.

[53] Bonaventure, *Itinerarium Mentis in Deum*, Prologus 3; ch. 4, secs. 1–8; ch. 7, secs. 1–6; Quaracchi V.295–296, 306–308, 312–313.

[54] For a wonderful discussion of Christological themes in Bonaventure, see Zachary Hayes, OFM, *The Hidden Center: Spirituality and Speculative Christology in St. Bonaventure* (Ramsey, NJ: Paulist Press, 1981).

enough. Bonaventure and the later Aquinas[55] reply that only the soteriological demand was decisive. Scotus replies, "First and foremost, God's goals in creation." On Scotus' scheme, human need for redemption does not function as a reason for Incarnation. Rather, only because the Incarnation is already in place (at the earlier instant of nature) does it seem wise and efficient (at the later instant of nature) for the Incarnate One to supply the remedy for sin.

Yet, these stances are open to them *only because they conceive of sin as optional.* With Augustine, they deny that sin is necessary for the perfection of the universe, and take it to be metaphysically possible for humans and angels to exist without ever sinning. This is how middle-third-of-the-thirteenth-century "Incarnation-anyway" authors can regard "if humans never sinned" as something other than contrary to necessary fact. Scotus is able to place Incarnation *prior* in the order of explanation to sin and its need of remedy only because he makes the same assumption. If sin were a naturally necessary consequence of the existence of rational creatures the way revolutions around the earth were supposed to be of the existence of earth and sun, then Divine decision to create the soul of Christ and other rational creatures in a world such as this would already include in it the inevitability of sin and its need of remedy. And the question "*Cur Deus homo*? Creation? Or Redemption?" would represent a false choice.

Like twelfth-through fourteenth-century Latin medievals, I believe that Incarnation is contingent, if for no other reason than

---

[55] In his *Sentence*-commentary III, d. 1, q. 1, a. 3, c (Parma VII.1.13A), Aquinas declares both answers to the question – would God have become Incarnate anyway, even if human beings had never sinned – defensible. He cites Augustine's and Pope Leo's tome that Scripture always links Incarnation to the remedy for sin, but does not there allow such *auctoritates* to trump opposing arguments that Incarnation exalts human nature and constitutes the consummation of the whole created universe. In *Summa Theologica* III, q. 1, a. 3, c and ad 1um, however, Aquinas leaves aside patristic exegesis of "cosmic Christ" passages to read Scripture as those *auctoritates* from Augustine and Pope Leo do. Thus, the later Aquinas concludes that, because Scripture always associates Incarnation with the remedy for sin, we should deny that God would have become Incarnate anyway apart from human sin.

that creation is itself contingent, a product of free and contingent Divine choice. But I contend that human horror-participation is inevitable given God's decision to create us in a material world such as this. And my cosmological hypothesis – that Divine love of material creation expresses itself in assimilative and unitive aims – implies that God's cosmic purposes can be achieved only if the soteriological plot resolves. Thus, *Incarnation is conditionally necessary on God's decision to create this world and realize such aims.*

Clearly, on my analysis, Christ is the Savior, the One in Whom the soteriological plot holds together. (i) The Word made Flesh, *Christ qua God and man*, participating in horrors in solidarity with us, establishes Stage-I horror-defeat. As the letter to the Colossians insists, this is a role that mere angels cannot share. Whatever their plight, they have no material aspect to run interference with their personal aspect, and so cannot share this dimension of human vulnerability to horrors. (ii) *Christ qua God and man* is the exemplar of our salvation: His horror-participation is Stage-I self-defeating. If His own horror-participation by definition *prima facie* defeats the positive significance of His earthly career, His own horror-participation gives His earthly career enormous positive significance because it Stage-I defeats ours. The *ante-mortem* excellent and *post-mortem* optimal collaboration of His human personality with His Divine Spirit means that He recognizes how His horror-participation establishes the Stage-I defeat of ours and thereby His human personality recognizes and appropriates many positive meanings in His human career (Stage-II horror-defeat). *Christ qua human,* crucified and risen in His human nature, now enjoys a non-toxic relation to material creation (proleptic Stage-III horror-defeat). (iii) *Christ qua Divine* is our Inner Teacher, the healer of our meaning-making capacities and principal orchestrator of Stage-II horror-defeat. (iv) *Christ qua Divine* is also cosmic Recreator Who renegotiates the relation of human being to its material environment (and so will accomplish Stage-III horror-defeat). Defeating horrors requires God to act through both Divine and human natures. Because Christ is the Divine person to Whom both natures belong, Christ is the One in Whom all of these contributions to the soteriological problem hold together.

Likewise, for me as much as for Anselm, twelfth-century Incarnation-anyway advocates, and Scotus, Christ is the key to the success of God's original aims in creation. Along with twelfth-century Incarnation-anyway advocates and Scotus but at odds with Anselm, I want to say that solving our non-optimality problems was not *the* decisive reason why God became human. There is the Lover's passion to unite with the beloved (what I have called God's unitive aim). But God's love for material creation cannot fail to be open-eyed. Divine desire to make matter as Godlike as possible allows material creation to work itself up into the personal. Divine desire to let matter be itself engenders a policy of permissiveness in which the material is mostly allowed to "do its" natural "thing." God commits Godself to *the material* by acting on these desires, and thereby accepts horrors as part of the cosmic package. But Divine desire to make matter as Godlike as possible also carries with it a matching commitment to *the personal*. God loves *us* as a way of loving material creation. Loving us, God aims to be good-to us, which involves solving our non-optimality problems and so requires the utter and ultimate defeat of horrors, not only within the cosmos as a whole but within the context of our individual lives. God's assimilative aim requires Incarnation, the object of God's unitive aim, as part of the cosmic package. Thus, on my hypothesis about Divine purposes, Christ is the One in Whom both cosmic and soteriological success hold together, because the two cannot not break apart.

My account definitely makes Christ integral and integrating both of the cosmos and of the soteriological plot. But does it really forward the primacy of Christ? Don't I instead identify a certain sort of cosmos as God's principal object and posit Christ as a necessary means thereto? Alternatively, don't I at least make cosmos and Christ coeval in Divine intention by seeing them as integrated into an organic whole at which God chiefly aims. Neither way would I seem to follow Scotus in putting Christ first, in making (the soul of)

Christ God's chief end in creation with everything else being made for Christ's sake.

Ready to hand though it was and is, this means/end conceptuality is misleading and does not capture my meaning. Material creation is not an end towards which assimilating and uniting (and hence Incarnation) are Divine means. Rather they are *ways* Divine love for material creation expresses itself. God loves material creation *by* assimilating it to Godself and *by* assimilating Godself to it. God loves material creation *by* uniting Godself to it in the most intimate ways metaphysically possible. Put otherwise, God creates us in this world because God wants to be a Lover of this sort of material creation. Christ *qua* God-man, sharing human horror-participation, is *how* God becomes and *Who* God is as such a Lover. *God creates this world because God wants to be Christ for a material world such as this!*

7. Unity and immanence – too much or too little of a good thing?

7.1. Idealist objections

Christ's cosmic preeminence is focal to the integrated realization of Divine purposes, and hypostatic union (see chapter 5) goes beyond the omnipresence of knowledge and power in making God metaphysically immanent in our world. Yet, if cosmic unity and Divine immanence are the desiderata, both might seem better satisfied by various forms of nineteenth-century idealist philosophy. Drawing on and developing ideas in neo-Platonism and Spinoza, these idealists held either that God *is* the cosmos (pantheism) or that the cosmos is *in* God (panentheism): God holds the universe together, is immanent in it either by *being* it or by *containing* it. (i) Both pantheistic and panentheistic theories make God *more immanent* because, whereas Incarnation metaphysically unites God to a particular individual within the universe, pantheism metaphysically identifies God with and panentheism makes God the metaphysical container of *all* of it.

(ii) Some pantheistic/panentheistic theories posit *greater unity* in the universe by giving a distinctive interpretation to the idea of organic unity.[56] They begin with Aristotle's notion that a biological organism is naturally prior to its parts: what it is to be a hand is defined by its function within the body, so that the hunk of flesh resulting when the hand is severed is not a hand. Organic parts cannot exist separated from the whole of which they are parts. So, too, some idealists insist that the state is an organic body politic. Citizens' identities are so defined in terms of their social roles that they owe their existence to the state and could not exist apart from it. Some such idealists go further still to contend that the cosmos is itself an organic whole. As a first approximation, this implies not only the trivial claim (i) that this very whole cannot exist without these very parts, but conversely (ii) that these very parts cannot exist without this very whole. (i) but not (ii) would be true even where parts are naturally prior to their wholes (e.g., a glass of water or a stack of pennies). However controversial (ii) might seem as applied to the cosmos as a whole, what these idealists really think is more radical still: viz., (iii) that organic wholes are so tightly integrated that the very attempt to think "parts" separately represents a falsifying abstraction from their essential relatedness to everything that the whole contains. Besides (1) the Identity/Containment Thesis and corollary to (2) the Organic Unity Thesis, is (3) the Necessity Thesis: everything that comes to be within the spatio-temporal order is developmentally necessary for cosmic realization (some take Hegel to mean necessary for the self-development of Absolute spirit).

---

[56] For an extensive discussion of British idealism and its impact on turn-of-the-twentieth-century British theology, see Alan P. F. Sell, *Philosophical Idealism and Christian Belief* (Cardiff: University of Wales, 1995). See also Edward Caird, *Hegel* (William Blackwood and Sons, 1883), ch. VIII, 151–185.

7.2. Idealisms and evil

My first response is that such idealisms have the vice of their virtues. According to (1) the Identity/Containment Thesis, God is metaphysically related the same way to everything in the cosmos, good or evil – to the genocides of Nazi Germany, Rwanda, and Darfur as to the spiritual icons of Polycarp and St. Francis, Mother Teresa and Martin Luther King, Jr. *Prima facie*, this would seem to make the problem of evil more difficult to solve. It would be wrong, however, to leap to an *ultima facie* conclusion. Such idealists would call on us to distinguish between *metaphysical* and *characterological* goodness. (1) The Identity/Containment Thesis implies that – *pace* Christian Platonists – what God *is*, or what God *contains*, is at most a complex good, a good that includes some evil (quasi-)parts whose negative value is defeated in the whole (see chapter 2). Moreover, (3) the Necessity Thesis entails the further (4) No-Power Thesis – viz., that Divine power does not include power to prevent or eliminate any and all evils. Global defeat combines with (4) the No-Power Thesis to block any automatic inference from evil metaphysical (quasi-)constituents to characterological evil in God.

(3) The Necessity Thesis makes (5) the Freedom Thesis – that God or creatures exercise incompatibilist freedom – difficult consistently to maintain, however. So process philosophical theologians, inspired by Whitehead, embrace an alternative (1) panentheism, which drops (2) the Organic Unity Thesis and insists that the creatures in God are, or are societies of, momentary incompatibilist free "occasions." Whiteheadian panentheism makes for less cosmic unity, insofar as any temporal segment of the universe is – due to (5) the freedom of its constituents – compatible with alternative futures. In exchange for (2) the Organic Unity Thesis, Whiteheadian panentheism wins the advantage of combining a high degree of Divine immanence with some measure of Divine transcendence. It allows that, while God could not exist without containing some creation or other, each created order is such that God could exist without it. So far as the

problem of evil is concerned, Charles Hartshorne appeals to (4) the No-Power Thesis on the ground that – because incompatibilist free creatures are uncoercible – God has only persuasive power, which God uses to lure the cosmos into an ever-increasing global harmony. God does not have coercive power to prevent or eliminate evils – horrendous or otherwise. Although ordinary psychological-sense persons do not survive – in the sense of having more experiences after – death, Divine persuasion endows their careers with ever greater significance within the global whole. Interpreting omniscience to include feeling or the capacity for sympathetic identification, Hartshorne adds (6) the Passibility Thesis – that God shares the suffering of all the creatures God contains. Hartshorne thus hopes to block any inference from (1) God's metaphysical containment of evils to any negative evaluation of God's character.

7.3. Alternative patterns of entrenchment

Idealisms that endorse (1) the Identity/Containment Thesis *do* permit a greater degree of Divine immanence than does medieval-style hypostatic union of God the Son with one individual human nature. Idealisms that endorse (2) the Organic Unity Thesis *do* allow for more cosmic unity than, say, Bonaventure's "centering" Christ affords. What this shows is that positions that affirm (7) the Real Distinction Thesis – that God and creatures are really distinct – and (8) the Independence Thesis – that God could exist without any and every created order – cannot consistently treat immanence and cosmic unity as pure perfections – like wisdom and beauty – that demand to be maximized. Given (7) the Real Distinction Thesis and (8) the Independence Thesis, Incarnation represents a *via media* between Divine immanence and Divine transcendence alternative to that struck by Whiteheadian idealists.

Put otherwise, my approach carries a limited commitment to cosmic unity and Divine immanence, because it is trying to harmonize a different set of entrenched beliefs. I start not with philosophical commitments to (2) the strict-sense organic unity of what there is, but with the phenomena of horrendous evils: with ordinary-sense individual human persons whose attempts to make positive sense of their lives have been shattered, leaving their subjective sense of self in pieces; with fragmented individual human persons and their sense of alienation from God. My engagement with horrors has led me to certain plausible but controversial interpretations. (a) First, I am committed to the existentialist assumption that meaning-making is an essential and distinctive function of persons. This drives me to the further conclusion (b) that there is enough to individual human beings metaphysically, that they have enough independence of the cosmos as a whole, to underwrite my demand that horrors be defeated, not only globally, but also within the frame of their individual lives. Likewise, I am assuming (c) that individual human persons have enough metaphysical independence of the cosmos for it to make sense for God to love them and to want to be good-to them in particular. Finally, my engagement with horrors and reading of the book of Job make me want to insist (d) that individual human persons are metaphysically distinct enough from God to relate to God person-to-Persons, and that individual human persons have enough functional initiative to have a quarrel with God and to be reconciled on the whole and in the end.

My hypotheses trace horrors to a series of systemic misfits in which we human beings are caught: between the material and the personal in human being itself, between human being and its material environment, and between creatures and God. But human social systems are also productive of horrors. This means both that our meaning-making frameworks are deeply social, and that horror-defeat requires individual human persons to be more independent of their societies than adherents of (2) Organic Unity allow. For my part, I have no wish to deny that humans are social animals. Normally, it takes a group to organize to feed, clothe, and protect ourselves against the physical environment. Normally, we require an environment of other human persons to realize our potential to be persons (feral human children cannot do this). Normally, we flourish as persons only in relation with others. Given that human individuals have a range of potentials best realized in social roles, I see no reason to deny that capacities for certain kinds of social interaction and functioning number among our "individuating" features.

What (2) organic-union idealists gloss over is the seemingly obvious fact that some of these social capacities – e.g., those for certain kinds of leadership by women or homosexuals or members of rejected racial groups – may be prevented from actualization by the societies in which the individuals actually live. Human social grids are often poorly matched to the proclivities and possibilities of the individuals involved. Environmental necessity, human tyranny, and incompetence all conspire to produce social systems in which the individual's potential is more thwarted than fulfilled, sometimes to the point that individuals reasonably feel it would have been better for them never to have been born.

My belief that horror-defeat is possible within the frame of the individual horror-participant's life leads me to the conclusion that individual human persons are not – contrary to (2) the Organic Union Thesis as applied to human social wholes – mere falsifying abstractions from the social wholes of which they are quasi-parts. Here we might take a page from Robert Merrihew Adams[57] and distinguish the metaphysical from the existential (or meaning-making) identity of human persons. So far as metaphysical identity is concerned, I contend – against (2) the Organic Union Thesis – that metaphysically the same individual human person can exist in different social systems. Consider the orphan who might grow up in Somalia or be adopted by an English couple and so come to understand him/herself in very different ways. Insofar as existential identities are deeply social, moving from one society to another that is

---

[57] Robert Merrihew Adams, "Existence, Self-Interest, and the Problem of Evil," in Robert Merrihew Adams, *The Virtue of Faith* (Oxford, New York, and Toronto: Oxford University Press, 1987), Part II, ch. 5, 65–76.

very different usually occasions an existential identity crisis (e.g., as asylum-seekers who moved from the Sudan to North Dakota discovered) which sometimes takes on horrendous proportions. But if it were impossible for metaphysically the same individual person to move from one society to another while winning through to some sort of existential continuity, it would be purely altruistic for any of us to work for foundational social change or to hope for the coming Kingdom of God which – unlike any merely human social systems – will feature a utopic integration of individual flourishing with the common good.

By prioritizing ordinary-sense individual human persons and their person-to-Persons relationship with God, my approach offers a soteriological payoff that goes beyond what Hegelian- and Whiteheadian-style idealisms can afford: viz., a Divine guarantee that each ordinary-sense individual human person will have a life that is a great good to him/her on the whole and in the end, and one in which any and all horror-participation is defeated, not merely globally, but within the frame of the individual horror-participant's own life. I see Stage-I horror-defeat as secured by Divine solidarity with individual human persons in horror-participation. Like Hartshorne, I endorse (6) the Passibility Thesis and affirm that God shares by participating in the suffering of suffering creatures. But God's feeling *in the Divine nature* all the pains that creatures feel will not constitute adequate solidarity with human horror-participants. Divine consciousness is of immeasurable scope. God's clear and comprehensive awareness of the Good that God *is* would radically recontextualize any creaturely pain and suffering that God might feel: what swamps a human consciousness would be a minuscule fragment of what occupies Divine attention. Moreover, what is distinctive about horrors is that they stump the meaning-making resources of the horror-participant. This is not possible where the Divine mind is concerned – a fact on which human salvation ultimately depends! To show solidarity with horror-participants, God must experience evils within the limits of a finite human consciousness, with a mind that can be "blown" and at least *prima facie* unable to cope with horrors. The two-natures theory, Incarnation of a Divine person into an individual human nature, fills this bill, but Hegelian and Whiteheadian idealisms do not!

7.4. Other incarnations?

Idealisms – whether Whiteheadian or such as endorse theses (1)–(3) above – are not the only way to spread Divine immanence equally throughout the created order. Having analyzed how alien assumption is possible for the special case of Christ's individual human nature, Scotus explicitly acknowledges that any and every created thing (*res*) could be assumed by (be hypostatically united to) a Divine person (see chapter 5). He thus concedes that (1) pantheism/panentheism is metaphysically possible![58] *A fortiori*, multiple incarnations are metaphysically possible, whether by the same or by different Divine persons.[59] Scotus did not think this possibility was actualized, however, because hypostatic union makes the created natures belong to the assumer, and makes the acts and changes in the assumed nature predicable of the assumer. Given the fact of evil, for God to assume all of the individual human natures that in fact exist would make God the subject of the morally vicious acts perpetrated by Hitler and Stalin and Pol Pot. This sort of metaphysical identification or containment carries with it a character ascription. The fact that the predication could be relativized to the assumed nature – "God commits moral atrocities with respect to this assumed human nature, but not with respect to the Divine nature" – did not keep the consequence from seeming too scandalous to embrace.

What if God had created a world in which personal creatures were not radically vulnerable to horrors? Would God have become Incarnate, would a Divine person have hypostatically united itself

---

[58] Scotus, *Op.Ox.* III, d. 1, q. 1, n. 10; Wadding VII.1.16.
[59] Scotus, *Op.Ox.* III, d. 1, q. 2, nn. 5–7; Wadding VII.1.36–37; III, d. 1, q. 3; Wadding VII.1.44.

to an individual substance nature in that world? If God's motive for creating is love that assimilates and unites itself to the creatures, then the answer would seem to be "yes."

Unity – One over Many, One integrating Many, One underlying Many – is an ancient, medieval, and perhaps modern preoccupation. But there is a competing principle of plenitude: the more, the merrier! What if God were to create, or even has created, other material systems of things that are not spatio-temporally continuous with ours, and/or systems of things made out of a different kind of matter? Would or has God become Incarnate in them as well? My logic would imply that God would or has, and that God participates in horrors in any such worlds in which created material persons do.

If there were or are multiple Incarnations, my motivational hypotheses do not – by themselves – entail anything about which Divine person or persons would be involved. If the cosmos were less unified than medievals thought (so that it involved systems of material things that were not spatio-temporally accessible to one another), then Christ *qua* God-man would not hold everything together in the way that they envisioned. If the same Divine person were Incarnate each time, then the worlds would be unified through having that same Divine person a member of them. If the matter were of the same kind in the mutually inaccessible systems, then the worlds might still be unified by shared natures. If not, then Christ would hold them together through His person and Divine nature alone. If the Divine persons shared the work of Incarnation, then it would be Godhead that held all the worlds together. But we would still be affirming that creation is organized by more than causal and excellence hierarchies. We would continue to say that God insists on investing Godself into whatever system of things God makes, that God demands to enter into intimate material connection with material creatures, to share in created natures so that we can be adopted into one another's families and function in the same body as parts.

8. Church as mediocosm

Bonaventure styles the universe as *macrocosm* of which human being is *microcosm*. My approach from horrors identifies Christ as the One in Whom all things hold together, the One Who becomes center of the macrocosm by hypostatically uniting Godhead to the microcosm. It also identifies Christ in the hearts of all people, laboring as Inner Teacher to become the center of each and every individual self. It remains to say something about the intermediate level, about the "mediocosm" which is the Church!

For Aquinas, Christ is the head of the Church because Christ holds the treasury of merits, and Christ is the fontal source from whom grace cascades down to all members of His Body. For Aquinas, the saving work of Christ is *objective*: Christ has made satisfaction for Adam's sin. For Aquinas, the benefits are *extensive*: Christ's voluntary acceptance of suffering to the glory of God has earned merit in quantities sufficient to extend to all possible humans and angels: to all actual members, to those who are not yet but will be in the future, to those who could be but never actually will be at all.

Twelfth-century Incarnation-anyway theologians say that, even apart from sin, God would have wanted to organize His rational creatures into a body-politic of which Christ was the head. Christ and we could be members of the same body because we share a nature, because Christ took our nature for His own. Even apart from sin and satisfaction, Christ would be *head* of the body as exemplar and teacher, and as the source of our justification, of those spiritual upgrades that transform us from mere images into likenesses of God.

On my view, Christ is primarily *head of the cosmos*: God makes the world in order to become Christ for it, shares the natures of the whole material universe by making Godself a member of the human race. On my view, there is no "anyway" to Incarnation, because God's making us in a world like this leaves us radically vulnerable to horrors. Besides this cosmic headship, Christ is in a special way *head of the whole human race*: for Christ shares our nature specifically; God the Son hypostatically united Himself to an individual human nature. By sharing the horrors (see chapter 3), Christ binds Himself to the human race in a mutuality of horror-defeat: Christ's horror-participation Stage-I defeats our horror-participation, and the fact that His defeats ours is what Stage-I defeats His! Within the macrocosm that Christ heads (the universe of all creatures), there is a mediocosm that Christ specially heads (the universe of all humans). It is with this mediocosm that I want to identify the Church.

Taken in its widest sense, "*the Church universal*" is the whole human race, all those human beings for whom Christ has established Stage-I horror-defeat. Membership in the Church universal is not mediated by human institutions. Membership in the Church universal is independent of whether or not the individual human beings believe that God exists, that God was in Christ, or that God in Christ has established Stage-I horror-defeat.

In a narrower sense, "*the wrestling Church*" is made up of all human beings who – despite the horrendous predicament of the human race, despite their own horror-participation – still believe in God enough to keep up the conversation; who are to some extent convinced that God is in Christ reconciling the world to Godself, who at least inchoately sense that in Christ God has accomplished Stage-I horror-defeat; and who wrestle to integrate this fact into the broken narratives of their lives and so win the blessing of Stage-II horror-defeat.

Members of the wrestling Church may be loners. But we may recognize "*the congregating Church*" as wrestlers who get together to articulate and to celebrate and to reinforce one another's confidence in Christ's Stage-I horror-defeat. The congregating Church also gives itself over to the study of Scripture and tradition, and to their practical application. Members of the congregating Church coach one another in wrestling, help one another to appropriate the significance of Christ's saving work for their own horror-participation (and so move towards Stage-II horror-defeat). Likewise, "*the missionary Church*" sends its members forth from the congregating Church to share its Good News with the world at large.

Heads act through their bodies. Bodies are distinguished by their functions. So we would expect the normative functions of Christ's body to be those that could be directed by or attributed to Christ the head. During His earthly career, Christ exercised a ministry of preaching and teaching, of healing (of horror-reversal) and solidarity (sharing the horrors). So, too, the primary functions of the Church are *testimony* and *solidarity*. The Church, both congregating and missionary, brings the fact of human horror out into the open, declares that horror-participation denies our worth as persons and brings Divine love for us into reasonable doubt. *And* the Church, both congregating and missionary, proclaims that God *does* love material persons as the crown of creation, that horrors *prima facie* defeat what God has in mind, but that in Christ God has trumped horrors by sharing them, by solidarity with us in horror-participation has Stage-I defeated them. Like the people Jesus healed – like the lepers, the blind, the deaf, the lame, and the demon-possessed – who ran all over Galilee and the Decapolis telling what Jesus had done for them, members of the wrestling Church who join the congregating Church, members of the congregating Church sent out by the missionary Church proclaim by who they are becoming as much as by what they say that Stage-II horror-defeat is possible. The wrestling Church and the congregating Church are communities of healing, where acknowledged horror-participants come alongside other horror-participants to bear witness to the reality of their problem and help them learn how to make the fact of Divine solidarity (of Stage-I horror-defeat) a centerpiece in making new sense of their lives. Likewise, the missionary Church steps outside in solidarity, publicly to protest horror-perpetrating individuals and institutional structures, to demand and work for changes in personnel and institutions that will bring horrors to a stop. Merely human solidarity with horror-participants is not enough to defeat horrors. Merely human efforts to change the system often do not so much eliminate as relocate horrors. Even when they fail to be concretely effective, however, solidarity and protest tell important truths: that horrors contradict the worth of persons, that they *prima facie* frustrate God's purposes, and that therefore they ought not to be!

Aquinas says that the head is the principal organ because it directs the body's movements. In the present world order, Christ directs His Church from the outside through the testimony, example, and achievements of His own *ante-mortem* career. Christ *qua* Divine directs His Church universal from the inside insofar as Christ dwells in the hearts of all human beings (see chapter 6). Because His direction is more effective to the extent that it becomes explicit and intentional, Christ's direction takes greater hold in His wrestling Church. The more people drop their defenses within Christ's congregating Church, the more the Spirit of Christ circulates between them, so that implicitly and explicitly, consciously and unconsciously, each becomes more affected by what the Inner Teacher is doing in the others. The more open they are with one another and the more regular in their gatherings, the more the Spirit of Christ binds them into a community with a distinctive common mission.

My analysis of ecclesial functions flows from my estimate of human non-optimality problems and my hypotheses about God's creative purposes. But all of these radically underdetermine institutional structures in which such functions might be housed. These might vary – indeed have varied – with place and time. The Church is headed by Christ and led by the Spirit of Christ, but the Church is human as well as Divine. The fact that we human beings are both social and socially challenged means that any human institution is apt to spawn horrors. However hard we work to improve our institutions, it is precisely their systemic character that makes them veer out of our control to produce effects beyond our powers to anticipate or prevent. History proves that the Church is no exception. The Church has been a horror-perpetrator: conspicuously, a sponsor of anti-Jewish pogroms, of the Crusades, and of the Inquisition. It has acquiesced in political oppression and sexual predation. This means

that the Body of Christ (whether Church or cosmos) is uncoordi-
nated and dysfunctional, both headed by Christ and directed by the
Spirit of Christ, and yet riddled with systemic evils and productive
of horrors. This ambivalence should keep members from turning
their ecclesial institutions into idols. It should make us humble and
vigilant, starkly self-critical, ready to repent and to seek God's help.
We will all have to live in this tension until God acts to bring horrors
definitively to an end.

8 | Resurrection and renewal: Christ the first fruits

1. Resurrection, another conditional necessity?

1.1. Thwarted evasions

What you think the non-optimality problems are determines what you think it will take for God to solve them. Reflecting on the history of soteriology, Paul Tillich distinguished: for the ancients, *death* was the problem; for the medievals as for both Protestant and counter-reformers, *sin* was the problem; for "modern man," *meaning* is the problem. In both this and my earlier book,[1] I take a page from Tillich and other neo-orthodox twentieth-century theologians to contend that *meaning* is the issue and *horrors* are the problem. I have defined horrors as evils participation in which makes positive meaning *prima facie* impossible for the participant. Like Tillich, I have seen the meaning-problem as a fundamentally *ontological* problem, one which underlies and *explains* our propensity to inauthentic choices and living, to our being and doing the kinds of things that medieval and reformed theology identified as sin (see chapter 2).

Twentieth-century neo-orthodox theologians set about to solve the meaning-problem without solving the death-problem. Either they did not believe that biological death – after bringing each of us to an end – would be overcome and itself be brought to an end; or they did not bring that belief systematically into play. Tillich urged stoic courage to be, held out the hope of new being, of living without

[1] M. M. Adams, *Horrendous Evils and the Goodness of God.*

anxiety in the face of finitude. Bultmann promised "a new self-understanding" which accepts and moves into the uncertain future that God will provide. C. H. Dodd urged that *realized* eschatology should replace *futuristic* eschatology, and found not only literal resurrection, but also life after death, to be inessential to the Christian faith.

By contrast with neo-orthodoxy, twentieth-century political and liberation theologies returned to the sin-problem. Their concentration on the systemic non-optimalities of political injustice and oppression led them to refocus on a very much *as-yet-un*realized eschatology. Their Marxian philosophical underpinnings spawned a stridently collective focus, which often dismissed concerns for individual salvation (much less bodily resurrection) in pejorative terms – as a product of Enlightenment individualism, capitalism, and/or right-wing evangelicalism. Pie-in-the-sky-by-and-by is politically pernicious, a rhetorical weapon used to keep the *hoi polloi* down. Their efforts to put the drama of salvation back into the concrete blood-and-gore of history where it belongs so immersed God in history as to make it impossible for God to act outside the seemingly inexorable historical process. As with much Hebrew prophecy, as with twentieth-century fascist and communist totalitarian states, the quest for individual meaning gets swallowed up in corporate hopes, which begin as concrete and historical but get displaced onto an ever receding future. Not infrequently, when the hope seemed too remote, liberation got dehistoricized and turned back into a regulative ideal.

Different as they are, opposed as they were often intended to be, both families of approaches represent the triumph of philosophical bias over soteriological exigency! Stoicism is deep and admirable. But stoicism is elitist – the spiritual exercises it commends are not something that many horror-participants are able to bring off. My own estimate is that for an omnipotent, omniscient, and perfectly good God, success with an elite isn't good enough; universal salvation is required. To be true to Godself, God must accomplish God's purpose in creation for each and every created person God has made. Likewise, experience and philosophy convince us that human beings are political animals. The Bible insists that Divine purposes for human beings are social. Establishing the Kingdom of God – a utopic society in which the interests of each are perfectly integrated into a common good – is thus necessary for the success of God's aims. Nevertheless, for an omniscient, omnipotent, and perfectly good God, a future just society isn't good enough. What about the countless individuals sacrificed on the slaughter-bench of history? An omniscient and omnipotent God Who loved human beings would make it up to them, would guarantee that there was enough positive meaning in it to defeat their horror-participation and make their lives great goods to them on the whole and in the end!

1.2. Facing the death-problem

My own view (already registered in chapter 2) is that God cannot solve the meaning-problem without solving the death-problem, because – for millions – *life after death* will be required for Stage-II horror-defeat. By definition, horrors stump our meaning-making capacities. Individual (as opposed to merely collective) horror-participation can break our capacity to make positive sense of our lives, can so fragment our sense of self and so damage our agency as to make authentic choice (such as ancient, existentialist, and neo-orthodox stoics require) impossible. No amount of whatever kind of psycho-therapy suffices to cure it. One experienced Los Angeles therapist, speaking of Cambodian immigrants from the killing fields, remarked: "Oh, we don't try to get them to remember and integrate. We are lucky if we can identify strategies that enable them to get through the day!" We cannot put Humpty Dumpty back together again. This condition of *prima facie* defeat is humanly incurable, and millions have taken it with them down into the grave.

The time has come to bring a further fact out into the open: *death itself is a horror!* Up to now, I have been complicit in covering up this grim truth or at least leaving it to lurk in the shadows. When I first defined "horrors" as "evils participation in the doing or suffering of which constitutes *prima facie* reason to believe the participant's life cannot have positive meaning," I was eager to contrast them with run-of-the-mill evils, whether of small, medium, or large size. Mumps, measles, toothache, losing a school sports match, not being invited to the prom, getting your second choice in college admissions, having to become a lawyer rather than a classicist to earn a living, breaking a leg or losing a gall bladder – these are among many other evils in life that we can work around, make up for by what we are or do, while learning profitable lessons from the experience. Despite our participation in run-of-the-mill evils, we can still have a good life. The burden of my earlier book and papers was that, however plausible traditional big-picture or free-will approaches to the problem of evil might seem where run-of-the-mill evils are concerned, they founder on the rock of horrors.[2] Yet, both here and in my earlier book, I have implied that some persons might be so fortunate as to get through life without *individual* horror-participation. Confronting death compels the confession: no human being escapes in the end!

Death is the one certainty for each and every human being. Death is the *natural* fate of animals. Insofar as human beings are personal *animals*, it is – *pace* Anselm – natural for us to die. Yet, human beings are *personal* animals. It is our vocation to *personalize* the material, thereby – so far as we know – making it as Godlike as it is possible for material to be. Death degrades by halting and reversing the process, by *depersonalizing* the material. Death either brings the meaning-maker to an end, or separates the soul from an appropriate body. Death proves that there is not enough to us to maintain

---

[2] Cf. M. M. Adams, "Theodicy without Blame," *Philosophical Topics* 16 (1988), 215–45; M. M. Adams, "Horrendous Evils and the Goodness of God"; M. M. Adams, "The Problem of Hell: A Problem of Evil for Christians," *Reasoned Faith: Essays in Philosophical Theology in Honor of Norman Kretzmann*, ed. Eleonore Stump (Ithaca, NY: Cornell University Press, 1993), 301–327; M. M. Adams, "Chalcedonian Christology: A Christian Solution to the Problem of Evil," *Philosophy and Theological Discourse*, ed. Stephen T. Davis (London: Macmillan Press, 1997), 173–198; and M. M. Adams, *Horrendous Evils and the Goodness of God.*

integrity, to hold body and soul together. It thereby *prima facie* defeats our efforts and obstructs the Creator's purpose. It is in our nature and our calling as human beings to strive against the forces that would undo us, and it is in our nature surely to lose.

Death mocks our personal pretensions. Atheist existentialist philosophers urge that death bids fair to reduce our meaning-making processes to an absurdity. The preacher of Ecclesiastes seems to agree: "vanity of vanities," "all is vanity and striving with the wind!" (Ecclesiastes 1–4). Atheist existentialists counsel rebellion against the basic conditions of our existence by making meaning anyway. Remembering that we are dust-to-dust-returning, we can for a little while insist that we are not only dust, and shake our fist at fate. The preacher of Ecclesiastes is more resigned: enjoy good things while you can, because neither they nor you will last forever! If death is a horror, and death is natural to human being, then to be human is to be headed for horror. In cultic conceptuality, human being is a *prima facie* cursed kind of thing to be.

To be sure, this bitter conviction is perennially resisted. A mere end, the finitude of our earthly career, has not always been thought to rob the career itself of positive meaning. If Genesis 2–3 sees death as a penalty, stories about the patriarchs and King David are told as brimful of significance, even though their heroes go down to their ancestors with no *literal immortality* in sight. Narratives, odes, and monuments may themselves bear witness to the idea that a meaningful career can be finite so long as it is *remembered and celebrated from generation to generation.*

In my judgment, such denial of the horror of death succeeds only by distracting us from the companion fact that our cultures, tribes, and nations are also transient and temporary. Even when we write in stone, whatever we store in time capsules or cyberspace, our monuments will fade into unintelligibility, their languages eventually become undecipherable. Worse still, we cannot count on the natural frame within which empires rise and fall. Eco-movements urge us to wake up to the fact that we are wrecking our environment, that planet earth may all too soon become uninhabitable by humankind. Cosmologists threaten that the universe is headed towards a state of entropy incompatible with organic life.

What we have here is a nesting of horrors corresponding to a nesting of meaning-making structures: individual, social, and natural. Each of them is radically vulnerable to undoing. Nature can evolve, human societies can organize, individuals can reproduce and rear personal animals. But nature, human societies, and individuals can stamp the material with the personal at most temporarily. Individual and collective human personal projects are doomed to dissolution. Matter by its nature is prepared to host the personal only for (what is in cosmological terms) a short stay.

(Incidentally, such nesting of horrors helps explain why terrorist attacks – such as the 9/11 attack on the World Trade Center in New York and the 7/7 attacks on a London bus and underground trains – are horrendous. At the individual level, the maimings and deaths were senseless the way any accidental death is senseless. Individuals' meaning-making activities were brought to a sudden end without regard to who they were *as persons* – to character or moral record, to age or gender, to sexual orientation or marital status, to race, creed, or national origin. The "selection-procedure" for victims was utterly indifferent to the projects and purposes that gave meaning to their lives.

Our feeling that terrorist attacks are worse than someone's being accidentally run over by a bus picks up on the fact that the terrorists' real aim is not at individuals but at the body-politic: it is the ethnic group, nation, or way of life that they hope to maim or destroy. Terrorists are out to degrade or destroy the body-politic by degrading and destroying random individuals who live and move and have their being within it. Moreover, unlike the hapless or reckless bus driver, terrorists *deliberately choose* perpetrating horrors on individuals as *a means* to the end of exploding the wider frame. Similarly, terrorist threats to poison water supplies or the air or to introduce lethal germs target the natural order within which society sets itself up, and so seek to undo us at an even more fundamental level.)

Still, have I not cautioned that what counts as horrendous is person-relative? Doesn't hagiography testify that death is not always horrendous? Recall stories of saints and martyrs (e.g., Polycarp, Perpetua, and Felicity) who were so certain of Divine favor that death and torture and dismemberment by lions did not seem to rob their lives of positive significance. On the contrary, their heroic faithfulness through these trials enhanced the positive meaning of their lives.

My reply is to emphasize the contrast between *prima facie* and *ultima facie* ruin. Horrors constitute *prima facie* reason to believe that the horror-participant's life lacks positive meaning. Context can defeat that *prima facie* presumption (what God has to do to defeat horrors is to change the context), but a defeated horror is one whose *prima facie* reason is not *ultima facie*, because a stronger reason for positive meaning has been found. A defeated horror still constitutes *prima facie* reason to doubt the positive significance of the participant's life. Torture and death are still horrors. The counterexamples cited are ones in which horror-participants recognized the presence of defeaters at the time of their horror-participation. Their experience of immeasurable Divine Goodness, their conviction that God was *for* them, their sense of being honored by a being a greater than which cannot be conceived, assured them that nothing their tormenters or the lions did could ruin their lives. Most horror-participants have to wait until later to put two and two – the horror with its outclassing defeater – together. Unlike such saints and martyrs, most horror-participants lack confidence to believe that there will be any "later" within which to reverse the degradation and to resolve the plots of their lives.

1.3. Resurrection and renewal?

Thus I hold fast to my conclusions that – for the vast majority of horror-participants – Stage-II horror-defeat requires life after death, while Stage-III horror-defeat demands universal human immunity to death. But – conceptually – life after death is not equivalent to resurrection. Many metaphysical dualists have advertised death as a good thing, because it sheds the body which drags us down. Remember how Socrates welcomes it in the *Apology*. Remember Origen's characterization of the body as a prison, or Ambrose's denunciation of the body as "a bag of shit," which it would be idiotic to want back![3] *Post mortem*, we will be able to concentrate on higher things – on Platonic forms, on God and the Divine ideas – unencumbered by sensory distractions. My estimates of human non-optimality problems and Divine purposes in creation pull in the opposite direction.

God's assimilative and unitive aims in creation find their focus in personalized material, personal animals, enmattered spirits – so far as we know, in human being. Human radical vulnerability to and inevitable participation in horrors *prima facie* reduces God's creative aims to an absurdity. To vindicate Divine prowess in creating, Divine Goodness and commitment to material creation, it is conditionally necessary for God to make good on the Divine project of *embodied* persons. To rip human personhood out of its material context would be to give up and admit defeat.

Moreover, since radical vulnerability to horrors renders embodied personhood in this world a *prima facie* curse, something which *prima facie* robs our *ante-mortem* careers of any positive significance, it is conditionally necessary that Divine goodness-to human horror-participants turn embodied personhood into an *ultima facie* blessing. We have paid prices to fill that role in God's plan. A God Who means to be good-to us would have to make it pay big dividends for us as well. For these reasons, horrors make human bodily resurrection conditionally necessary for the fulfillment of Divine purposes.

---

[3] Ambrose, *De excessu Fratris Sui Satyri*, II.20 (Corpus Scriptorum Ecclesiasticorum Latinorum 73, 260), quoted in Caroline Walker Bynum, *The Resurrection of the Body in Western Christianity 200–1336* (New York: Columbia University Press, 1995), Part I, ch. 2, 61.

Merely human effort cannot harrow the hell of horrendous evil, because horrors are a product of systemic and structural mismatches: between God and creature; between the material and the personal; between the material and the spiritual within human being; between human nature and our material environment of real and apparent scarcity; between what God is and what we are. The human condition cannot become optimal or even excellent unless God is able and eventually ready and willing to "change the system" and establish a new world order. The completion of Stage-II and Stage-III horror-defeat requires Divinely instigated cosmic renovation!

Notice that I am not saying that God is compelled by the necessity of the Divine nature to re-create us or to renew the material cosmos. Both creation and re-creation are a matter of God's free and contingent choice. Rather, just as Anselm argues that a God-man is conditionally necessary, given Divine purposes for humankind and given human sin, so I want to say that resurrection and cosmic remodel are conditionally necessary, given God's love for material creation and given God's love for human being(s).

GRACE

1.4. Appeals to authority

Scripture and tradition also bear witness to resurrection and renewal. How can Christology miss the centrality of Christ's resurrection in the New Testament texts? C. H. Dodd himself identifies death–resurrection–ascension as the kernel of the earliest Christian sermons: enemies crucified Jesus, but God vindicated Jesus by raising Him up to sit at God's right hand. The Synoptic Jesus repeatedly predicts the scenario of crucifixion followed by resurrection. All four Gospels include resurrection–appearance stories. St. Paul digs deeper theologically: because death is the last enemy (I Corinthians 15:26), the meaning of Christ's resurrection is not merely individual, but prototypical. "Christ is the first fruits," but "at His coming all who belong to Christ" shall be raised. "As in Adam all die, so also in Christ shall all be made alive" (I Corinthians 15:20–23).

Both the Apostles' and Nicene creeds reassert the doctrine of parallel destinies: we believe in the crucifixion and death, resurrection and ascension of Jesus; *and* we believe in the general resurrection of the dead and the life of the world to come. Apocalyptic visions picture ritual cleansing by cosmic conflagration (II Peter 3:7, 10), the descent of the new Jerusalem, a new heaven and a new earth (Revelation 21:1–2). Plenty of plain-sense and scholarly readings of the New Testament agree with explicit credal clauses: in the Savior, God is at work to solve not only the sin-problem or the meaning-problem, but also the death-problem. Twentieth-century theologians who deny it (Dodd and Bultmann among them) have had a lot of texts to explain away!

My argument – negatively from soteriology, and positively from Divine purposes in creation – for resurrection and renewal is strong, but controversial. Indeed, one might question whether I can consistently endorse some of its substantive assumptions. Before reflecting more concretely on what the new world order and our risen embodiment might be like, I need to pause over several of these in turn.

2. Divine agency

Most twentieth-century theologians who reject literal resurrection – both Christ's in the past and ours in the future – find the idea incredible, something no modern person formed and informed by a scientific worldview could believe. On their diagnosis, my systematic arguments lead to manifestly false conclusions because they presuppose unacceptable claims about Divine power and Divine policies:

(T1) that God has power to intervene in, obstruct, and/or reorganize causal interactions among creatures; and

(T2) that God does not have overriding reasons never to do so.

2.1. The scope of Divine power

For medieval Latin school theologians, adherence to (T1) was necessary to underwrite the miraculous in this world, general resurrection and cosmic renewal in the world to come. I have already (in chapter 3) registered my judgment against the stridently anti-miraculous stand of much of twentieth-century theology: viz., that it is philosophically parochial and overestimates what science requires. Once again, philosophical positions are inherently controversial. As a philosopher, I have not yet been shown cause why I should assign presumptive weight to the Kantian, post-Kantian, Hegelian, and neo-Marxian approaches that reject (T1) instead of the many rigorous medieval and contemporary systems that accept it. Neither does the integrity and autonomy of science require us to reject (T1). Scientific inquiry may deploy some sort of uniformity assumption as a working hypothesis. But the project of scientific investigation and the utility of its results do not depend on actual exceptionless conformity. Aristotelian not-always-but-for-the-most-part conformity will do. After all, Newtonian mechanics was worked out for an idealized world without friction, and remains useful even though it requires to be imbedded in an Einsteinian frame. So long as miracles are rare, (T1) can be true, God can have raised Christ from the dead, and science can be as accurate and useful in this world as we experience it to be.

Cosmic renewal on the scale needed for Stage-III horror-defeat means permanent and systematic interference of a different order of magnitude, however – one that would render some discoveries or discoverables of this-worldly science no longer applicable. If it didn't, the remodels wouldn't be drastic enough to take away our radical vulnerability to horrors. (T1) is strong enough to underwrite this soteriological desideratum. That the new world order would leave this-worldly science in need of extensive revision is no argument against it; it is just what we would require and exactly what we would expect.

215

2.2. Divine policies

Those who think (not-T1) that Divine interference in the created order is metaphysically impossible *a fortiori* deny that God purposes anything that requires such intervention. Others (e.g., Maurice Wiles[4]) deny (T2), because such Divine meddling – though metaphysically possible – would be immoral in not treating like cases alike – rescuing some horror-participants and not others. Such Divine interference would also be unmannerly, like disrespectful parents trying to control the lives of their adult children. It might seem, however, that my own soteriological analysis is incompatible with (T2) the same way, insofar as I postulate a Divine love for material creation that wants it to be as Godlike as possible *while still being itself.* In trying to explain what God might have been thinking in creating us in a world like this, I have supposed Divine love for material creation to be permissive – a love that produces material stuff and lets it "do its thing," allows it to interact and evolve in whichever ways. This hypothesis has explanatory value for my purposes precisely because such a permissive policy inevitably results in some material things ruining others: lions devour lambs; swallows eat bugs; human biochemistry interacting with our present environment wrecks and distorts before it destroys human personality. Since it is not part of my view that God ever ceases to love material creation, how can I think God will suddenly interfere with and obstruct it, not only by raising us from the dead, but by instigating a cosmic overhaul?

One medieval answer would be that God can be constant in loving material creation and yet have *priorities* – indeed changeable and changing priorities – within this love. Aquinas argues that God's role as providential governor of the universe means that God will look first to the good of the universe as a whole and be willing to

---

[4] Maurice Wiles, *God's Action in the World: The Bampton Lectures for 1986* (London: SCM Press, 1986).

accept defect and imperfection in individual parts if the whole is enhanced thereby. Species diversity perfects the whole, even though the natural functioning of one (lions or swallows) destroys or interferes with the natural flourishing of another (lambs or bugs). Scotus recognizes a hierarchy of natures. According to Aristotelian science, plants and animals have "mixed" bodies, constituted from all four elements. The elements have their natural places, however, and hence a natural tendency to fly off in different directions (earth to the center of the universe, fire to the outer rim, water and air in between), thereby pulling the mixed body apart. Because in the essential order of eminence, plant and animal natures are more excellent than the elements, it is appropriate for the natural tendencies of the elements to be subordinated to the natural ends of living things. The elements are violently obstructed from "doing their thing" so that plants and animals may exist and "do their" more excellent "thing."[5]

Several metaphors and analogies suggest how a lover – while yet loving – might mutually restrict one beloved in the interests of another. (i) *Sibling harmony?* Parents who deliberately beget a second child do not thereby automatically prove diminished love for the first, even though the older will have to learn to share benefits with the newcomer, and the younger will have to adjust to a world already occupied and shaped by the needs and desires of others.

(ii) Hagiographies of St. Francis identify *courtesy* as a way of heralding God's kingdom. Courtesy consists of symbolic behaviors that show honor to others, that signify that they are welcome in the world, entitled to space and time, the means to survive, the opportunity to function and flourish. Courtesy is considerate and appreciative of the other, to one degree or another anticipates and provides for the other's needs, makes room for its desires and pleasures. Courteous acts not only assert the worth of others, but also

[5] Scotus, *Op.Ox.* IV, d. 49, q. 13, n. 13; Wadding X.591; IV, d. 49, q. 14, n. 12; Wadding X.604.

imply the worth of their agent, that there is enough to him/her, that s/he is so self-possessed, that s/he can afford to be generous and to focus on the worth and well-being of someone or something else. Thus, courtesy presumes secure abundance, or at least the pretense of it, on the side of the agent.

Francis *knew* the Heavenly Father to be Boundless Goodness, and regarded all God's creatures as brothers and sisters. Francis' daunting asceticism was a form of extravagant courtesy that refused to relate to others as means only. Because Francis knew himself to participate in Goodness from a boundless source, he was free not to demand that other creatures meet his needs, but to let them be, to the honor and glory of God. Other stories tell how Francis occasionally asked them to return the favor. Singing birds in the wood reminded Francis that it was time for vespers, whereupon he asked the birds to be quiet for a while, to give the human beings their turn.[6] When doctors decided to cauterize Francis' temples in a bizarre attempt to cure his blindness, Francis first praised the fire that was about to scar his flesh, but then asked it to be gentle with him, presuming that such a noble creature could afford to be mannerly, that it would have no need for maximal self-assertion at all times. Reportedly, the fire burned the flesh, but Francis felt no pain.[7]

(iii) Another biblical and Franciscan image, also forwarded by C. S. Lewis who lived and worked in that nation of pet-lovers, is that of *domestication*. Pet owners love their pets in part for their *wildness* that doesn't neatly fit into a human way of life. Yet, because pet owners *love* their pets, they want to live together with them and so bring them into their own human households. Domestication involves raising the pet to a style and level of life for which it is not naturally suited. Nature is not erased – once again, that's part

[6] Bonaventure, *Legenda Sancti Francisci*, ch. VIII, secs. 7–8; Quaracchi VIII.528–529; Thomas of Celano, *St. Francis of Assisi: First and Second Life of St. Francis with Selections from the Treatise on the Miracles of the Blessed Francis*, trans. Placid Hermann (Chicago: Franciscan Herald Press, 1963), Second Life, Book II, ch. 130, sec. 170, 273–274.
[7] Thomas of Celano, Second Life, Book II, ch. 125, sec. 166, 271.

of what the pet owner loves. But its expression is curtailed – dogs and cats have to give up biting and scratching and hunting – to get along with human beings. The pets get something out of it, but they also lose something. It may be controversial where the right balance lies.[8]

To these thoughts and images, add biblical dispensationalism, according to which the cosmos is organized very differently in one period and another. In particular, recall the two-age theory according to which God first allows wickedness to do its worst, to run its course, to evacuate its vilest by-products, to exhaust its ruinous power; and then God reverses all of its effects and establishes a new world order.

Borrowing from all of these, I suggest that Divine love of material creation expresses itself in two stages. In this present age, Divine love for material creation is permissive: for the most part (some miracles do happen), material stuff is allowed to "be itself," to exercise its powers without Divine interference. The personal is allowed to spring up in the household of the material, but the material ravages it. In the age to come, Divine love for material creation will express itself by domesticating the material into the household of the personal, so that persons do not become – by intimate association with it – radically vulnerable to horrors.

3. What *are* human beings (Psalm 8:4)?

The metaphysics of human being – the "mind–body" problem – is and ought to be perennially controversial. Well-formulated versions of idealisms, dualism, hylomorphism, functionalism, eliminative materialism, are impossible to refute philosophically, because counterarguments involve premises that would be problematized

---

[8] See my article "Courtesy, Divine and Human," in "Three Great Theological Ideas from the Middle Ages," *Sewanee Theological Review* (Easter 2004), 47:2, 145–163.

by the position under attack. Likewise debatable and ever debated is the question whether it is good-for human beings for mind and body to be functionally interactive. Already noted is the fervent conviction of some dualists (Socrates and some Church fathers) whose answer is "no."

Most medieval Latin school theologians agreed that ultimate human happiness would be found in the beatific vision and enjoyment of God. But they insisted that the human being could not be maximally happy if its soul were separated from its body. For one thing, the soul has *a natural inclination* to its body.[9] Aristotle had argued – against real or imagined dualists – that, because souls are or naturally give rise to functional powers, they cannot animate any body whatever but only those with organs suitable for the functions in question:[10] e.g., cow souls can animate only bodies that have eyes for seeing and ears for hearing and double stomachs for cud-chewing digestion; human souls, only reasonably normal human bodies. Medieval Aristotelians went further to insist that a given human soul has a natural inclination to *its very own particular* body.[11] Aquinas holds that souls are individuated by their inclinations to *this* hunk of matter as opposed to that, and that a soul cannot be united to a numerically distinct body from the one it had.[12] Bonaventure compares the resurrection soul in search of a body to a man confronted by two equally beautiful and virtuous women: each will prefer union with the one it/he had intimately known before.[13] Bernard of Clairvaux compares soul and body to unequal friends who

---

[9] Bonaventure, *Sent.* IV, d. 43, a. 1, q. 1; Quaracchi IV.883–4; Aquinas, *Sent.* IV, d. 43, q. u, a. 1; Parma XXII.416; d. 44, q. 1, a. 1; Parma XXII.418; d. 49, q. u, a. 4; Parma XXII.433; Aquinas, *Summa Contra Gentiles* IV, ch. 79.

[10] Aristotle, *On the Soul* II.II 414a 15–29; text 26.

[11] Bonaventure, *Sent.* IV, d. 43, a. 1, q. 4; Quaracchi IV.888–889; Bonaventure, *Breviloquium*, Part VII, ch. 5, sec. 5, ch. 7, sec. 4; Quaracchi V.287, 290.

[12] Aquinas, *Sent.* IV, d. 43, q. u, a. 2; Parma XXII.417; Aquinas, *Summa Contra Gentiles* IV, ch. 84; Bonaventure, *Sent.* IV, d. 43, a. 1, q. 4; Quaracchi IV.888–889.

[13] Bonaventure, *Sent.* IV, d. 43, a. 1, q. 5; Quaracchi IV.894.

worked together and helped each other in their *ante-mortem* pursuit of a shared and lofty goal.[14] Because the human being's *ante-mortem* career is a product of their collaborative agency, they must be resurrected and reunited so that the same agent can receive punishments or rewards.[15] Even if Bonaventure,[16] Aquinas,[17] Scotus,[18] and Ockham[19] do let natural science problematize whether and how – given that humans eat each other or eat food grown in soil fertilized by human remains – the resurrection body can be altogether materially the same, they still want to insist that it is enough the same!

Medieval Latin school theologians insist that maximal human happiness involves happiness for *both* soul and body. The soul has an infused vision of the Divine essence and is confirmed in uprightness of will. Some suggest separation from the body would make a difference to the soul's subjective experience, that it will be consciously dragged down by the awareness that its natural inclination is frustrated.[20] Others probably do not understand it to make a subjective difference because the soul's natural inclination is in effect unconscious.[21] Nevertheless, beatific vision and enjoyment will be metaphysically less perfect because its subject will be metaphysically incomplete if there is no soul–body reunion.

I have already signaled – in chapter 5 – my preference for a tighter human mind–body connection than dualisms seem to afford. I have argued that Divine love of material creation, its assimilative and unitive purposes, find their focus in personified matter, enmattered

[14] Bernard, *De diligendo Deo*, ch. 11, paras. 30–33; *Opera* III.144–147; William of St. Thierry, *De Natura Corporis et Animae*, II (Patrologia Latina 180, cols. 707–726).
[15] Bonaventure, *Sent.* IV, d. 43, a. 1, q. 1; Quaracchi IV.883–884; IV, d. 43, a. 1, q. 2; Quaracchi IV.886; Bonaventure, *Breviloquium*, Part VII, ch. 5, sec. 2; Quaracchi V.286; Aquinas, *Sent.* IV, d. 43, q. u, a. 2; Parma XXII.417; IV, d. 47, q. u, a. 1; Parma XXII.427.
[16] Bonaventure, *Sent.* IV, d. 44, p. 1, a. 2, q. 2; Quaracchi IV.911–912.
[17] Aquinas, *Summa Contra Gentiles* IV, chs. 80–81.
[18] Scotus, *Op.Ox.* IV, d. 44, q. 1, n. 17; Wadding X.117.
[19] Ockham, *Quaest. in IV Sent.* q. 13; OTh VII.257–276.
[20] Bernard, *De diligendo Deo*, ch. 10, para. 29–ch. 11, para. 33; *Opera* III.143–147.
[21] Aquinas, *Summa Contra Gentiles* IV, ch. 79.

spirits, personal animals, embodied persons – so far as we know, in human beings. It is as embodied persons that God has purposed us, and embodied persons is what we are. Whether or not we can exist between death and resurrection as ghosts (whether as disembodied spirits or as souls attached – *pace* Aristotle – to some fragment of matter but not to a human body through which it could act in significant ways), we would not be happy remaining ghosts. Our knowledge and appreciation of the world, of one another, and of God are carnal. We are acquainted with our material environment through sense perception. Unlike dogs and earthworms, we are *intelligent* perceivers, but our medium of contact is *sense* perception all the same. During this passing lifetime, embodiment is the medium of our personal connection. We have carnal knowledge of one another – the infant nursing its mother, the fraternal hug, the collegial handshake, the lover's kiss, face-to-face recognition of one another on the path. We have carnal knowledge of one another when with lumps in our throats and tears in our eyes, with heartburn, headaches, and the bowels of compassion (diarrhea?), we sympathize, take into our own bodies one another's anxiety and pain. Our knowledge of God is likewise carnal, when we bend our bodies to postures and shape our mouths to blasphemy and defiance, to prayer and praise. And we spend our artistic creativity to shape other materials – stones and plaster into statues and buildings, colors and canvass into paintings, vibrations of the air into music – into further expressions of these sentiments. Julian of Norwich prayed to have carnal knowledge of Christ's suffering by feeling in her own body the pains that He suffered when He died on the cross.[22] Some ninth- to eleventh-century theologians insisted that we have carnal knowledge of God in holy eucharist when we eat Christ's flesh and drink Christ's blood (see chapter 10). When we stop to think about it, do we really have any notion of how *we* could be ourselves, be personally connected with one another and our lived worlds, and yet be disembodied? How – I

---

[22] Julian of Norwich, *Revelations of Divine Love*, ch. 3, 66.

ask – could anything merely immaterial be more than a fragment of *us*?

4. New creation, what sorts of changes?

What you think the non-optimalities are determines what you think needs fixing. Scripture and tradition conceptualize both in a variety of ways.

4.1. Hebrew Bible pictures

Dominant in the Hebrew Bible is a collective focus that spotlights shortages and shortness of years, agricultural vulnerability to plagues and bad weather, political injustice and poverty, threats of foreign domination and deportation, and poor Divine–human communications. God's answer will be an end to scarcity, agricultural abundance, a land overflowing with milk and honey, supernatural produce (a year's supply of wine from a single grape); an end to premature death, primordial length of years; an end to bodily dysfunctions (the eyes of the blind opened, the ears of the deaf unstopped, the lame walking). God's Messiah will effect a social revolution: justice will roll down like waters; poverty will be a thing of the past (each person will be able to occupy his patriarchal allotment, to live from the fruits of his labor; there will be no more enslaving debt). God's dwelling on Zion will make it impervious to foreign attack; exile will be reversed. Not only Israelites but all the nations will stream to Jerusalem to worship the evident glory of God. Overall, God will usher Israel into a secure and flourishing, communal this-worldly life, in a city flooded with Divine presence. The envisioned transition between old and new world orders will be apocalyptic, traumatic, and cataclysmic, comparable to cosmic catastrophes and geological upheavals. The juridical turning point will be the great Day of the Lord from which those deeply invested in the old world order will have a lot to fear.

4.2. New Testament transformations

The New Testament revises Hebrew Bible and pseudepigraphal pictures from two principal sources: from Christ's earthly ministry, and from the risen Christ Himself. Jesus preaches a Reign of God full of reversals in which the dishonored will be honored, and the excluded will be brought in. The Reign of God will mean an end to disabling physical and psycho-spiritual conditions, an end to stringencies, the beginning of feasting. The risen Christ is invulnerable to death (Romans 6:9). His body is still wounded, but His torn flesh implies no dysfunction. He is not a ghost but eats and renews table fellowship with His friends. His body is solid and touchable but unobstructed by closed doors, visible but with unusual powers to appear or disappear (Luke 22:17–18; 24:28–42; John 21:9–15). These, along with His ascension, suggest different and enhanced capacities for mobility. Apocalyptic passages foretell the transition from this age to the next with images of cosmic catastrophe (Mark 13, Matthew 24) culminating in conflagration (II Peter 3:7, 10) and a last judgment in which Christ the judge separates the elect from the damned who are thrown into the lake of fire prepared for the devil and all his angels. The new Jerusalem will be an unending scene of Divine presence and joyful worship (Revelation 4:2–11, 5:6–14, 21:10–27).

4.3. Medieval reframings

Medieval Latin school theology divided the difficulties into ontological and juridical. God created a cosmos subject to generation and corruption, in order to produce enough human beings to fill up heaven, and to provide an arena within which they/we could exercise our free choice to forge careers that God would count as worthy of eternal punishment or reward. The world as we know it will end when that purpose has been accomplished. The world to come will feature *an end to ontological instability*: first and foremost, *a cosmos-wide end to generation and corruption*: the heavens cease to move; the elements no longer interact and undergo substantial change; mixed bodies are not allowed to corrupt. Aquinas and Bonaventure go so far as to say that mixed bodies (and hence all plants and animals) other than the human body will no longer exist in reality, and the contrary qualities of the elements – that are interactive and productive of generation and corruption – will be annihilated.[23] Moreover, all human beings will be raised into a state of permanent *ontological completeness*. The human soul will be inseparably reunited to its complete body, this time in prime (thirty-year-old) condition.[24] Where the elect are concerned, the soul will be infused with a vision of the Divine essence, and the will confirmed in justice – in loving God above all for God's own sake and love of neighbor as oneself.[25] Likewise, ungodly orientation of will and appetite will be confirmed in the damned. An end to corruption does not mean that *all* changes cease.[26] Locomotion will be easier than before. Changing thoughts and choices, sensations (at least vision and hearing), are allowed so long as they are not naturally corruptive and/or are obstructed from producing corruptive effects. But the soul will no longer engage in its vegetative functions: nutrition involves destroying the food to turn it into the eater; reproduction involves the substantial change of materials in the mother into the bodies of new members of the species.

---

[23] See Aquinas, *Sent.* IV, d. 47, q. u, a. 4; Parma XXII.428; IV, d. 48, q. 2, a. 2; Parma XXII.430–431; Aquinas, *Summa Contra Gentiles* IV, ch. 97; Bonaventure, *Sent.* IV, d. 47, a. 2, q. 1; Quaracchi IV.975–976; Bonaventure, *Breviloquium*, Part VII, ch. 4, 1–7; Quaracchi V.284–286. These views are critiqued by Scotus in *Op.Ox.* IV, d. 48, q. 2, n. 13; Wadding X.318; d. 48, q. 2, n. 16; Wadding X.320; d. 49, q. 13, nn. 2–3, 7–8, 9–11; Wadding X.578–579, 583, 587.

[24] Bonaventure, *Sent.* IV, d. 44, p. 1, a. 3, q. 2, Dubia I–II; Quaracchi IV.917–918.

[25] Aquinas, *Sent.* IV, d. 49, q. u, aa. 1–2; Parma XXII.431–432; Aquinas, *Summa Contra Gentiles* IV, ch. 92; Bonaventure, *Breviloquium*, Part VII, ch. 7, secs. 7–8; Quaracchi V.290–291.

[26] Scotus, *Op.Ox.* IV, d. 48, q. 2, n. 13; Wadding X.318; IV, d. 49, q. 13, n. 8; Wadding X.583; IV, d. 49, q. 13, n. 11; Wadding X.587–588.

Clearly ruled out are ageing and diminishment, which are partially corruptive changes and precursors of death.[27]

Ontological stability and completeness not only vindicate the Re-creator's prowess, but also serve God's juridical agenda. The world to come will not be a place of trial and achievements. Rather it will begin with the last judgment and continue with the eternal suffering of punishments or enjoyment of rewards. Each individual human being must rise into ontological completeness of body and soul, because justice demands that the very same agent who lived the career – body and soul, not soul alone – be the one who stands trial and reaps the consequences (see section 7).[28]

4.4. Horror-defeating criteria

My own systematic assumption – that the human condition generally and Divine–human relations are alike non-optimal because God has set us up for horrors by creating us as personal animals in a mate-rial environment of real and apparent scarcity – issues in a *negative* criterion for salvation: that it should put an evident end to human radical vulnerability to and participation in horrors. My further sys-tematic hypothesis – that God loves material creation, and that this love expresses itself in assimilative and unitive aims – yields a *positive* criterion: that we should be as Godlike as it is possible for material to be, and that we should enter into personal union with God. Since God's love for material creation finds its focus in humankind, God's love for material creation implies a love for us that translates into a determination to be good-to each and every created person God has made. Divine goodness-to each and every created person consti-tutes a further positive measure. And this implies first that we should

---

[27] Aquinas, *Sent.* IV, d. 44, q. 1, a. 3; Parma XXII.420; Aquinas, *Summa Contra Gentiles* IV, ch. 83; Bonaventure, *Breviloquium*, Part VII, ch. 4, sec. 7; Quaracchi V.289–290.

[28] Aquinas, *Sent.* IV, d. 47, q. u, a. 1; Parma XXII.427; Aquinas, *Summa Contra Gentiles* IV, ch. 79; Bonaventure, *Sent.* IV, d. 43, a. 1, qq. 1–2; Quaracchi IV.883–886; Bonaventure, *Breviloquium* VII, ch. 1, secs. 1–2; Quaracchi V.281–282.

flourish as personified matter, that we should be brought into a state of harmonious functioning as embodied persons; second, that we should be brought into a state of beatific enjoyment of God and of our fellow human beings. My negative criterion implies only an end to the worst that we can suffer, be, or do. My positive criteria for end-time changes include this, but are more comprehensive.

5. No more horrors!

If definitive horror-defeat is the soteriological reason for believing in a world to come, then surely, whatever else may be true about it, it will be a horror-free zone.

5.1. Domesticating biochemistry

I have already argued (in section 1) that death and vulnerability to death should be the first to go. Since what is at stake in getting rid of horrors is clearing our path of obstacles to positive meaning, surely biochemical conditions that distort, degenerate, and destroy our meaning-making capacities (e.g., severe clinical depression, schizophrenia, Alzheimer's) would come a close second. Already on this side of the grave, modern medicine has discovered drug therapies that reverse, delay, or diminish the effects of some of these conditions. Surely the Creator will know how to adjust and stabilize brain chemistry so that we are no longer assailed by mental illness. In cases such as depression, schizophrenia, and Alzheimer's, there is usually an individual personality that has been formed before the effects of the disease have taken full hold – a personality that can be recovered and brought to flourishing. More difficult are cases in which biochemistry has limited the individual's meaning-making capacities from the beginning. If traditional theology held that those who die in infancy will rise as adults, should we think that people with Down's syndrome or other mentally challenged individuals will rise with normal IQs? Would such a change preserve enough meaning-making continuity for the individual, so that this change would be a favor to *her* or *him*? For that matter, not all such genetically induced conditions are clearly horrendous: individuals with Down's syndrome do not appear to have lives devoid of positive meaning, even if the positive meanings that they make are more childlike in scope than those of normal adults. What about individuals whose mental capacities are so severely challenged that they have never been meaning-makers? Will the world to come supply these deficits so that they can function as persons for the first time?

5.2. *No more social dysfunction!*

We human beings are both socially imbedded and socially challenged. Humanly contrived social systems institutionalize invidious distinctions, enshrine tribalism, nationalism, racism, caste systems or class distinctions, sexism and homophobia. Family systems lock themselves into abusive dynamics. These pervert our meaning-making systems and beget many and ghastly horrors. Plot-resolution into a happy ending means that dysfunctional social systems must come to an end.

Yet, God can no more solve the social-dysfunction problem by isolating us in heavenly hermitages than God can fix mind–body friction by saving our souls without our bodies. On the contrary, God made us social animals. According to the Bible, God was out to form Godself a people, to gather us into the Kingdom of God to live under God's most blessed reign. God made us to adopt us as God's children, to domesticate us into God's household. God cannot make a success of Divine purposes without ushering us into a utopic society – one that integrates the well-being of each into the common good. Likewise, this built-in social propensity has proved costly for us, because it has made us radically vulnerable to, inevitable participants in, many and ghastly horrors. A God Who loved us, Who meant to be good-to each created person, would want to make social life enjoyable for us, an ineffable blessing in place of unspeakable curse.

Traditional Christian theology has mostly agreed with the reasoning but restricted the conclusion. In the world to come, God will organize an ideal society for the elect, but arranges hell, a polar-opposite society under devilish management, for the damned. Medieval Latin school theologians imagine hell as a place of darkness, of continual pain and frustration; a place where inmates teeter-totter between isolation and tormenting personal engagement. If horrors destroy positive personal meaning *prima facie*, consignment to hell ruins lives *all things considered*.

In the past, I have faulted the traditional notion that God separates winners from losers on the basis of their *ante-mortem* moral performance and their general conformity to Divine commands.[29] I have argued that it errs in assigning human agents enough competency to bear responsibility – through their own beliefs and choices – for their own and others' eternal destiny. Ignorance diminishes the voluntary. We cannot get our minds around *ante-mortem* horrors that we have not experienced. How much less the torments of hell and everlasting separation from God!

Traditional doctrines of hell err again by supposing either that God does not get what God wants with every human being ("God wills all humans to be saved" by God's antecedent will) or that God deliberately creates some for ruin. To be sure, many human beings have conducted their *ante-mortem* lives in such a way as to become anti-social persons. Almost none of us dies with all the virtues needed to be fit for heaven. Traditional doctrines of hell suppose that God lacks the will or the patience or the resourcefulness to civilize each

---

[29] Bonaventure, *Sent.* IV, d. 44, p. 2, a. 1, q. 1–p. 2, a. 3, q. 2; Quaracchi IV.920–933; Bonaventure, *Breviloquium* VII, ch. 6, secs. 1–6; Quaracchi V.287–288; Aquinas, *Sent.* IV, d. 44, q. 1, a. 4; Parma XXII.420–421; IV, d. 45, q. u, a. 1; Parma XXII.423; IV, d. 50, q. u, aa. 1–2; Parma XXII.433–435.

and all of us, to rear each and all of us up into the household of God. They conclude that God is left with the options of merely human penal systems – viz., liquidation or quarantine![30]

Traditional doctrines of hell go beyond failure to hatred and cruelty by imagining a God Who not only acquiesces in creaturely rebellion and dysfunction but either directly organizes or intentionally "outsources" a concentration camp (of which Auschwitz and Soviet gulags are pale imitations) to make sure some creatures' lives are permanently deprived of positive meaning.

My own view is that *ante-mortem horror-participation is hell enough.* Horrors constitute the *prima facie* destruction of the positive meaning of our lives; a destruction that we lack knowledge, power, or worth enough to defeat; a destruction that reasonably drives many to despair. For God to succeed, God has to defeat horrors for everyone. We have all been to hell by being tainted by horrors *ante-mortem.* We all will meet the horror of death at the end. For some, life has been one horror after another between the dawn of personhood and the grave. In millions of cases, these horrors have been spawned by the systemic evils of human societies. To be good-to us, God will have to establish and fit us all for wholesome society, not establish institutions to guarantee that horrors last forever in the world to come!

6. Embodied enjoyment

For God to make good on God's creative projects with material creation involves so adjusting *prima facie* metaphysical misfits to one

[30] I have opposed conventional doctrines of hell throughout my career, in sporadic occasional pieces: "Universal Salvation: A Reply to Mr. Bettis," *Religious Studies* 7 (1971), 245–49; "Hell and the God of Justice," *Religious Studies* 11:4 (1975), 433–447; "Divine Justice, Divine Love, and the Life to Come," *Crux* 13 (1976–1977), 12–18; and "The Problem of Hell: A Problem of Evil for Christians."

another that they can abide together in peace and harmony.[31] For the human condition to be optimal, human being needs to become enjoyable, and that enjoyment needs to be secured. Insofar as we are *embodied* persons, it would seem that our bodies should be in excellent condition. Insofar as we are personal *animals*, plot resolution would seem to involve flourishing animal functioning. Yet, whatever may be the case for cows and donkeys, flourishing human being requires animal functioning to be domesticated into personal housing. By the same token, for Divine–human relations to become optimal, created personality has to be domesticated into the household of God. Many parameters are worth pondering.

6.1. Bodily being

Karl Rahner recognizes that, for the *human* condition to be optimal, the relation between our personal and material dimensions needs to be renegotiated. His suggestion is that *post mortem* we will cease to be specially connected to a particular finite human body and instead have an enjoyable relation to the material cosmos as a whole. Ancient Roman pagans imagined that after death we would get new bodies that were perfectly spherical, that being – in their estimation – the most perfect of shapes.

Whatever may be said for these ideas, they do not strike me as a way for God to make good on the Divine project of *human* being. *Ante mortem* the attachment of our personhood to particular human bodies is important in differentiating us from one another. The fact that we have boundaries that contain us puts us in a position to decide whether or not and how to make contact with others who are

---

[31] For helpful discussion of these topics, I am grateful to Wendy Boring, Alice Chapman, Shannon Craigo-Snell, Christine Helmer, Connor Lynn, and Christian Swayne. I also profited from the senior project of Carol Wade at the Institute of Sacred Music, Yale University, 2002.

also thus defined and allows the body to be a medium of personal intimacy. Likewise, faces dynamically embody our personalities and personal interactions in ways that perfect spheres could not. For God to make *human* being good-for humans, God needs to give us new and improved *human* bodies. *Ante mortem*, the adolescent or young adult body is very different from that of the infant or toddler or grammar-school child; yet the later body is recognizable to a person as her/his own, even as that towards which the earlier phases of her/his body were tending. So also perhaps the resurrection body will be transformed, but recognizable as ours, as the one in which we can be our truest selves.

To be a perfect specimen would seem to require a complete human body, all parts present and in working order, properly positioned and proportioned, requisitely sized and strengthened.[32] From this, it would seem to follow that risen bodies would not have missing or twisted or arthritic limbs, shrunken or hydrocephalic heads, hunchbacks, cleft palates, blind eyes or deaf ears. Such deficits not only *concretely* interfere with optimal functioning, they *symbolize* the ultimate deficit of death and dismemberment. Surely, human bodies will be freed from them, restored whole and wholesome in the life to come! But what if bodily deformities dug their way deeply into the individual's *ante-mortem* identity, not only negatively but positively by becoming integral to the way they served Christ? Do deformities then become like Christ's own glorified wounds, which still tear His body but with transformed significance? Would they no longer signal death and curse and excommunication, but advertise Divine Goodness, Power, and resourcefulness to defeat all of these things?

Bodies are naturally extended in space, and capable of moving through space, so that they occupy first one position and then another. Aristotle made bodily motion a differentia of the genus animal; bodily motion is one test of whether an animal is still alive.

---

[32] Bonaventure, *Sent.* IV, d. 44, p. 1, a. 1, q. 2; Quaracchi IV.909–910; IV, d. 44, p. 1, a. 3, q. 1; Quaracchi IV.915.

Moreover, animal bodies are in some sense self-moving, so that where they go is to some extent directed by the animal's own perception and appetites. New Testament resurrection narratives suggest that Christ's risen body enjoyed supranatural upgrades in both departments. Christ's risen body was able not only to be extended in places not occupied by other bodies, but also in the same place at the same time as doors to rooms (Luke 24:36; John 20:19, 26). Reasoning backwards from the premiss of Mary's perpetual virginity, medievals inferred that Christ's body had this capacity even before His death and resurrection, at the time of His birth. Glorified bodies, they thought, would enjoy a new way of being in space, so that one body would not have to elbow out another to be there or to pass through. Bodies *qua* bodies would have a tendency to impenetrability, and would usually put up resistance to one another then as now. But they would not *have* to do so, and would not if a human being willed to be where something else is at the same time.[33]

Animals move one bodily part by first moving another. Moving takes effort to shift out of inertial rest, uses energy, can be painful at the time and leave muscles sore afterwards. *Ante mortem*, even athletes in excellent physical shape know the feeling. Medievals imagined that, in the world to come, bodies would move without effort to overcome such internal resistance, wherever the individual willed to go.[34] Athletes speak of a rare experience in which their bodies are fluid in their movement with no pain at all; in which they, their bodies, and their instruments are so in harmony as to be able to move with perfect timing and coordination to execute the maneuver with outstanding beauty and grace.[35] Dancers are able to flex and extend remarkably many muscles individually and on purpose, and to coordinate their movements in dramatic ways. Medievals imagine that in the

---

[33] Scotus, *Op.Ox.* IV, d. 49, q. 16, n. 19; Wadding X.621.

[34] Aquinas, *Sent.* IV, d. 44, q. 1, a. 3; Parma XXII.420; Scotus, *Op.Ox.* IV, d. 49, q. 14, n. 8; Wadding X.596; IV, d. 49, q. 12, n. 7; Wadding X.574.

[35] I rely here on Christine Helmer, a theologian and an Olympic trial athlete.

resurrection such ease and grace of motion will be within reach of all of the elect (as is perhaps signified by the lame leaping for joy in Acts 3:1–10; see Isaiah 35).

Will we also be able to move in ways for which humans are not naturally suited – say to fly, or to leap tall buildings with a single bound, or to swim for long periods of time without coming up for air? Human artists equivocate, portraying Christ's risen body as ascending on its own, but the Blessed Virgin Mary's as born aloft by humanoid winged angels. Should we deny that Christ's human nature receives any special *post-mortem* power to fly, but maintain that His Divine power is able to make His human body ascend? Does St. Paul imagine that He will do the same miracle for the elect who will meet Jesus in the air (I Thessalonians 4:17)? Will Divine power do it repeatedly for *post-mortem* athletes who would enjoy it?

Medieval expectations that resurrection bodies will be beautiful extends to their static qualities. Inspired by Gospel transfiguration and resurrection narratives as well as by hagiographies, some expect resurrection bodies of the elect to shine like the sun.[36] Scotus instead interprets *claritas* in terms of maximally appropriate coloration for the different body parts with their different textures, shapes, and surfaces.[37] Beauty is in part a matter of fit. Should we say that eventually, after positive meaning-making has taken significant hold, we will have bodies and faces that aptly express the wholeness of the persons we are coming to be?

6.2. *Carnal knowledge*

Optimal animal functioning involves sense perception and correspondingly appropriate sensory appetites. Medievals thought that domesticating the animal to the personal within human being would mean the subordination of sensory appetites to the government of

---

[36] Aquinas, *Sent.* IV, d. 44, q. 1, n. 3; Parma XXII.420.
[37] Scotus, *Op.Ox.* IV, d. 49, q. 15, a. 2; Wadding X.606.

right reason. While all acknowledged as an obvious fact that much of our *ante-mortem* knowledge depends on sense-perception, some speculated that this might change in the world to come, when we are raised up into the high society of the Blessed Trinity. Either this would be because the blessed would see all things in God and therefore not require any causal interaction with the objects themselves, whether sensory or otherwise; or because material objects would no longer be obstructed from acting on the intellectual soul directly. Aquinas brings us back to the point that – whether or not sense perception will be needed to acquire information – human flourishing will require the natural functional activity of its intellectual powers, and these latter require images derived from sense perception. Certainly, it would not be unreasonable to infer that if human happiness requires soul–body reunion, it would include the best of the functions of which they are together the subject. This claim also has warrants in Scripture, in the prophecy that, when Messiah comes, the eyes of the blind shall be opened and the ears of the deaf unstopped (Isaiah 35:5–6) – which would be pointless if they were no longer of any use.

Taking a page from twelfth-century Incarnation-anyway theologians, we can affirm that part of the body's happiness is seeing God's own body (viz., Christ's human body) through the bodily eye.[38] So far from an intellectual vision of God making sense perception of God and other bodies superfluous, they would be mutually reinforcing. Seeing God with the mind's eye puts the mind in a better position to appreciate the varying Godlikenesses of material creatures and to love that of God in each of them; seeing and recognizing that of God in each of them would intensify our desire to praise our common Maker.[39]

Medieval authors tend to focus on sight and hearing, because they believe that touch and taste may involve generation and corruption,

---

[38] Grosseteste, *De cessatione legalium*, Part III, sec. 1.24, 129.

[39] Arguably, this is how Bonaventure sees our *ante-mortem* spiritual assignment in the *Itinerarium*.

which on their view will have utterly come to an end. But *ante-mortem* touch and taste are dominant media of personal connection, so much so that we speak metaphorically of "getting" or "keeping in touch" or "making contacts." Between the newborn infant's nursing at its mother's breast and the lover's kiss, there are hugs and handshakes of greeting and comfort, of reassurance and joy. If bodies give the human person sensible boundaries that enable us to differentiate ourselves from one another, the meeting of bodies is also a powerful partic-ipating symbol of *personal* connection. More fundamentally, touch grounds our sense of reality. As Berkeley noted, seeing shouldn't be believing if visual were not so regularly correlated with tactile sensa-tions. Certainly, there can be meaningful personal intimacy without touching. But this is so much the exception that we tend to be sus-picious of it. We usually measure how much we have been together by its approach to touch: seeing is normally better than a phone call, because it proves we have been spatially proximate; the handshake or hug "clinches it" that *real* contact has been made. If this is so in our dangerous world *ante mortem*, how much more for embodied persons in the world to come, where the Inner Teacher has so brought us up that abusive touch will be a thing of the past!

6.3. Eating

Medievals contended that Death would come to an end and shortages would be irrelevant, because God would bring about an end to all generation and corruption. They concluded that there would be no eating and drinking in heaven, because the eater fragments, degrades, and destroys what s/he eats in order to turn it into her/himself.[40] St. Francis and Gandhi might have hoped for an end to eating because it would be more courteous to other creatures if human beings didn't have to destroy anything else in order to keep body and soul together!

---

[40] Aquinas insists that resurrection bodies are impassible: *Sent.* IV, d. 44, q. 1, a. 3; Parma XXII.420; *Summa Contra Gentiles* IV, ch. 83.

By contrast, the Bible and pseudepigrapha imagine a great end-time banquet, in which the elect eat together at the marriage feast of the Lamb (Revelation 19:9; 22:17; cf. Matthew 22:1–13, 25:1–13). The Bible does not envision a time when we will not need to eat, but a time in which there will always be enough for everyone to eat. Starvation is prevented not by ending all generation and corruption, but by a bountiful food supply. Shared food is not a mere symbol; it is a *participating* symbol, an embodiment of shared life. In seasons of scarcity, we share food with those whose lives are so bound up with ours that we have nothing to lose by giving to them and nothing to gain by withholding. In seasons of abundance, feasting together is a fit way for embodied persons to celebrate their common life. The marriage feast of the Lamb shows God's largesse, acts out how God has enough to give without stinting and still has as much as before. It celebrates Boundless Goodness pouring forth on creatures, making possible fruitful and harmonious relations with one another. We will be able to live together in peace and unity because God gives so much that envy and jealousy, greed and competition, will become obsolete. Luke's Jesus does not say that He will never drink wine again, but that He will not drink it until the Kingdom of God comes (Luke 22:18). The risen Jesus actually resumes table fellowship with his friends (Luke 24:13–43; John 21:9–14). This suggests that we will not only be able to eat and drink in God's presence, like Moses and Aaron, Nadab and Abihu (Exodus 24:9–11); at the marriage feast of the Lamb, we will eat and drink with God in a literally shared meal.

7. Meaning and fulfillment

7.1. The Last Judgment, definitive verdict

Medieval Latin school theologians think the world to come will bring not only resurrection into ontological completeness for each and every human being, but also a definitive interpretation of the meaning of each person's life. They conceive of such "meaning-completion" under the rubric of "the Last Judgment." *Ante-mortem* people *do not* get what they deserve: the righteous suffer and the wicked prosper. *Ante-mortem* people *could not* get what they deserve, because sin against God deserves an everlasting punishment and per-severance to the end merits an everlasting reward. Medievals insist that Divine justice requires that *the very same* agent who acted *ante mortem* be rewarded or punished *post mortem*.[41] Since it is the human (soul–body) composite that is the subject of action and passion, it must be the human composite that is rewarded or punished in return. Consequently, for Divine justice to be executed and manifested, the human dead must rise.

Moreover, Divine judgment will be public:[42] the thoughts of every heart are revealed, so that the good deeds of the wicked and the bad deeds of the just may manifest Divine mercy, while the bad deeds of the wicked and good deeds of the good manifest Divine justice. What we meant and what God meant during our earthly careers will be made fully explicit, so that God knows and each and every created person knows, and each knows that the others know. Whether spoken or merely mental, infused into our minds, whether general or minutely itemized, the Last Judgment will bring full disclosure.

Medievals were convinced that Divine judgment will be *final*. According to Divine statutes, death will end human chances to merit and demerit.[43] The meaning of one's earthly career will be focussed along a single parameter: whether it was or was not requisitely

---

[41] Aquinas, *Sent.* IV, d. 47, q. u, a. 1; Parma XXII.427; Aquinas, *Summa Contra Gentiles* IV, ch. 79; Bonaventure, *Sent.* IV, d. 43, a. 1, qq. 1–2; Quaracchi IV.883–886; Bonaventure, *Breviloquium* VII, ch. 1, secs. 1–2; Quaracchi V.281–282.

[42] Aquinas, *Sent.* IV, d. 47, q. u, a. 1; Parma XXII.427; Bonaventure, *Sent.* IV, d. 43, a. 1, q. 3; Quaracchi IV.887; IV, d. 43, a. 2, q. 3; Quaracchi IV.898–899; IV, d. 43, a. 3, q. 1; Quaracchi IV.900–901; Bonaventure, *Breviloquium* VII, ch. 1, sec. 3; Quaracchi V.281–282; Scotus, *Op.Ox.* IV, d. 47, q. 1, n. 5; Wadding X.294.

[43] Aquinas, *Sent.* IV, d. 50, q. u, a. 1; Parma XXII.433; Scotus, *Op.Ox.* IV, d. 47, q. 1, n. 4; Wadding X.293.

conformed to God's will; the Godward orientation of the elect is "confirmed" by God, and the turning away from God by the wicked is made permanent as well. Verdicts will be immediately followed by rewards and punishments – eternal life for the elect, and eternal damnation for the reprobate.

Inspired as they were by Scripture, medieval accounts posit a *juridical* connection between our earthly careers and our *post-mortem* status, in that – within the framework of Divine statutes of merit/demerit – the former explains aspects of the latter. Nevertheless, they also posit a discontinuity: merit-earning, the period of *posse peccare/posse non peccare*, of moral effort, etc., is confined to our *ante-mortem* careers; *post mortem* there is the enjoyment or suffering of the consequences. We rest on our laurels or sink into our depravity. Thus, death is the deadline for moral or religious achievement.

7.2. Meanings, multiple and collaborative

My own systematic assumptions take me away from the idea of a momentary final verdict pronounced from without. Rather, redemption from horrors involves the recovery and appropriation of positive personal meaning from the worst that we can suffer, be, or do. Stage-II horror-defeat requires God to heal and enable our meaning-making capacities. Follow-through on the Divine design of human nature will involve God in enlisting the collaboration of the created person in reconstituting his/her fragmented self, and this suggests a *process* – if *ante-mortem* psychotherapy is an analogy, a long and arduous process – rather than a "twinkling-of-an-eye" declaration. Stage-II horror-defeat requires God to overcome our fear that God hates us. For Divine–human relations to become optimal, or even excellent, many radical misunderstandings of Divine intentions will have to be cleared up. If *ante-mortem* psycho-spiritual experience is an analogy, the cure might come through a dramatic "breakthrough" experience of the bigness of Divine Goodness followed by the labor of integrating of this datum into the rest of the horror-participant's life. This task of setting the "breakthrough" experience up against the experience of horrors, and of questioning and disputing God for their meaning, is one that itself occurs in the presence of the Goodness, of the Inner Teacher Who is increasingly recognized as God's own self.

Rather than waiting aeons for the number of the elect to be fulfilled, it seems more apt – on my systematic assumptions – for God to "break through" as soon as possible after the horror-participant's death, to be so obvious and present as to convince at least some fragments of him/herself of the following general truths: that love is, was, and always will be God's meaning; that beloved-by-God is who we are, have been, and always will be; that horrors never were and never will be final; that God was never aloof from our horror-participation, neither was, is, nor ever shall be aloof in relation to us, because we are created for mutual indwelling; that God is powerful enough and resourceful enough to make the plots resolve, so that everything will be all right. The particular meanings that flow from these are something that God and the creature make together, to begin with, as the creature enters into the significance of Divine solidarity with us in horror-participation (Stage-I horror-defeat), and comes to appreciate and appropriate the good God has brought out of the worst aspects of our lives. Nor will meaning-making in heaven be merely retrospective. If the world to come is a rest from horrors, it does not bring an end to the enjoyment of shared creativity in which we collaborate with God and other creatures as friends. As Gregory of Nyssa urges, it will not mean an end to discovery. Godhead will be eternally fascinating because however much we know and love of God, there will always be more. Intimacy with the Trinity will eternally unfold in surprises about who we are to God and to one another.

7.3. The great judgment seat of Christ

Revelation 1:7 looks forward to the day on which Christ returns, His authority and power obvious to everyone. The epistles repeatedly warn that we must all stand before the great judgment seat of Christ. But Christ is one person with two natures. Medievals explain that everyone will see Christ according to His glorified human nature, but not everyone will see Christ according to His Divine nature; Christ's Divinity is something that the reprobate will have to infer.

Medievals ask whether Christ is judge according to His human nature, or only according to His Divine nature.[44] They answer that, while the soul of Christ could know (by Divine revelation) whatever it needed to know to render the verdicts, the human will of Christ is not omnipotent and so not efficacious in carrying the sentences into effect.[45]

My own view is that Christ is judge according to His human nature. The manifestation of His resurrected and glorified wounds publishes the truth about our *ante-mortem* human condition, and the truth about God's everlasting ability, resourcefulness, and intentions to restore human being thereby. Christ as God-man is judge, the One Who renders the final verdict on God's projects in material creation, because Christ is the One in Whom Stage-I, Stage-II, and Stage-III horror-defeats hold together.

---

[44] Aquinas, *Summa Theologica* III, q. 59, a. 2; Aquinas, *Sent.* IV, d. 48, q. 1, a. 1; Parma XXII.429. Cf. Bonaventure, *Breviloquium* VII, ch. 1, sec. 4; Quaracchi V.281–282.

[45] Scotus, *Op.Ox.* IV, d. 48, q. 1, nn. 4–9; Wadding X.307–310.

9 | Horrors and holocausts, sacrifices and priests: Christ as priest and victim

1. Cultic reconnection

Horrors threaten to ruin human lives. Horror–participation strains Divine–human relations to the breaking point. Cult condenses cosmos, becomes a focal scene of Divine–human relationship development. It is a scene of close encounters: even if God is supposed to be everywhere, Divine presence and influence certainly not confined to temple precincts, there is still the notion that by coming to the holy place one is *drawing near* to God. Cult is a scene of obstacle-removals: most notably, cult defines the etiquette that allows humans and divinities to share the same social space, furnishes ritual remedies by means of which offenses and disabling conditions can be recontextualized and removed. Cult is a scene of covenant-making, of covenant-renewal, and of payment of vows. It is also a scene of thanks and praise, of celebration and consummation.

In the Bible, patriarchal religion linked theophany with cereal and animal sacrifice. Tabernacle, shrine, and temple focussed worship in sacrificial rites, and codified elaborate rules and regulations as to who, what, when, where, how, and why. Nor was this an Israelite invention. Sacrificial emphasis was widely taken for granted and crossculturally shared. Nor was this a fleeting cultural phenomenon. Despite critiques, sacrificial cult – including the offering of animals – remained entrenched in majority-report religion in the Roman empire until Constantine. Christians and Jews (after the destruction of the Second Temple in 70 CE) stood alone in refusing any longer to participate in the sacrifice of bulls and goats, birds and lambs.

Yet, even where and when temples ceased to be scenes of animal slaughter, sacrifice did not become a thing of the past. The conceptuality of sacrifice remained entrenched, within ready reach for easy transfer to alternative and wider contexts. New Testament writers used it to frame our soteriological predicament generally and to give positive meaning to the death of Jesus (Romans 3:25; Matthew 20:28; Mark 10:45; and Hebrews *passim*). St. Paul joined other rabbis in using notions of temple and sacrifice to frame their ideals of human life devoted to God (e.g., II Corinthians 2:14–16; 6:16). From the beginning, Christian practice and theological reflection subsumed the dominical sacrament of the breaking of the bread under a variety of sacrificial categories. Indeed, the instinctive dynamics of sacrifice remain alive and well at the unconscious level – so deeply rooted, some maintain, as to be archetypal, like Kantian categories, naturally built-in ways that humans organize their experience.[1] We bump into them when we "scapegoat" someone, or when we offer young people for slaughter on the battlefields of war. Surely, they underlie our subliminal sensibility that the Pentagon is *holy* ground and not merely a useful social agency. Some argue that we are the more readily driven by the dynamics of bloody sacrifice *because* we know not what we do![2]

My contention is that even if – perhaps partly *because* – the category of sacrifice is too deep for words, it provides an excellent conceptual frame for the Divine–human predicament in a horror-strewn world. In any event, the notion is not utterly ineffable. In what follows, I will draw on ancient texts, history, and social anthropology to make some logics and varieties of sacrifice explicit. Then I will map cult

---

[1] See John Dunnill, *Covenant and Sacrifice in the Letter to the Hebrews* (Cambridge: Cambridge University Press, 1992), Part II, ch. 2, 43–63.

[2] René Girard, *Violence and the Sacred* (Baltimore: Johns Hopkins University Press, 1977).

back onto cosmos to exhibit our world as a scene of sacrifice: one in which sacrifice is what humans and God offer, one in which sacrifice is what God and humans require of one another.

2. Logics of sacrifice

2.1. Definitions and dichotomies

Sacrifice is a ritual in which human beings make the material stuff of their lives the medium of exchange in the hope that their offering, things about which they are specially concerned, they themselves will be transformed by supranatural power.[3] The profane and sacred are distinguished as two realms or spheres. The profane needs the creative power of the holy, and yet the holy threatens danger to profane order. What is required is access to supranatural power that is beneficial rather than harmful.[4] Religious rites define ways of approach, so that the profane can draw near and transact for blessing rather than for ruin.

Because human experience of the cosmos and the supranatural is ambivalent, supranatural power is conceptually cut by double dichotomies: positive-versus-negative, personal-versus-impersonal.[5] Thus, in the Bible, the holy sometimes gets represented as an *impersonal* force that can "break out" on humans for good (as when power flows from Jesus to heal the hemorrhaging woman) or ill (as when Uzzah touches the ark [I Samuel 6:6–11], when Nadab and Abihu offer unauthorized incense before the altar [Leviticus 10:1–3], and when God descends on Sinai warning the people to purify themselves and keep their distance, lest He "break out" upon them

---

[3] Godfrey Ashby, *Sacrifice: Its Nature and Purpose* (London: SCM Press, 1988), ch. 2, 5–25.

[4] Dunnill, *Covenant and Sacrifice in the Letter to the Hebrews*, Part II, ch. 3, 73–90.

[5] J. H. M. Beattie, "On Understanding Sacrifice," in *Sacrifice*, ed. M. F. C. Bourdillon and Meyer Fortes (London: Academic Press, 1980), 29–44, esp. 36–39. Cf. Dunnill, *Covenant and Sacrifice*, Part II, ch. 3, 77–79.

and they die [Exodus 19:10–24]). Likewise, priestly and holiness code writers conceive of impurity as an *impersonal* force that is contagious not only by contact (as when someone steps on a grave or touches a menstrous woman) but also at a distance (as when sins committed elsewhere pollute the temple precincts – unwitting sins, the outer altar; high-handed sins, the holy of holies itself).[6] At the same time, the Bible also understands supranatural power as *personal*, with New Testament demons causing diseases, madness, and bad weather, and God acting both for good and for ill, both to build up and to destroy. Notably, the Bible associates both impersonal and personal supranatural force with Divine agency and with Jesus, allowing it to operate both outside and within personal voluntary control.[7]

To these dichotomies, Beattie adds another – conjunctive-versus-disjunctive – and combines it with personal-versus-impersonal to make an *a priori* division of sacrifices into four classes: (i) *personal conjunctive* sacrifices, which aim to obtain and maintain closer contact with supranatural personal spirits; (ii) *personal disjunctive*, whose purpose is to ward off or insure some degree of separation from such spirits; (iii) *impersonal conjunctive*, which attempt to give access to supranatural power, impersonally conceived; and (iv) *impersonal disjunctive*, which try to achieve separation from or the removal of impersonal supranatural forces.[8]

In the Bible, the sacred/profane distinction gets multiple (and, once again, apparently incompatible) mappings, corresponding to contrary problematics. On the one hand, the psalmist declares that the whole world is filled with the glory of God, and regards the entire

---

[6] Jacob Milgrom, *Leviticus 1–16: A New Translation with Introduction and Commentary* (New York: Anchor Bible, 1990), 2 vols., vol. I, 257–261, 1033.

[7] Milgrom boasts that the Hebrew Bible does not posit personalized evil in the form of demons, even though he is not fully comfortable with impurity as an impersonal "miasma" that acts at a distance (*Leviticus 1–16*, vol. I, 730, 1051–1052). In any event, personified evil returns to the stage in force in the Gospels.

[8] Beattie, "On Understanding Sacrifice," 38–39.

cosmos as sacred precincts, with everything in them "devoted" to sacred use. Human beings are trespassers on Divine turf, with no entitlement either to being or to well-being, with no right to life, whether to our own or to those of other animals or plants. Rites are required so that space can be cleared and stuff appropriated for common use. On the other hand, the world here below is seen as fundamentally profane, so that rites must be deployed to set aside (whether temporarily or permanently) places for God to visit or inhabit, and to define how humans may safely draw near. In the Hebrew Bible, God chooses particular stones or mountains, trees or bushes, as places of theophany, and the patriarchs respond by setting up pillars or altars to mark the spot as holy ground.[9] Again, God gives Moses elaborate instructions for the layout and decoration of the tent of meeting, the liturgical hardware, vestments, and rites for Divine–human transaction.[10]

Both mappings are fueled by twin but opposite fears – that the sacred will annihilate the profane, and that the unclean will drive out the holy – and contrary estimates of relative strength. Thus, priestly and holiness-code writers suggest that impurity is an impersonal force that can act at a distance to drive a Holy God out of temple or land, although Divine departure is sometimes restored to God's control as a matter of freely chosen Divine policy.[11] Yet, these same authors also represent holiness as an impersonal force lethal to the profane or impure who "draw near," and understand the holiness of ordained priests as able to overpower the impurity of the sin-offerings they eat.[12] Likewise, the Gospels presuppose that Jesus' holiness is "catching" by contact – more powerful than the defilement of lepers, bleeding women, and dead bodies that He touches and restores.

---

[9] See Genesis 12:7–8, 13:18, 28:20–22, 32:22–32, 35:9–15. *Pace* Milgrom who is eager to distance Hebrew Bible conceptions from naturalistic animism (*Leviticus 1–16*, vol. I, 730; vol. II, 1711–12).

[10] Exodus 25–32; Leviticus *passim*; Numbers 1–19, 28–29.

[11] Milgrom, *Leviticus 1–16*, vol. I, 316–317, 454, 724, vol. II, 1353–1354, 1371, 1398–1399.

[12] Milgrom, *Leviticus 1–16*, vol. I, 616–617, 624–625, 636–639.

2.2. The dynamics of transaction

In their pathbreaking study,[13] Hubert and Mauss distinguish three factors in sacrifice. The *sacrifier* is the individual or collective person who bears the expenses of the sacrifice, the one to whom the benefits of the sacrifice accrue and/or the one who undergoes its effects.[14] The *thing sacrificed*, or victim, is the intermediary between the sacrifier or the object which is to receive the practical benefits of the sacrifice, on the one hand, and the divinity to whom the sacrifice is addressed, on the other. The assumption is that humans and divinities are not in direct contact.[15] The *object of sacrifice* is that for whose sake the sacrifice takes place. Often there is a double effect: one on the object of the sacrifice, and the other on the sacrifier him/herself.[16] Hubert and Mauss insist that, at every stage, sacrifice involves someone or some thing *representing* others (e.g., as king or chief the sacrifier may act on behalf of the whole nation or tribe; the quantity of grain offered may stand in for the whole crop of that species).

Turning to the dynamics, Hubert and Mauss maintain that sacrifice involves *consecration*: something passes over from the common/profane to the religious/sacred domain. Some sacrifices affect only the consecrated thing sacrificed. Others affect the sacrifier or the objects of the sacrifice, so that they acquire a positive or lose a negative spiritual force or character.[17] Hubert and Mauss see the consecration as progressive, so that – by virtue of the rite – the religious force or character is transferred to and concentrated in the victim, raised to a peak intensity, and then released. On their analysis, killing the animal dispatches its spirit to the sacred realm and with it the excess of positive spiritual force that would be destructive to humans,

---

[13] Henri Hubert and Marcel Mauss, *Sacrifice: Its Nature and Function*, trans. W. D. Halls; forward by E. E. Evans-Pritchard (Chicago: University of Chicago Press 1898/1964).

[14] Hubert and Mauss, *Sacrifice: Its Nature and Function*, ch. 1, 12.   [15] Ibid.

[16] Hubert and Mauss, *Sacrifice: Its Nature and Function*, ch. 1, 10.

[17] Hubert and Mauss, *Sacrifice: Its Nature and Function*, ch. 1, 9.

so that the animal's material remains can be approached and handled with fewer precautions. Burning or eating by priests completes the removal of the victim from the profane to the sacred domain. When the sacrifier eats a portion of the animal, s/he receives a beneficial dosage of spiritual force. When the spiritual force is negative, then the material remains must be eliminated whether by fire or by priestly consumption, so that the sacrifier or his object are plagued by it no more.[18]

Given this account, it is unsurprising if Hubert and Mauss insist that *destruction* of the thing sacrificed is *essential* to sacrifice. They understand killing the animal to be a key step in its consecration, and the elimination of its material remains as a further means by which the victim passes on the religious power accumulated in its consecration to the sacred sphere and to the profane sphere to which the sacrifier belongs.[19] It is controversial, however, whether – in the Bible – killing the animal was conceived of as part of the consecration or preparatory to the sacrificial blood rite.[20] Again, what seems essential to the logic of sacrifice as they present it is the *elimination* of negative force or excess positive force. But undesirable spiritual forces can be removed from the sacrifier's or the object's profane world by banishment (as when the scapegoat is sent off to the wilderness, or one of the birds in the leper's cleansing offering is released to fly away), even when the offering is not killed, burned, and/or eaten.[21]

---

[18] Hubert and Mauss, *Sacrifice: Its Nature and Function*, ch. 1, 9, 12–13, ch. 2, 44.

[19] Hubert and Mauss, *Sacrifice: Its Nature and Function*, ch. 1, 12–13.

[20] Milgrom points to the fact that it was the lay sacrifier's job to kill, skin, quarter, and wash the animal, as evidence that it was preparatory. At the same time, he sees the animal as set apart at the moment when the offering is accepted (*Leviticus 1–16*, vol. I, 156–159).

[21] See Milgrom, *Leviticus 1–16*, vol. I, 1051. Interestingly, the debate over whether destruction is essential to sacrifice was lively in sixteenth- and seventeenth-century Spanish Roman Catholic sacramental theology. Cf. Darwell Stone, MA, *A History of the Doctrine of the Holy Eucharist* (London, NY, Bombay, and Calcutta: Longmans, Green, & Co, 1909), 2 vols., vol. II, ch. XIV, sec.I.i, 362–466.

Based on their understanding of the logic of sacrifice, Hubert and Mauss *a priori* distinguish sacrifices into three categories. (i) *Neutral beginning*: The sacrifier and/or victim start in a neutral state and make ritualized entry into the sacred world to obtain a positive religious charge which may also carry with it certain prohibitions due to its new citizenship (e.g., priests by virtue of their ordination). (ii) *Negative beginning*: The sacrifice has the goal of removing a negative religious character (expiation) of the sacrifier or the object, and so communicates the impurity to the victim and eliminates the impurity by destroying (or banishing) the victim. (iii) *Positive beginning*: The sacrifice has the goal of desacralization (e.g., of releasing nazarites from their vow, of the spirit of life from the crops) so that the thing/person will be able to return to ordinary life or be available for common use. Whichever way, the rite concentrates the religious force and carries it along.[22]

2.3. Rites of passage

Hubert and Mauss focus on the human need to traffic with the sacred to secure the necessities and/or the good things of life, and on the role of the victim as mediator conducting spiritual "charge" from one domain to the other in either or both directions.[23] Dunnill draws on anthropological analyses of rites of passage to underscore the transgressive character of sacrifice. Borrowing from E. R. Leach and Victor Turner, Dunnill takes initiation rites to have a three-stage action that constitutes a symbolic death and rebirth through an inversion of normality. The initiands who have been occupying one set of social roles are temporarily removed to a marginal place for a specified time, within the frame of which norms are inverted and special rules of behavior, dress, etc. are allowed, the better to empower the initiands to return and reenter society in new roles with fresh energy. Dunnill

[22] Hubert and Mauss, *Sacrifice: Its Nature and Function*, ch. 3, 60.
[23] Hubert and Mauss, *Sacrifice: Its Nature and Function*, ch. 6, 97.

sees sacrifice as conforming to this pattern: it is "an *effective action*" involving "a temporary transfer of the subject (or a representative) into the sacred marginal sphere, by which a *consecration* occurs, a transformation through sacred power."[24] The killing, burning, and eating that happens in animal sacrifice within that sacred space-time involves a "ritual inversion," insofar as normally such destruction of life would be imprudent husbandry at best, at worst cosmos-disrupting murder. Ritual converts what is normally outlawed into a system-empowering source of life.[25]

3. Types and varieties of sacrifice

Social anthropologists arrive at their conceptual grids by analyzing different kinds of data, including not only the practices of living societies, but also various sorts of literature – quasi-historical treatises, sacred writings, tales, and mythologies – from the past. In New Testament and patristic times, when Christians first began to theologize about the significance of Christ's death and the meaning of holy eucharist, sacrifice was very much a living religious institution – within Judaism until the destruction of the Temple in 70 CE, within the dominant cults of Greco-Roman society, as also within so-called mystery religions that flourished in the later Roman empire. In forwarding Christ's death and the breaking of bread as Christian sacrifices, it was natural for apologists to relate them to types of sacrifices with which their intended audiences were already familiar. In her very useful books,[26] Frances M. Young charts how Christian

---

[24] Dunnill, *Covenant and Sacrifice*, Part II, ch. 3, 76. Ashby agrees: *Sacrifice: Its Nature and Purpose*, ch. 3, 47–48, ch. 5, 74.

[25] Dunnill, *Covenant and Sacrifice*, Part II, ch. 3, 75. Cf. Milgrom, *Leviticus 1–16*, vol. I, 711–712, vol. II, 1352–1353.

[26] Frances M. Young, *The Use of Sacrificial Ideas in Greek Christian Writers from the New Testament to John Chrysostom* (Philadelphia: Philadelphia Patristic Foundation, 1979); and Young, *Sacrifice and the Death of Christ* (London: SPCK, 1975).

writers defended their refusal to participate in further animal sacrifices by eclectic appeals, now to Jewish, now to Gentile, sacrificial categories. A brief review of these overlapping but not fully congruent classifications will strengthen our conceptual grip by giving content to the formal logics of sacrifice just outlined. It will also prepare us to understand crucifixion and horror-participation as a many-sided sacrifice and holy eucharist as the sacrament of the altar.

3.1. Hebrew Bible sacrifices

Most familiar to the earliest Christians were Jewish sacrifices prescribed by the Torah. Although cereal offerings numbered among them, bloody sacrifice loomed large. The theology behind blood rites is elusive, but holiness-code writers drop at least two hints on which commentators seize. The first comes in Leviticus 17:14:

> For the life of every creature is the blood of it; therefore I have said to the people of Israel, You shall not eat the blood of any creature, for the life of every creature is its blood; whoever eats it shall be cut off.

The explicit premiss – that the life is in the blood – combines with the suppressed premiss – that life belongs to God – to motivate the concluding taboo – that Israelites are not to consume the blood of any animal. Most commentators understand this reasoning to explain the rubric governing almost all livestock sacrifices – that blood from the sacrificed animal be splashed against the basin of the outer court altar – as a way of returning the animal's life to God and hence as an expiation for taking its life.

The second hint comes a few verses earlier (in Leviticus 17:11) and bears on the use of sacrificial blood as a ritual detergent to absorb and/or ward off pollution:

> For the life of the flesh is in the blood; and I have given it for you upon the altar to make atonement for your souls; for it is the blood that makes atonement, by reason of the life.

Holiness is incompatible with pollution, and life is opposed to death. Correlating the pair of binary oppositions, commentators reason that if blood is the life of the animal, then to say that blood is stronger than impurity is to assert that life is stronger than death, and God than what is unholy.[27] Conversely, sacrificial blood can also absorb positive supranatural force by contact with the altar, and so become efficacious against virulent impurities (such as corpse contamination) and dangerous to (too highly charged for) non-priestly handlers.[28]

Leviticus catalogues occasional sacrifices as to types and procedures. (1) *Holocausts* (Leviticus 1:1–9) are sacrifices in which the altar fire (supposed to be of Divine origin) consumes by turning the whole offering into smoke and thereby transfers it to the sacred realm.[29] The animal is slaughtered, its blood drained into a bowl and splashed around the base of the outer altar, and its carcass burned "as a pleasant odor" to God. On the one hand, holocausts are the best sort of gift offerings, because no part of it is held back for human use. On the other hand, in biblical narratives, holocausts sometimes function to propitiate Divine wrath and to bring an end to the punishments set in motion by Israel's transgressions.[30]

(2) *Cereal offerings* (Leviticus 2:1–16) were partly burned and partly eaten by the priests. Probably they were originally a distinct type of sacrifice, during Temple days became ancillary to meat offerings and/or the poor man's substitute for meat offerings, and after the Temple's destruction continued to be offered on the Temple site and elsewhere.[31]

(3) *Well-being offerings* (Leviticus 3:1–17; 7:11–18) involved killing of the animal and throwing its blood against the base of the altar,

[27] Milgrom, *Leviticus 1–16*, vol. I, 711–712.

[28] Milgrom, *Leviticus 1–16*, vol. I, 443–444. Thus, those who burn the red heifer and collect its ashes are contaminated by it, but not the priests who use the ashes to purify others of corpse contamination.

[29] Milgrom, *Leviticus 1–16*, vol. I, 157, 160–161.

[30] Milgrom, *Leviticus 1–16*, vol. I, 174–176.   [31] Milgrom, *Leviticus 1–16*, vol. I, 195, 197.

burning the prescribed parts on the altar to provide a pleasant odor for God, distributing the appointed shares for the officiating priests, and eating the rest of the meat by the worshiper and his party. Commentators think that because the life is in the blood and life belongs to God, secular animal slaughter was originally disallowed. Meat meals meant offering the animal at a local shrine and (in the beginning) eating it within the sanctuary precincts. Laypersons had to be ritually clean to partake of the sacrifice (Leviticus 7:19–21), partly because it was being eaten within the sacred precincts,[32] and partly because the animal's carcass would have "caught" the positive supranatural charge communicated to its blood by contact with the altar.

Priestly theology holds that Israelite impurity pollutes the sanctuary. It distinguishes different sorts of impurities as to act-type or condition: severe physical impurities (e.g., hemorrhages that last more than seven days), *unwitting* transgression of God's *prohibitive* commands (e.g., against working on the Sabbath or taking God's name in vain), unwitting violation of God's *performative* commands (e.g., to perform certain rituals, to pay tithes to the Levites, to let the poor thresh the edges of your fields), and witting or brazen violation of such commands. Impurities vary as to polluting-power depending upon the *social role* – whether a layperson, the ruler, the whole congregation, or the priest – and the *intentionality* of the agent – whether he did it on purpose, knowing what he did. Thus, the individual layperson's impurities pollute the courtyard altar; those of the high priest or entire community penetrate to the shrine; witting, brazen, unrepented sin pierces the veil to pollute the very throne of God. Impurities also differ as to sacrificial remedy. Originally, there was none for witting or brazen sins. But priestly theology invented a legal device for reducing witting or brazen sins to the status of unwitting sins via repentance, reparation (where relevant), and confession.

---

[32] Milgrom, *Leviticus 1–16*, vol. I, 217–221.

(4) Hatta't *offerings*: Priestly theology (Leviticus 4:1–31) allows these only for specified physical impurities and the inadvertent violation of God's prohibitive commands. Numbers 15 extends *hatta't* remedies to inadvertent violation of performative commands as well. Where the offending party is the priest (Leviticus 4:1–12) or the whole congregation (Leviticus 4:13–21), the required offering is a young bull. Because such sins pollute the shrine, the bull's blood is sprinkled seven times before the veil of the sanctuary, and daubed on the horns of the incense altar within the tent of meeting. The rest of the blood is poured out as usual at the base of the outer altar of burnt offerings. Its fat and other prescribed portions are burned on the altar of burnt offerings. Because the rest of the carcass will have "caught" the potent degree of pollution absorbed by its blood, or alternatively too high a degree of holiness from the blood's contact with the inner shrine (Leviticus 6:30), it is too dangerous for any human – even a consecrated priest – to eat. Moreover, the holiness of the priest is not enough to consume his own sins that way. Therefore, the carcass has to be carried outside the camp, and the lingering pollution eliminated by burning.[33]

For the offending ruler and the impure common layperson, the offerings are different: a male goat and a female goat or lamb, respectively. But because the pollution-power of the agents' impurity is the same, reaching only the outer altar of burnt offerings, the liturgical procedure is the same as well. The animal's blood is daubed on the horns of the altar of burnt offering, and the rest is poured out at the base of that altar. The fat and other prescribed parts are burned on the altar of burnt offering. As before, the carcass will "catch" any negative or positive supranatural charge its blood absorbs by virtue of contact with the altar. Yet, because both are significantly less virulent, the remaining meat is safe for the consecrated priests (infused with their own positive charge via ordination) to eat. By consuming these sin offerings, the priests bear the sins of the people by

---

[33] Milgrom, *Leviticus 1–16*, vol. I, 263, 638–639.

"disappearing" the pollution they cause (Leviticus 6:24–30, 10:16). Once again, holiness swallows impurity, as life defeats death.[34]

(5) *Graduated* hatta't *sacrifices* (Leviticus 5:1–13) are prescribed for a variety of cases not covered by *hatta't* sacrifices, properly speaking. Failure of an offender (of whatever type) to avail himself of the prescribed purification procedures within the specified time increases the polluting-power of the original offense. Even if the original condition could have been remedied by a bath, delay now means a sacrifice to cleanse the sanctuary-pollution it has caused.[35] Another case involves forgetting to fulfill an oath or a vow, which is the violation of a performative command. Still other cases involve *witting* violations: withholding evidence when called upon to give it under oath, taking a false oath, hearing but doing nothing to turn back the blasphemy (boomerang its negative spiritual force) onto the original blasphemer.[36] Here priestly theology innovates, allowing these deliberate violations to be reduced – by remorse, repentance, *and confession* – to the status of unwitting ones that are susceptible of sacrificial remedy.[37] Where there is a breach of faith with another human being, restitution must also be made to the person defrauded, and an extra fifth of the value paid to the priest. Here the prescribed offerings are "graduated" according to the offender's socioeconomic status – from a female goat or lamb or ram, to two turtledoves or two pigeons, to a tenth of an ephah of flour.

(6) Preeminent among Israel's purification sacrifices are the rites mandated for *the Day of Atonement* (Leviticus 16), which are supposed to cover all of Israel's sins – corporate and individual, priestly or lay, royal or common, witting as well as unwitting. The liturgy divides into two main parts: a purification offering – a young bull

---

[34] Milgrom, *Leviticus 1–16*, vol. I, 638–639. Milgrom speculates that originally the leftover carcass of all *hatta't* offerings would have been burned outside the camp, and that it is a priestly innovation to allow priests to eat the remains in the case of *hatta't* offerings by rulers and ordinary laypersons (vol. I, 636–637).

[35] Milgrom, *Leviticus 1–16*, vol. I, 311.   [36] Milgrom, *Leviticus 1–16*, vol. I, 315.

[37] Milgrom, *Leviticus 1–16*, vol. I, 301–302, 374.

for the high priest and his house; two goats for the people – and a holocaust – a ram for Aaron and his house; a ram for the people. Since the main point of the liturgy is to cleanse the sanctuary, the purification offering comes first. Since the holiness of the priesthood serves as a shield between the people and excess spiritual force, the sin-offering of the priest is made first, and that of the people second. Since the liturgy of the day is supposed to "cover" *all* Israelite sins, and since the witting sins of the individual layperson as much as the unwitting sins of the priest pollute the shrine, the blood of the sin offerings is not merely splashed against the base of the outer altar and daubed on its horns. Rather the blood of *each* offering is first sprinkled seven times before the mercy seat itself. Then the high priest comes out and puts blood (a mixture of the bull's and goat's blood) on the horns of the outer altar of burnt offering to purge it, and sprinkles the altar with blood seven times to reconsecrate it.[38] For the same reason, the carcasses of both the priest's sin offering and the people's sin offering are so highly charged that they must be burned outside the camp, and they pollute those who handle them.

The people's sin offering is complicated, insofar as it involves *two* goats. Both are presented before the Lord, and lots are cast – one for the Lord, and one for Azazel.[39] The one for the Lord is killed, its blood used in the purification rite, and its carcass disposed of as above. The other one is presented alive, the priest lays both his hands on the goat's head and confesses all the transgressions and sins, both witting and unwitting, thereby transferring those in the former category to the latter category.[40] The goat is then banished to the wilderness, taking the sins of the people with it. Milgrom insists that the scapegoat's job is not so much to take away the pollution (the blood rituals do that), but rather to "disappear" the *cause* of

---

[38] Milgrom, *Leviticus 1–16*, vol. I, 1037–1038.

[39] "Azazel" could mean just "the one who carries away evil," or "a rough and difficult place," or it could be the name of a demon. Cf. Milgrom, *Leviticus 1–16*, vol. I, 1020–1022.

[40] Milgrom, *Leviticus 1–16*, vol. I, 1042–1043.

the pollution, the wrongs themselves, are taken out of reach, in the wrong realm or too far away to pollute the Temple. At least once, however, Milgrom relates the two parts of the service another way: the blood rite releases the accumulated sanctuary impurities, so that they can be transferred to the head of the live goat by the priest's confession.[41] Perhaps it was thought that *both* Israel's impurities *and* the resultant sanctuary impurities are piled on the goat's head! Only after the scapegoat actually enters the wilderness, so that Israel's sins cannot undo the purification of the altar and sanctuary, does the high priest offer the burnt offerings and the fat of the sin offerings on the freshly cleansed altar.

With one eye on Hittite rites and the other on Christian typologies, Milgrom denies that the Bible's scapegoat has anything to do with substitution or appeasement. He sees a closer analogy with exorcisms.[42] Hubert and Mauss would surely see a parallel: just as the Day of Atonement rite concentrates impersonal negative spiritual force on the goat's head, so belief in demons condenses negative spiritual force into personal beings. Either way, the negative spiritual force needs to be banished and quarantined somewhere – the underworld or the wilderness – that puts both the sacred and the profane beyond reach. Of course, this reflection complicates the religious geography to give us the three-story universe of the Synoptic Gospels about which Bultmann vigorously complained![43]

(7) *First-fruits* offerings were mandated for the morning after the concluding Sabbath of the feast of unleavened bread, and fifty days later on Pentecost. The earlier offering (Leviticus 23:9–14) involves a sheaf to be waved, an unblemished male lamb and flour mixed with oil to be burned for a pleasant odor, and wine to be poured out. The stern warning – "You shall not eat parched or fresh grain

---

[41] Milgrom, *Leviticus 1–16*, vol. I, 1033–1034, 1044–1046.

[42] Milgrom, *Leviticus 1–16*, vol. I, 1071–1072.

[43] Rudolf Bultmann, *Jesus Christ and Mythology* (New York: Charles Scribners' Sons, 1958).

until you have brought the offering to God!" – fits with Hubert and Mauss' hypothesis: that the offerings represented the entire crop, and that the sacrifice functioned to desanctify the rest of the yield and release it for common use. The Pentecost offerings (Leviticus 23:15–21) involved more produce and several types of sacrifice: two loaves of baked leavened bread to be waved; seven yearling lambs and one young bull and two rams with accompanying cereal and drink offerings as a *holocaust* for a pleasant odor; and one male goat for a *purification* offering and two yearling male lambs for a *well-being* offering. In this case, the priest gets to eat the lambs and the bread. Holiday get-togethers with God transact many kinds of business at once.

(8) *Covenant sacrifices* get noted in narrative more than legal materials, evoke many sacrificial categories, but invariably "seal the deal" in blood. God confirms the Divine promise to Abram three times: with the hacked-in-two-animals/smoking-fire-pot ritual (Genesis 13:7–21); with the requirement of circumcision to cut the covenant into the flesh of every male (Genesis 17:9–14); and with the testing, the command to sacrifice Isaac, and the eventual provision of the ram (Genesis 22:1–19). Commentators have been quick to link the last two with Passover (Exodus 12) via Exodus 4:24–26 which tells how YHWH, Who has just drafted Moses to represent Israel's cause before Pharaoh (Exodus 3), meets Moses on the way and tries to kill him, only to be warded off when Zipporah circumcises her son and touches the foreskin to Moses' feet, making him a "bridegroom of blood." This dark story, like the Akedah and the Passover, puts Divine ambivalence front-and-center: the God Who covenants blessing appears as the Destroyer to be warded off. Here, as in Genesis 17, circumcision (cutting the generative member) symbolizes and substitutes for death as a blood-provider. In Genesis 22 and in Exodus 12, beloved sons are redeemed by Divine provision – the ram in the thicket and the Passover lamb. Once again, sacrificial categories are straddled: the Akedah is a holocaust, while the Passover lamb not only provides blood for the door-lintel to avert Death,

but meat for the family (as in a well-being sacrifice) to celebrate its deliverance.

The covenant sacrifices at Sinai (Exodus 24:3–8) are referred to as holocausts and well-being offerings (24:5), but the blood rite is varied: first, half of the blood is thrown against the altar; then the book of the covenant is read out for the people to hear; then the other half of "the blood of the covenant" is thrown on the people (24:6–8). Does this signify kinship ("blood relations") mediated by the sacrificial animals (see Exodus 4:24: "Israel is my first-born son")?[44] Does the blood thrown against the altar "catch" its positive spiritual force and communicate that sanctifying charge to the rest of the blood, which makes Israel a holy people for a holy God? This ceremony is immediately followed by Moses and Aaron, Nadab and Abihu, and the seventy elders going up to see God and to eat and drink (presumably the well-being sacrifice) not *with* God, but in God's presence (Exodus 24:9–11).

With these narratives in mind, it is easy to recognize Day of Atonement rites as – among other things – a covenant-renewal ceremony: the sin offerings, the blood rites and scapegoat, take away the pollution of Israel's past covenant infractions, while burnt offerings on a freshly cleansed altar constitute a new beginning.

3.2. Sacrificial categories in Greek religion

Gentile and perhaps even diaspora Jewish audiences would have been more familiar with the sacrifices of Greco-Roman religion. From ancient primary and contemporary secondary sources, Young abstracts five varieties of Greek sacrifice, the first three of which are "personal conjunctive" in nature, insofar as they seek, repay, or celebrate a positive connection with supranatural powers. (1) *Votive sacrifices* offered by the worshiper in payment of a vow made to enlist the deity's aid (e.g., if you will heal me of this disease, I will offer such

---

[44] As Ashby suggests: *Sacrifice: Its Nature and Purpose*, ch. 3, 40–41.

and such in thanks and praise). The operative principle is *do ut des*. (2) *Thank offerings or gift offerings* brought by the worshiper on occasions of rejoicing and feasting. Animals were sacrificed, with parts burned on the altar and parts eaten by the worshiper and his family and friends. In at least some times and places, it was thought that the gods relied on sacrifices for food and consumed (in the sense of eating) them by fire, so that thank or gift offerings spill over into the category of (3) *communion sacrifices*, in which those gathered shared a common meal with the god(s). Although the evidence is debatable,[45] some scholars understand the cult of Dionysius to have eaten raw flesh from a live bull thought to be an embodiment of the deity himself, thinking to participate in the very nature of the deity thereby.

By contrast, the other two are "disjunctive" in character. (4) *Holocausts*, in which the whole offering was burned or buried, were brought to ward off demons that cause disease, old age, and death, and to remove pollution. (5) *Placatory sacrifices* were offered to appease the offended deity and/or to distract the suprahuman power from its anger (e.g., Agamemnon's sacrifice of Iphigenia to appease Artemis' wrath over the poaching of a stag).[46]

3.3. Composite taxonomy

In a further effort to integrate and systematize these unruly materials, Young imposes a threefold summary classification: (1) *Communion sacrifices*: Here the worshiper shares in a meal at which the god is the unseen guest of honor. Part of the animal is offered to the god on the altar – whether or not the god is thought thereby to "eat" and "drink" it. Thanks and praise are also offered to the deity. Some evidence suggests that, in some Greek versions, the worshipers were thought to eat the very substance of the god.

---

[45] See Ashby's scepticism about reports of Bedouins eating the flesh of live camels (*Sacrifice: Its Nature and Purpose*, ch. 2, 14).

[46] Young, *The Use of Sacrificial Ideas*, ch. 1, 11–14.

(2) *Gift sacrifices*: Here the thing sacrificed is given to the god as a present. In some Greek versions, this was a *do ut des* transaction, while in some Jewish ideals they were ways of expressing the highest possible thanks and praise. In Judaism, the holocaust is offered to the Supreme God, whereas in Greek religion it was offered to propitiate demons.

(3) *Sacrifices for sin*: The sacrificial repertoire includes three different ways of dealing with sin or pollution. First, in Judaism, sin offerings were expiatory, to remove the pollution of sin. Second, some Greek sacrifices for sin were intended to avert the spirits who caused evil, to remove the pollution of sin, and to appease the powers of the underworld. Third, some Greek sacrifices for sin were offered to propitiate angry deities.[47]

4. Cautions and objections

At a high level of abstraction (as in section 2), the conceptuality of sacrifice seems apt for soteriology, because it front-and-centers traffic between the profane and the sacred, the means and obstacles thereto, the potential dangers and benefits therefrom. Considered in the concrete, in its material details and praxis (as in section 3), numerous ancient authors already find it far from theologically salutary. On the contrary, they charge, the practice of sacrifice is based on and encourages false conceptions of the nature of things and of what is at stake between us and God (the gods)!

4.1. Philosophical problems

Looking to the nature of the universe in general, some philosophers argued that sacrifice and prayer are unable to affect the course of things, because the world is governed by *impersonal* chance or fate or a strict deterministic causal network, beyond the reach of divine

---

[47] Young, *The Use of Sacrificial Ideas*, ch. 3, 72–73.

or human *personal* beings to influence or control. Pointing to the dignity of be-souled animals, Porphyry rejected bloody sacrifice on the ground that it is wrong to kill animals, and speculated that the practice must have arisen during times of famine when a vegetarian diet was scarce!

Turning to the nature of deity and the character of the gods, Sophists declared that sacrifices should not be offered because the (mythological) behavior of the Greek pantheon proved them unworthy of worship. Forwarding a different understanding of deity, others argued that the gods are not the sort of beings who need to be fed by humans (whether because they have their own food, eat foods of a different type, or are immaterial and so not the kind of beings that eat at all), or do not have the sort of nature (because immutable or impassible and so beyond anger or influence) or character (because just and upright) to be influenced by gifts or bribes (*do ut des* gifts or placatory sacrifices). Neo-Platonizing philosophers recognized a "great chain of being" and contended that only the lowest level of gods is appropriately worshiped by material offerings; spiritual offerings are required for "drawing near" to the supreme God! Thinking that evil demons cause famine, crop failure, earthquakes, and other natural disasters in order to get bloody sacrifices, Iamblicus recommends aversion sacrifices as the prudent course, while Porphyry disagrees because feeding them with such offerings would strengthen them for their mischief. So far as human being is concerned, the offerings that befit our nature are neither grains nor barnyard beasts, but prayer, thanksgiving, and virtuous living.[48]

4.2. Biblical reservations

Biblical prophets and psalmists also pronounce it mistaken and insulting to think that Divine being or well-being depends on

---

[48] Young, *The Use of Sacrificial Ideas*, ch. 1, 15–33.

animal or cereal sacrifices. Moreover, what interests God about human being is our *personal* dimension. Prophets and psalmists find animal or cereal sacrifices *insufficient* apart from obedience, praise, and thanksgiving; compared with the latter, such cultic exercises are *less important*. The Synoptic Jesus leaves the same impression (Matthew 6 and 23 *passim*, esp. Matthew 23:23). After the destruction of the Temple, the rabbis can declare good deeds, repentance, fasting, prayer, and study of the Torah *equivalent* to sacrifice, so that agricultural offerings, most notably bloody sacrifices, are *not necessary* after all.[49] Humans look to the outward act, but God looks on the heart!

5. Martyrdom: sacrifice, bloody and personal

Ironically, what cements bloody sacrifice into the conceptuality of Christian theology is not the temple slaughter of bulls and goats, but the hardest case, so far scarcely mentioned: human sacrifice, in particular, the martyr's voluntary self-offering of his/her own life. A martyr is simply a witness: in the sense relevant here, someone who gives testimony about a person, some events, or an ideal, and who is made to pay a price for doing so. The price a martyr is willing to pay is a measure of his/her love for and loyalty to that to which s/he bears witness. In highly hostile circumstances, ultimate *personal* devotion to God (which both biblical prophets and philosophical critics commend) may carry the cost of *animal* bloodshed and death (which the Temple cult required).

---

[49] Young, *The Use of Sacrificial Ideas*, ch. 2, 57–66. Milgrom insists that the prophets do not oppose the cult itself, but only its misuse and separation from moral living (*Leviticus 1–16*, vol. I, 483–484). Young notes that the Gospels record no outright rejection or even extensive critique of the Temple cult by Jesus. His cleansing of the Temple and prediction of its destruction can be placed within the tradition of prophetic critique (Young, *The Use of Sacrificial Ideas*, ch. 4, 79–80).

5.1. Paradigms and precedents

IV Maccabees brings its theology of martyrdom close to the surface in its stories of the martyrdoms of Eleazar (5:4–6:30) and of the seven brothers (8:3–18:24) under the Hellenizing pogroms of Antiochus Epiphanes. Taking a page from holiness-code and prophetic writers, it affirms that *widespread and flagrant disregard of Divine commands eventually provokes Divine wrath which sets a variety of collective punishments in motion.* To the usual list – bad weather, pestilence, and crop failure; military siege, cannibalism, and exile – IV Maccabees adds religious persecution. Just as God moved Babylon to destroy and deport, so also God has raised up Antiochus Epiphanes to require Jews to eat pork, to renounce Divine law and their ancestral traditions, on pain of being brutally tortured to death. But *the stead-fast loyalty of observant individuals developed and/or exhibited in the course of their being tortured to death may win God's mercy towards His people.* In the story, Eleazar conceptualizes this in three ways. First, he prays, "let our punishment suffice for them" (IV Maccabees 6:28): let what the martyr bravely endures count as *a representative punishment* adequate to turn away Divine wrath from the nation. Second, Eleazar petitions, "Make my blood their purification" (IV Maccabees 6:29). Because his own individual obedience to the law is unblemished, he qualifies as a fit *purification offering or expiatory sacrifice.* Third, Eleazar asks, "take my life in return for theirs" (IV Maccabees 6:29) – recalling a complex tradition according to which all first-born male animals are holy to the Lord, although – according to some passages – human first-born sons may be *redeemed* by substituting another life (i.e., that of an unblemished lamb).[50] The narrator speaks of the martyrs' offering as *a ransom* for the sin of the nation (IV Maccabees 17:21), evidently paid to Divine wrath to restore the people into the arms of Divine mercy. Again, the author confirms,

---

[50] See Jon D. Levenson, *The Death and Resurrection of the Beloved Son: The Transformation of Child Sacrifice in Judaism and Christianity* (New Haven: Yale University Press, 1993).

the blood of the devoted ones and their death is an *expiation* for the nation (IV Maccabees 17:22). The Maccabean martyrs concede the justice of Divine punishment, implicitly acknowledge and confess national iniquity, and thereby render even Israel's high-handed sins eligible for sacrificial remedy.

Eleazar emphasizes that his self-offering is *voluntary*: "You know, O God, that though I might have saved myself, I am dying in burning torments for the sake of your law" (IV Maccabees 6:27). The narrator and the seven brothers sound the theme that such violent persecution is *a test*, through which devout reason, godly training, and virtue will triumph (IV Maccabees 6:21–23, 9:7–8, 31–32, 10:10). The author recognizes how emotionally repugnant it will be to consent to human sacrifice – either one's own or – as in the case of the mother – that of one's children (IV Maccabees 16–17). Disciplined reason and religious zeal are (or should be) strong enough to overcome.

Not only is the nation preserved for renewed covenant observance, peace at home, and military ascendancy. *Divine wrath will turn on Israel's enemies* (e.g., Antiochus Epiphanes) *who will be punished on earth and eternally tormented in the age to come* (IV Maccabees 9:8, 24, 31–32, 12:12, 17, 18:5). By contrast, *the martyrs will "have the prize of virtue" and endless life with God for whom they suffer* (IV Maccabees 9:8, 16:25, 17:11, 18, 18:23–24).

Throughout their long history of pogroms, Jewish communities came to read their own martyrdoms and the Akedah (the Genesis 22 story of the binding of Isaac) over against one another. In the Bible story as we have it, God commands Abraham to sacrifice Isaac on Mt. Moriah, but calls it off and provides a ram in the thicket when God sees that Abraham is prepared to obey. When Abraham takes up the knife to kill Isaac, God forbids the patriarch to lay a hand on Isaac or do anything to him. Isaac does not die. Many current commentators write the whole episode off as a test of faith in which Abraham learns that YHWH does not demand child sacrifice. For the Jewish community, repeated Gentile persecutions raised the question: does God after all require the sacrifice of Israel, His first-born son (Exodus

4:22)? Midrash retells the story, in some versions casting Isaac not as a boy but as a 37-year-old man who voluntarily consents to the sacrifice, is killed and burned, so that his blood and ashes are on the altar, to remind God on the Day of Atonement to show mercy to Israel. In some versions Isaac is resurrected, in some taken to Paradise to recover from the wounds Abraham inflicted. During the Middle Ages, when cornered Jews steeled themselves against their emotions and sacrificed one another for the sanctification of the Name rather than be killed and defiled by Gentile mobs, their communities wondered whether such martyrdoms would – why they would not – bring the pogroms to an end![51]

5.2. Transferred usage, altered rubrics!

Striking for present purposes is the fact that such traditional treatments of martyrdom do not replace sacrificial understandings of what God requires with merely moral ones. On the contrary, martyrdom *is* human sacrifice. The sacrificial conceptuality is transferred, but remains fundamental and is made to house the personal performance. The personal dimension dominates in dictating the rubrics, and the sacrificial precedents look back to patriarchal times.

The Torah sets down Divine specifications for sacred space, lays out the liturgical calendar, draws up the rota of clergy, and retails the costumes, hardware, and ritual actions. Animal sacrifices accomplish their purposes, are beneficial rather than lethal, only if Divine directions are followed in every detail. Where the *animal* dimension of martyrdom is concerned, the martyr usually will not (as with Eleazar and the seven brothers) get to decide where, when, how (with what weapons and by whose office) bloodshed and death occur. So

---

[51] Shalom Spiegel, in his remarkable book *The Last Trial: On the Legends and Lore of the Command to Abraham to Offer Isaac as a Sacrifice; the Akedah* (Woodstock, VT: Jewish Lights Reprints, 1993), retails how these varied midrashim developed through the times of the medieval Crusades.

far from a highly sanctified priesthood, the martyr's killers may be highly irreligious; their instruments of torture and murder, devoted to desecration. Where the *personal* dimension of martyrdom is concerned, however, the martyr him/herself is the sacrifier. *Every* Israelite is enjoined to love God with his/her whole heart, soul, strength, and mind. *Everywhere and always* are appropriate occasions to offer oneself without reservation. Thus, the *personal* sacrifice of martyrdom is valid and acceptable to God, wherever and whenever it occurs.

The Torah dictates that sacrificial animals be *physically* unblemished, that they be of a certain birth order, age, and gender. Where martyrdom is concerned, the purity-requirements are not physical but *personal*: viz., unqualified loyalty that loves God more than life itself.

According to Levitical legislation, sacrifice does not aim at the death of the animal. Rather its death is a side effect of separating the blood to be splashed against the altar (in all offerings), and daubed and sprinkled (in purification offerings). Likewise, the animal's death is a precondition of the burning or eating that transfers its carcass from one realm to another and/or communicate tolerable doses of positive spiritual charge to the sacrifier. Such burning or eating is also one means of eliminating negative spiritual force from the sanctuary and from the sacrifier's world.

Death is not the aim in martyrdom either. As sacrifier, the martyr purposes total devotion, to give him/herself to God without reservation. The martyrs' enemies threaten torture and death in order to get them to renounce their deepest loyalties. Martyrs (such as the seven brothers) greet such threats as a challenge, as an occasion of faith development, as an opportunity to strengthen their commitments and to exercise greater resolution than ever before. It is because we humans are personal *animals* that we are susceptible to torture and death. Indeed, the epistle to the Hebrews identifies human fear of death as what gives the devil power to pervert us as *persons*. This power is defeated by the martyr's *personal* perseverance despite *animal* vulnerabilities. Thus, the martyr's *personal* performance turns an occasion of attempted degradation and death into an acceptable *animal sacrifice*! Conversely, martyrdom becomes a paradigm of animal sacrifice because it is precisely where the animal and personal are integrated!

Note that if martyrdom as sacrifice transfers the usage from cult to cosmos, medieval Jewish martyrs did not experience it as removed very far. Like Eleazar and the seven brothers, they were about to die for their faith due to Gentile pogroms. Unlike Eleazar and the seven brothers, medieval Jewish martyrs had the luxury of a little time. Stepping into the priestly role of Father Abraham, they attempted to follow as many of the primary-context rubrics as they could.

5.3. Onward, Christian martyrs!

Against such a background, it was easy to identify Jesus – like the suffering servant of Isaiah 53, like the midrashic Isaac – as a prototypical martyr, whose "obedience unto death on a cross" has decisive *expiatory* significance. So long as Christ's death was believed not to cover post-baptismal sin (an idea clearly presupposed in the epistle to the Hebrews, but eventually dropped), the deaths of Christian martyrs were thought to provide further expiation. Thus, in *The Martyrdom of Polycarp*, Polycarp speaks of himself as a *ransom* for the Christians at Smyrna and prays that in death he be poured out as *a drink offering*. Likewise, Ignatius of Antioch represents his impending death as a sacrifice and encourages his fellow believers to imitate his offering. *The Martyrdom of Polycarp* and Origen's treatise focus on martyrdom as a complete self-offering, and in that respect a *holocaust* in which nothing is held back, not even life itself, and so the most extravagant *gift offering* or *sacrifice of praise and thanksgiving*.[52] Much later, post-Reformation Spanish Jesuits valorize martyrdom as an expression of total devotion which sets oneself apart – like temple hardware –

---

[52] Young, *The Use of Sacrificial Ideas*, ch. 5, 108–109, ch. 6, 130–131.

for holy purposes and utterly withdraws oneself from profane or common use.[53]

5.4. Stoic sacrifices, elite solutions

The stories in IV Maccabees forward not only a theology, but also a *philosophy* of martyrdom, one of a broadly stoic nature. Human beings may not be able to control what happens on the outside: e.g., whether Antiochus Epiphanes conquers Palestine, instigates a pogrom, and threatens "apostacize, or be tortured to death." But human beings do have a capacity for inward self-control. While acknowledging that some particular provisions of Jewish law may seem petty or arbitrary (e.g., "don't eat pork"), Eleazar insists that the law as a whole is useful, because following it teaches us how to "master all pleasures and desires," "trains us in courage, so that we may endure any suffering willingly," "instructs us in justice, so that in all our doings we act impartially," and "teaches us piety so that with proper reverence we worship the only real God" (IV Maccabees 5:19–24). Reason teaches us to obey; devout reason will enable us to conquer and choose the right thing at any price. By presenting the martyrs as heroes of faith and exemplars, the author of IV Maccabees at once urges others to imitate them and at the same time acknowledges that heroic performance is rare. Hence, the martyrs' prayers that their tortured deaths may *substitute* for the punishment of the people at large! Yet New Testament appropriation of this ideal (e.g., in the epistle to the Hebrews) implies that every Christian is expected to muscle up to it, that for believers who apostacize there is no further remedy against Divine wrath (see Hebrews 4:1–13; 12:25–29).

Once again, I find these stoic paradigms deep and worthy of great respect, but elitist. Even if martyrologies exaggerate, I have no wish to deny that some humans put in some truly impressive individual performances. But experience shows such perseverance to be out of

---

[53] See Stone, *A History of the Doctrine of the Holy Eucharist*, vol. II, ch. XIV, sec.I.ii, 374.

psycho-spiritual reach for many (perhaps even most) human beings in sufficiently desperate circumstances. Wartime horrors expose deeply rooted ordinary-time virtues as ineffectual defenses against betraying one's deepest loyalties. Even if the Spirit of Christ indwells us, many-to-most of us have not learned to cooperate well enough to offer the sacrifice of heroic martyrdom either in this world's torture chambers and death camps or on the altar of our hearts.

Corollary to such philosophical overestimation of human agent-competence, this *theology* of martyrdom identifies the root of our non-optimality problems as sin, our individual and collective refusal to keep God's commandments. After the second destruction of Jerusalem in 70 CE, the author of IV Ezra challenges this. God knows whereof we are made, how the evil *yezer* is more powerful than the good. God knows that, even if a few individuals succeed, the nation as a whole will not be able to keep Divine laws. For God to cut a covenant with Israel, one that makes such curses consequent upon national apostasy, is for God to set Israel up for ruin![54]

6. Horror-participation as bloody sacrifice!

My own sympathies lie with IV Ezra. Throughout this book, my contention has been that the problem of sin is real but derivative, that the root of our non-optimality problems is that God has set us up for horrors by creating us personal animals in a world such as this. Individual heroic moral records and/or escape from individual (as opposed to collective) horror-participation do nothing to change the basic horrendous conditions of *ante-mortem* human existence and so are insufficient to secure the possibility of positive meaning for other merely human beings. What I want to urge is that horror-participation is another paradigm of human sacrifice, one which puts animal and personal sacrifice together another way. When the

[54] IV Ezra 3:3–36.

conceptuality is thus transferred from cult to cosmos, human horror-participation is seen both to resemble and to invert the categories of bloody sacrifice, while Divine participation in horrors bears witness to deep truths about us and God.

6.1. Apt categories

Human horror-participation bears strong analogies to bloody sacrifice. First, in sacrifice, the medium of Divine–human exchange is the material stuff of human lives. God relates to humankind through the medium of material creation, the environment in which God has placed us. God relates to humankind first and foremost through the medium of human nature – personal animality, enmattered spirituality, personified material – itself. Eventually, God relates to humankind through the medium of God's own humanity, in the Word made flesh and crucified. Reciprocally, the material stuff through which human beings relate to God is preeminently the material beings that we are; secondarily, the material stuff of our surround. My suggestion is that the horror-participant is the victim in a human sacrifice.

Second, Hubert and Mauss insist that *destruction* of the victim – its elimination or disappearance – is essential to the sacrifice, insofar as it transfers the victim to another realm, effects its passover from the profane to the sacred, or its banishment from the profane to the cursed (as in aversion sacrifices offered to demons). Post-Reformation Catholics debate the sense in which something must be destroyed in the sacrifice: Suarez says what is important is that the object be presented in God's honor; De Lugo argues that degradation of the sacrifice is from a living and sometimes personal being to the status of food; still others contend that some sort of change will suffice.[55] Material creation evolves personal animals and *presents* them in God's honor. Horror-participation *degrades* embodied persons by

---

[55] Stone, *A History of the Doctrine of the Holy Eucharist*, vol. II, ch. XIV, sec.I.ii, 369–375.

prima facie destroying their personhood, by furnishing *prima facie* reason to believe that no positive sense can be made of their lives.

Third, horror-participation, indeed radical vulnerability to horrors, does not so much transfer as confine and condemn human being to the realm of curse. So far from being fundamentally profane so that room must be made for the sacred, or essentially sacred, so that safe space must be cleared for the profane, the created world of our experience is unclean, because dysfunctionally heterogeneous and self-defeating.[56] God created the material world with the aim of entering into intimacy with it and with the purpose of matter's becoming as Godlike as possible while still being itself. But human being, the personal animality on which these twin goals converge, is – by itself – a dysfunctional hybrid that so misfits the material environment that evolved it as to be radically vulnerable to horrors. The material environment that gives rise to human being also *prima facie* destroys the personhood of human being, *prima facie* reduces this aspect of God's creative purpose to an absurdity, and *prima facie* renders human being in this world a curse from which no merely created sacrifice can deliver us.

Fourth, seeing horror-participation as sacrifice should dispel modern bewilderment at the idea that impersonal material things could possess a positive or negative religious "charge" that might be lethally contagious when the wrong persons draw near in unauthorized ways. We human beings experience this world as apt to "break out" on us unexpectedly and ruinously, without regard to our intentions, personal character, moral record, or religious devotion, and

---

[56] Mary Douglas in *Purity and Danger: An Analysis of the Concepts of Pollution and Taboo* (London: Routledge and Kegan Paul, 1966), explains that "dirt" is "stuff out of order" and – among other things – correlates purity with fitting precisely into a category. Linsey-woolsey, partly leprous limbs, or partly mildewed walls are unclean because they are not wholly and completely of one kind rather than another. But the fact that any animal can be clean shows that impurity is not simply a matter of having heterogeneous parts, but of heterogeneity that lacks wholesome functional organization (of the sort that a healthy animal has).

yet in such a way as to stultify or pervert them all. Metaphysically, this is because of what I have called the "misfit" between personal and material. The philosophical majority report gets at the same point when it rejects any "type–type" reduction of the psychological to the material. Epistemologically, the two types of explanation are not congruent with one another, so that – as stoics note – the material order grinds on in a way indifferent to human personality. Moreover, human understanding of the material world remains fragmentary, despite the impressive achievements of natural science. The result is that we can be salient members of causal chains whose effects amplify into consequences we could never have anticipated. We, our personal choices, are inserted into a material system beyond our ken, with the result that – much to our peril – we know not what we do!

Fifth, like Levitical priests drawing near to the sanctuary, we humans in this world experience the risks of ambivalent Divinity. God is responsible for our *prima facie* ruin, and yet God is the only One Who can save us from degradation and despair. God has set us up for horrors by creating human being in a world like this, and yet God – Who God is, What God is – is the only good great enough to defeat horrors and restore us to positively meaningful lives. What we need is a transaction that puts the "bigness" of God on our side, and channels its power to transform our relation to the material world of which we are a part.

6.2. Offering up humanity

If horror-ridden human being is the victim, the sacrifiers are two. On the one hand, material creation offers up human sacrifice to God: as *a communion sacrifice* insofar as by evolving human beings material creation becomes capable of personal intimacy with God; as *a holocaust* insofar as it not only destroys bodily life, but – in *prima facie* ruining human capacity for personal meaning – it does not retain any meaning-making capacities for itself; as a *best-fruits* (on analogy with *first-fruits*) offering insofar as personal animals are the best that material creation has produced. On the other hand, God sacrifices humankind on the altar of Divine cosmic purposes – among others, to have a material creation, to enter into intimacy with it, to make matter as Godlike as possible while still being itself. God can be said to offer human beings as *holocausts* insofar as death and horrors are known if unintended side effects of Divine creative policies.

6.3. *God as sacrifier, priest, and victim*

God sacrifices humankind by setting us up for horrors. God defeats horrors by sacrificing God's own self. But sacrifice requires material stuff, and Divinity is immaterial. To make this offering, God must become Incarnate, the Word (or some other Divine person) must be made flesh!

6.3.1. Reversing the direction of travel, averting the powers of darkness

Priestly and holiness-code writings chart the rubrics for human beings attempting to establish and/or maintain a relationship with the sacred by means of some sort of transfer from the profane/impure world to the sacred world. The direction of travel is reversed when God is the sacrifier who takes the initiative to repair relationship obstacles with our horror-strewn world. God has to draw near to our dwelling place, enter into the world in which we are *prima facie* cursed, to purify it and make us whole. In priestly and holiness-code texts, entry into the Holy of Holies could prove dangerous to the high priest's health, because the Holy could "break out" on unrubrical approaches. Likewise, entry into a horror-cursed world proved dangerous to God, because the curse not only threatened, but *prima facie* succeeded in destroying or banishing God from the face of the earth. Just as the Levitical high priest enters the Holy of Holies on the Day of Atonement, so God enters the most cursed part of our cursed world, by taking on our human nature in both material and personal aspects. Just as the Levitical high priest does not dare to enter the shrine without the blood of purification to absorb and ward off impurities, so God does not enter our world without an *aversion sacrifice*, an offering for the powers of darkness – i.e., the horror-producing powers of material creation – to consume, not by fire or literal eating, but by crucifixion. The Blessed Trinity sends God the Son, the Divine Word to take our human nature. God offers the Word made flesh up for horror-producing powers to do their worst, to destroy His life materially and to appear utterly to defeat the positive meaning of His human life. Then the ironic reversal takes hold: God the Son's becoming a horror-participant, having the positive meaning of His human life *prima facie* destroyed, defeats the power of horrors to destroy the positive meaning of our lives, and so fulfills the positive purpose of His own human career.

6.3.2. Sacrificing Godself to us

God also sacrifices Godself – the Word made flesh, a material offering made holy by virtue of hypostatic union – *to us*. Certainly Emmanuel, God-with-us, counts as a *communion sacrifice*; so also as a *gift sacrifice*, a sweet smelling savor to honor us by His visitation. Strictly speaking, God cannot make *sin offerings*, because – without obligations to others – God cannot sin no matter what God does. Nevertheless, because radical vulnerability to, inevitable (at least collective) participation in horrors, is a harm to human being for which God is *responsible*, God's offering of the Word made flesh to us bears analogies to *sin offerings*. Recall that in priestly and holiness-code legislation, *hatta't* sacrifices are offered for unwitting violations of God's prohibitive (and, in Numbers, also performative) commands, while graduated *hatta't* offerings can be brought for witting as well as unwitting transgressions. Insofar as horrors and horror-participation are not the creative *purpose* at which God aims, these harms can be seen as somehow incidental – which makes God's offering of the Word made flesh as a sacrifice to us analogous to the *hatta't* sacrifice. Insofar as these consequences are *known*, however, God's sacrifice is more like a graduated *hatta't* or Day of Atonement offering. Recall how priestly legisla-tion allows witting sins to become eligible for sacrificial remedy via repentance, confession, and reparation. Although God, as naturally impeccable, cannot confess sin, God can do something analogous by acknowledging Divine *responsibility* for creating us in a world like this. Thus, God's offering of the Word made flesh can be compared to the sin offering sacrificed for the people on the Day of Atonement. Insofar as the responsibility for Divine creative policies is laid "on the head" of the Word made flesh, the Word made flesh can be com-pared to the scapegoat, "disappeared" by being banished outside the city gates. According to priestly and holiness-code legislation, "high-handed" sins defile not just the outer court and altar, not just the altar of incense, but the Holy of Holies itself, thereby threatening to drive God out of temple and land. Similarly, horror-participation does not do merely peripheral damage to personal meaning-making systems; it disables the core of that system, stalemating the person's attempts to make positive sense of his/her life. The blood of bulls and goats, merely human sacrifice, would be ineffectual to purify (restore wholeness to) human horror-participants, because no pack-age of merely created goods could defeat horrors. The only remedy is for God to offer Godself: the Word (or some other Divine person) made flesh is the only human sacrifice that will defeat the horror-participation of others, of merely human beings within the context of their individual lives.

Israel carried out Day of Atonement rites to protect the nation from Divine wrath. But God comes into our world *in order* to expose Godself to human wrath. Thus, God's offering of the Word made flesh functions as a *propitiation*. In human propitiatory sacrifices to the gods, anger is turned away by offering them something they like to distract their attention from what made them angry. The Lamb of God is offered to calm our anger by showing solidarity, by becoming human to share the costs of horror-participation, the better to declare that God does not ask more of us than God asks of Godself. But the Lamb of God is offered not simply as a distraction *from* our anger, but as a target *for* our anger. Psychological displacement (acting out on a substitute) never gives full satisfaction. Because God is the One Who is ultimately responsible for human vulnerability and horror-participation, acting out our anger on God, letting it do its worst to God, ultimately will give satisfaction. God in Christ crucified stretches out loving arms on hard wood to absorb our anger – the very worst that human beings can suffer, be, or do – into God's own flesh.

God's offering of the Word made flesh as a sacrifice to us can also be seen as a *covenant sacrifice* (Mark 14:24; Matthew 26:28; Luke 22:20). In contracting with Abram, God commanded him to hack in two a heifer, goat, and ram, and to offer a turtledove and young pigeon (Genesis 15:7–21). In "sealing the deal" with Abraham (Genesis 17:9–14) and later Moses (Exodus 4:24–26), circumcision – a symbolic sacrifice, a shedding of human blood – was required. At Passover, a lamb was to be slain and its blood daubed on the entrance to the house (Exodus 12:1–13). At Calvary, God offers God's own self; in the tradition of the Akedah, the Trinity offers God's only begotten, God's first-born Son, the Word made flesh to be "hacked in two" (His flesh torn by whips, thorns, nails, and spear), to be killed (as an *aversion sacrifice*) by the destroying angel, to become cursed and thereby to have the positive meaning of His human life *prima facie* destroyed. Christ our Passover does protect us from the destroying angel insofar as Divine horror-participation entails that ours wrecks the possibility of positive personal meaning *prima facie* but not all things considered.

God's offering of Godself to us is analogous to *the martyr's self-offering*. God has to offer up God's whole self in God's human nature to the worst that we can suffer, be, or do. Thereby God bears witness to the truth about human being in this world, to our horrendous predicament, and testifies to the truth about Divine responsibility for it. To show ultimate loyalty, to go all the way with us, God has to take the curse on Godself (Galatians 3:13). By so doing, God also testifies to (at least gives evidence of) the truth that God is *for* us after all. God's self-offering is a *gift sacrifice* to honor us. It is also a *thank offering* to express Divine gratitude to us for living a human life in this horror-ridden world.[57]

7. Horrors as gift?

7.1. The dynamics of gift-giving

Yet another angle on soteriological ironies is furnished by Marcel Mauss' analysis of the gift as a system of economic exchange (alternative to that of market economies) based on a threefold obligation: the obligation to give, the obligation to receive, and the obligation to reciprocate.[58] Gifts are neither free nor disinterested, but a way of establishing and maintaining social connection (across families, clans, or tribes) and solidarity.[59]

Gifts engage the honor of all parties. The gift symbolizes how much there is to the giver; the greater, the more generous, the gift, the higher the rank claimed.[60] A gift also represents a challenge to the honor of the one to whom it is offered: to accept a gift from a peer is for the receiver to claim that there is enough to him (the social group he represents) at least to reciprocate in kind, if not something of greater value. To refuse the gift is to refuse the attendant social connection and so either to insult the giver – "you aren't of a high enough status for it to be worthwhile for me to establish bonds with you" – or to lose face by conceding that one does not have the resources to respond at

---

[57] Julian of Norwich says that, when we get to heaven, God will welcome us with gratitude: "Thank you for your suffering, the suffering of your youth" (*Revelations of Divine Love*, ch. 14, 85).

[58] Marcel Mauss, *The Gift: The Form and Reason for Exchange in Archaic Societies*, trans. W. D. Halls, forward Mary Douglas (London and New York: W. W. Norton, 1990).

[59] Mary Douglas, Forward, in Mauss, *The Gift*, vii, x; Mauss, *The Gift*, ch. 1, sec. 1, 8–14, ch. 2, sec. 1, 19, ch. 2, sec. 2, 27–29, ch. 2, sec. 3, 33, ch. 2, sec. 3, 39–42, ch. 3, sec. 2, 59.

[60] Mauss, *The Gift*, ch. 2, sec. 3, 39–40, ch. 4, sec. 2, 75.

the required level.[61] To reciprocate with a greater or equal gift is both to meet the challenge of the gift received and to counterchallenge, thereby continuing the connection.[62] A gift of the same value produces a stable system of statuses. If the return gift must be of greater value, this produces an escalating competition for honor.[63] Failure to reciprocate within the expected time frame carries a loss of status.[64] Where there is a stable hierarchical order between giver and receiver, the donor would be expected to reciprocate something scaled to his station, and to receive in turn something befitting the higher-up's station. Thus, one answer to Mauss' question – what keeps the system going? – is the dynamics of the Honor Code.[65] (Mauss proposes a further energizer: that the gift is really part of the giver, bears the giver's honor, and carries the giver's spirit or even the spirit of the tribe or their ancestors or some sort of religious character that acts upon the receiver to cause him to reciprocate and/or to punish his not doing so.[66] But later research has called this interpretation of the Maori practices into question.)

In the highly competitive North American potlatch, donors not only bestow ever more extravagant gifts on their guests; they also destroy wealth with abandon. This makes two powerful symbolic statements. First, it declares that there is "so much to" the donor tribe that it can afford to throw wealth away. Second, since what is destroyed is not given to human receivers who would be obligated to make return on it, it boasts that the donor tribe is so rich that it can afford to dispose of wealth without expecting to receive anything

[61] Mauss, *The Gift*, ch. 1, sec. 3, 13, ch. 2, sec. 3, 41.

[62] Mauss, *The Gift*, ch. 1, sec. 3, 14, ch. 2, sec. 3, 42.

[63] Douglas, Forward, in Mauss, *The Gift*, viii.

[64] Douglas, Forward, in Mauss, *The Gift*, ix; Mauss, *The Gift*, ch. 2, sec. 2, 23, ch. 2, sec. 2, 26.

[65] Mauss, *The Gift*, Introduction, 3.

[66] Douglas, Forward, in Mauss, *The Gift*, ix; Mauss, *The Gift*, ch. 1, sec. 1, 8, ch. 1, sec. 2, 11–13, ch. 1, sec. 3, 14, ch. 2, sec. 3, 37–38, ch. 2, sec. 3, 46, ch. 3, sec. 2, 55.

back.[67] Third, and inconsistently, destruction of the wealth is a way of offering their wealth back as a gift sacrifice to the gods with whom the donor tribe is not in competition and from whom it may expect a still more abundant return.[68] Mauss speculates that alms – giving to the poor who have no possibility of reciprocating – also both amplifies the donor's status and constitutes a sacrifice to the gods who have no need of gifts and pass them on to others.[69]

7.2. Divine–human gift exchange

God is a being a greater than which cannot be conceived, infinite being and goodness. That Divine worthiness of honor immeasurably outclasses that of anything else possible is a necessary and immutable metaphysical fact. God has neither need nor obligation to get into a cosmic gift exchange. Yet, Goodness Itself inclines to share the wealth. Moreover, God can afford to be generous. Divine resources are limitless. No matter how much God gives, no matter how much God destroys, God can always create more. And so God confers being and goodness on a vast array of creatures. God gives human beings extravagant gifts to bind us together socially – that receiving all that we are and have, we might render our whole selves, the world over which we share dominion, back to God. Not content to donate law and prophets, God gives us the only gift that can be extravagant relative to Divine resources: the Word-made-flesh, God's own self. Yet, human beings collectively refuse these gifts – disobey the law, persecute the prophets, and (according to His human nature) destroy the God-man, God's well-beloved Son – thereby insulting God by refusing social ties.

When God's people were persecuted by ethnic and religious pogroms, thereby calling into question God's power and faithfulness

---

[67] Mauss, *The Gift*, ch. 2, sec. 3, 37.

[68] Mauss, *The Gift*, Introduction, 6, ch. 1, sec. 4, 14–17, ch. 4, sec. 2, 74.

[69] Mauss, *The Gift*, ch. 1, sec. 4, 18.

as a patron, martyrs and their communities saved God's face by reconceptualizing their situation: God is using the Gentiles to punish Israel's national apostasy, and the martyrs are offering sacrifice to God (see section 5). My suggestion is that at Calvary God returns the favor. When human beings attempt to divorce themselves from God by destroying God's best gift, God reconceptualizes our murder of the God-man as a connection-reinforcing gift sacrifice. Moreover, God counts it as a case in which – for once – creatures give as good as they get, for we return by destroying the very same gift that God offered: the Word-made-flesh, God's own self!

Martyrs see themselves as worthy offerings by virtue of their personal integrity. Horror-participation usually robs human beings of their capacity for integrity, by destroying their capacity to make positive sense of their lives. My suggestion is that the lens of gift exchange allows God to accept horror-participants as worthy offerings for the same reason. Their deaths and/or destruction of their meaning-making capacities return to God the very gift that God offered in the first place: the gift of being a personal animal, an enmattered spirit in a material world such as this. Horrors for horrors! No wonder Mauss feels compelled to remind us of the ambiguity of the letters: what in English signifies gift in German means poison![70]

---

[70] Mauss, *The Gift*, ch. 3, sec. 3, 62–63.

10 | Christ in the sacrament of the altar: Christ in the meantime

1. Interim exercises

Futuristic eschatology promises that, in the life to come, the plot will resolve for everyone: all shall be well, all shall be well, all shall be very well![1] But what about in the meantime? Horrors, the attendant alienation from self, God, and others, are a heavy cross to bear.

Christianity advertises a God Who wants to help us in the meantime. Traditionally, sacraments are means of grace, liturgical rites through which participants appropriate *ante-mortem* benefits of the Savior's work. Like birth, baptism is once and for all and acknowledges our adoption as God's children. By contrast, the second sacrament – the Lord's supper, holy eucharist, the sacrament of the altar, the sacrifice of the mass – is oft-repeatable, a rite to which we regularly return throughout our lives, and so a scene of Divine–human relationship development. For horror-participants who have not given up on God altogether, for the wrestling and congregating Church, the second sacrament is particularly promising because it puts horrors front and center. By Christ's own command, its explicit purpose is "to show forth the Lord's death until He comes": "do this in remembrance of me!" My suggestion is that this makes the second sacrament an apt place for horror-participants to begin to "learn the meanings": to enter into an ever deeper recognition of how Stage-I horror-defeat is accomplished through Christ's Incarnation and passion, and thereby to take some steps towards Stage-II horror-defeat.

[1] Julian of Norwich, *Revelations of Divine Love*, ch. 27, 103–104.

Perhaps because the second sacrament digs so profoundly into our sense of personal meaning, of who we are to God and who God is to us, it has repeatedly been the subject of virulent theological conflict (e.g., in Europe, in the ninth century, again in the eleventh century, and in the sixteenth-century Protestant Reformation), so much so that it is difficult to identify it otherwise than by polemically loaded names. Conflicts raged over whether and/or in what sense the Body of Christ is really present in the eucharist, over whether the eucharist is in any way a sacrifice or is only a commemoration or sign of one, and over eucharistic participation – whether access should be easy or tightly restricted. Horrors invite a distinctive stance on these controverted issues. Horrors push us to replace emphasis on worthy reception with a policy of permissive participation, and to embrace a strong doctrine of corporeal presence. Horrors also figure-ground shift us into the recognition of cult, like cosmos, as a scene of human sacrifice in which not only Christ but we are both priest and victim!

2. Material rites: easy access for embodied persons!

2.1. Material versus personal?

Sacraments are the material cult of Christians; they are "outward and visible," *material* "signs." Even "low-church" ceremony has stage and props and costumes, prescribed gestures, characteristic intonations and patterns of speech; if not a script, at least a predictable dramatic structure and topical order. Yet, as often as the material aspect of Christian worship has been elaborated and ornamented, it has been critiqued and downplayed. The counterargument lies on the surface: God is personal, and we are personal; therefore, we should focus on meeting God person-to-person rather than on choreography, smells, and bells. Proof texts from psalms (Psalm 51:16–17), prophets (Jeremiah 7), and Gospels (Matthew 6) warn that God doesn't care about being honored with outward ceremony and ritual. God wants us to observe the first and second great commandments (Matthew 22:37–40; Mark 12:28–34; Luke 10:25–28). God looks on the heart!

In worship, however, it is not just any person, it is *God* Whom we are meeting! Biblical authors dramatize their appreciation of the metaphysical size-gap by representing God as an aloof monarch, whose palace is divided into outer courts and inner sanctum, whose servants are allowed varying degrees of access by rank, and then only when the court etiquette of costume, gesture, and timing is meticulously observed. Transposing such outward and visible to inward and moral requirements has tended to generate extremely demanding admission standards. Witness the elaboration of the 614 commandments within Pharisaic Judaism! Writing in the middle of the seventeenth century, the Anglican divine Jeremy Taylor carries on the tradition when he insists that to receive holy communion is not merely to approach, but to attempt to *become*, the Holy of Holies, to offer oneself as sacred space in which the Holy Spirit might dwell.[2] Preparation for it involves "an heap of duties,"[3] beginning with rigorous self-examination. Taylor declares that we are not fit to communicate unless we are fit to die[4] – i.e., unless our state of soul is such as would withstand the final judgment and gain entry to heaven's gate. Again, we are not fit to receive holy communion unless our souls are in a condition to persevere through fiery trials or have already stood the test of persecution.[5] More particularly, the worthy communicant must have a zealous love for God (strong enough to die or pay significant penalties for God's sake)[6] issuing in a warm and earnest desire and longing to converse with Christ. *And* these sentiments must be strong enough and stable enough to have borne

---

[2] Jeremy Taylor, *The Worthy Communicant*, vol. VIII in *The Whole Works of the Right Rev. Jeremy Taylor, DD* (London: Longman, Brown, Green, and Longmans, 1854), Introduction, 7, ch. 2, sec. 1, 54–55, ch. 5, sec. 2, 158–159.

[3] Taylor, *The Worthy Communicant*, Introduction, 7–8.

[4] Taylor, *The Worthy Communicant*, ch. 5, sec. 4, 172.

[5] Taylor, *The Worthy Communicant*, ch. 2, sec. 1, 55–56.

[6] Taylor, *The Worthy Communicant*, ch. 2, sec. 3, 70.

fruit in *action*.[7] Faith is required, not only in the sense that only the baptized are eligible, but also that the baptized must have actual and exercised faith.[8] Prayers must come from the heart and inform the life.[9] The whole of human life must be continual repentance.[10] *All* sinful affections must be discovered, and crucified, so that the passions are under the dominion of grace, the command of reason, and the rule of the Spirit.[11] Great fear or anger, any lasting and violent, unreasonable and transporting passion, is sufficient to exclude one from the table.[12] *Prima facie* disqualifying are the inability to accept the defeat of one's purposes or to be at peace with those who thwart them.[13] Taylor emphasizes that, worthy communicants must have perfectly renounced all sinful affections, firmly purposed amendment of life, and made good on their intentions with a significant record of performance.[14] Taylor comments,

> the grace of God in the sacrament usually is a blessing upon our *endeavors*; for spiritual graces and blessings of sanctification do not grow like grass, but like corn; not whether we do any husbandry or no; but if we cultivate the ground.[15]

Equally stern if more economical is the invitation to confession in the 1662 *Book of Common Prayer*, which teaches that we dare approach the sacrament only after rigorous self-examination, only if we

---

7 Taylor, *The Worthy Communicant*, ch. 2, sec. 2, 59–61.

8 Taylor, *The Worthy Communicant*, ch. 3, sec. 1, 87.

9 Taylor, *The Worthy Communicant*, ch. 2, sec. 4, 73–75.

10 Taylor, *The Worthy Communicant*, ch. 5, sec. 2, 158.

11 Taylor, *The Worthy Communicant*, ch. 2, sec. 5, 77, 79, ch. 5, sec. 3, 161, 164; cf. Taylor, *The Rules and Exercises of Holy Living*, vol. III in *The Whole Works of the Right Rev. Taylor, DD*, ch. 4, sec. 10, 215–216.

12 Taylor, *The Worthy Communicant*, ch. 2, sec. 5, 77–78.

13 Taylor, *The Worthy Communicant*, ch. 2, sec. 5, 78.

14 Taylor, *The Worthy Communicant*, ch. 5, sec. 3, 168–169; cf. Taylor, *The Rules and Exercises of Holy Living*, ch. 4, sec. 10, 215.

15 Taylor, *The Worthy Communicant*, ch. 1, sec. 4, 35.

truly and earnestly repent of our sins, are in love and charity with our neighbors, and intend to lead new lives following the commandments of God and walking from henceforth in his holy ways.

Such requirements effectively restrict eucharistic reception – like stoic martyrdom (see chapter 8) – to a spiritual elite of mature adults already possessed of a high degree of moral integrity. Martin Luther and John Calvin seem lenient by comparison, refusing as they do to see holy communion as a merit badge or prize for moral achievement. Nevertheless, they usually link worthy reception to saving faith, which believes the promises of God to be true and refuses to accuse God in any way.[16] This criterion would count out any individual horror-participants, for whom the existence and trustworthiness of God, Divine goodness-to-them, are precisely what horrors call into question.

Happily, the book of Job bears contrary witness, front-and-centers the metaphysical misfit between Divine and human being to draw an opposite moral. The Holy does not need to be protected from the unholy; Divine majesty does not require to be shielded from the relentless accusations and insults of horror-participants. Quite the reverse: God *does* consider the source and rewards persistent blasphemy with a vision of God's face![17]

Equally fundamentally, horrors expose this recurrent dichotomy between the personal and the material as entirely bogus where human being is concerned. Horrors force us to take our status as personified

---

[16] Against Rome, Luther argues that faith is necessary for sacramental efficacy and that faith is sufficient without it (*The Pagan Servitude of the Church*, in *Martin Luther: Selections from His Writings*, ed. and intro. John Dillenberger (Garden City, NY: Anchor-Doubleday, 1961), 274–275, 298–304). Likewise, Calvin says that the most appropriate posture is to despair of our worthiness and cast ourselves on God's mercy (*The Institutes of the Christian Religion*, Library of Christian Classics, vols. XX–XXI, trans. Ford Lewis Battles (Philadelphia: Westminster Press, 1960), Book IV, ch. XVII, secs. 41–42, vol. II, 1418–1420).

[17] For a fuller development of this interpretation of Job, see my "In Praise of Blasphemy," *Philosophia: Philosophical Quarterly of Israel*, 36: 1–2 (2003), 1–17.

matter seriously, because it is our nature as personal animals or enmattered persons that exposes us to degradation by horrors in a material world such as this. We *are* by nature *embodied* persons, personified matter, enmattered spirit; both poles are brought together in our very selves. Moreover, the attempt somehow to detach or abstract the personal from the material in human being and bring the personal to God while leaving the material behind would constitute a betrayal of the human vocation. On my cosmological hypothesis, one leading reason for personifying matter is so that God can relate to the material world in personal intimacy. This makes it our calling as human beings to return to God as personified representatives of the material world, so that loving us can be one way God loves material creation!

2.2. *Family focus, liturgical rough-and-tumble*

Without denying such rigorous sixteenth- and seventeenth-century spiritual exercises their time and place, I want to insist that they are not the measure for all persons or seasons. Beginning with horrors suggests an alternative model, where cult is not the throne room of the King of the universe, but a family room where adoptive children are reared up in the knowledge and love of the God and Father of Our Lord Jesus Christ!

To be pedagogically effective, sacraments must be adapted to the real condition of human beings in this world, and so need to take the personal, the material, and their interaction into account. Looming large is the fact that as personal animals human beings are *developmental*: we start full of potential that has to be evoked and actualized by stages over a lifetime. Likewise, human being is *multidimensional*: we include the bodily and biological, the sensory and intellectual; psychologically, the cognitive and the affective, the unconscious as well as the conscious. These evolve in different orders, at varying rates, in and out of phase with one another. They are differently affected by life's eventualities and interact with one another in complex ways. Thus, although we in some sense share body, biology, and sensory faculties with cows and donkeys, it is not as if these were of exactly the same sort in humans, with personality as an isolable "add on." Rather (as Aquinas already noted) each and all of these faculties is personified by their personal context, just as personality is formed and informed by biological and sensory dimensions. Human flourishing requires the maturing of each and all of these dimensions in appropriate coordination with one another. Our vocation before God is to offer them integrated into a Christocentric functional whole. Even apart from individual horror-participation, such growth to maturity involves a long struggle and is a difficult task in which the Inner Teacher is our constant (if often silent and unacknowledged) helper.

Horrors go beyond developmental messiness to create a major crisis. Horrors are personally fragmenting by definition, because they stalemate participants' abilities to make sense of their lives overall. Wartime trauma, sexual abuse, physical deformities, and ghastly surgeries may trigger an attempted divorce of person from body, further caricaturing who the individual was meant to be. Horrors provoke psychological "splitting" off and storing of good and bad experiences – not least of really present Divine Goodness and of horrendous evil – in different psychological closets, to keep them from confronting and devouring one another, and/or to conceal one or both from conscious view.

Thus, if what God especially wants with us is enmattered personhood, personified matter, "ourselves, our souls and bodies," one would expect God to sponsor *a material cult that engages human beings in every dimension and that has something for everyone at whatever stage of life.* Infants can feel the water poured and chrism smeared on their heads, taste the salt under their tongues and wine in their mouths. Children can bend themselves to postures, take bread in their hands, form their mouths around the responses, watch processions and pageantry, take in the colors and candles with wonder, learn the stories, more and more listen to sermons, sooner and later probe with questions as to what it is all about.

Especially important for fragmented horror-participants is the fact that adults who regularly put themselves in the pew, who avail themselves of incense and holy water (à la Pascal), expose their unconscious selves and senses to being formed and informed by symbolically loaded liturgy, with or without much conscious faith or good will towards God. *Pace* Protestant reformers, such structured repetition is not vain in religion any more than it is in the pedagogy of mathematics and language-learning. Just as memorizing multiplication tables or declensions and conjugations set the pupil up for understanding, so downloading Christ into the body and sensory faculties, establishing habits, and setting up conscious and unconscious associations prepare the way for greater commitment of intellect and will. Moreover, liturgical repetitions foster a sense of safety, lead to a gradual dropping of defenses and an opening of the self to experience the real presence of God even when it is not yet consciously recognized or named. The fact that a person's faith response remains dis-integrated, that the religious investments of the various dimensions remain unsynchronized with one another for a long time, does not mean that the religious practice is unfruitful. On the contrary, the "conversion" of a great many of the psycho-spiritual pieces to Christ prepares the way for a fuller Christocentric, I-not-I-but-Christ reintegration (see chapter 6).

3. Corporeal presence, embodied encounters

3.1. Manifold objections

From the ninth through the fifteenth centuries, the western theological majority report held that when in the course of the eucharistic prayer the officiating clergy says the words of institution – "This is my body!," "This is my blood!" – the Body and Blood of Christ come to be literally located where the eucharistic bread and wine were and still appear to be. Yet, this medieval consensus was vigorously challenged in the sixteenth century by Reformed and reforming theologians – including Zwingli, Bullinger, and Calvin – on multiple grounds.

First, they contended, it was *unsupported by Scripture.* Zwingli among others ridiculed Aquinas' and others' literal reading of "This is my body" as rhetorically naive. The Bible is full of figures of speech! Moreover, everyone agrees that sacraments are signs; how could Aquinas so blatantly fail to observe the distinction between the thing signified and the sign?[18]

Second, they insisted, transubstantiation and other school theological theories *fly in the face of reason and experience* – of philosophy, physics, and common sense. The senses testify to the continued presence of bread and wine; moreover, such perceptions survive all the usual tests to rule out sensory illusions. Doesn't everyone know, don't philosophy and science agree, that it is impossible either for two bodies (e.g., the bread and the Body of Christ) to be in the same place at once, or for a single body to be in two places at once (e.g., the Body of Christ in heaven at the right hand of God and on each altar where the eucharist is being celebrated)?[19]

Third, they charged, belief in corporeal eucharistic presence is *pragmatically pernicious.* Combined with the (anti-Donatist) *ex opere operato* provisions of medieval sacramental theology, it turns the eucharist into a magic trick in which the priest mumbles the secret formula – "*hocus pocus*" was a popular contraction of the words of

---

[18] Zwingli, "On The Lord's Supper," in *Zwingli and Bullinger*, ed. G. W. Bromiley (Philadelphia: Westminster, 1953), 188–193. Cf. Zwingli "An Exposition of the Faith," in *Zwingli and Bullinger*, 265; Calvin, *The Institutes*, Book IV, ch. XVII, secs. 1–2, vol. II, 1359–1363, secs. 21–23, 25, vol. II, 1385–1390, 1391–92; Calvin, *Three Forms of Exposition: Short Treatise on the Holy Supper of Our Lord Jesus Christ*, in *John Calvin: Selections from His Writings*, ed. John Dillenberger (Atlanta: Scholars Press/AAR, 1975), secs. 15–16, 515–516, sec. 39, 528.

[19] Zwingli, "An Exposition of the Faith," 255–258, 261. Cf. Zwingli, "On the Lord's Supper," 186; Calvin, *The Institutes*, Book IV, ch. XVII, secs. 13–18, vol. II, 1379–1381, secs. 26–27; vol. II, 1393–1395; Calvin, *Short Treatise*, secs. 41–42, 529–530.

institution *"hoc est corpus meum"* – to summon the presence of a thing whose occult powers work effects for good or ill apart from faith and beyond our knowledge.[20] Besides superstition, such conviction fosters the putative idolatry of eucharistic veneration and the popish pomps of Corpus Christi processions.[21] Enlightenment Anglicans deplored bad consequences of a different sort, pointing to their own history of religious bloodshed, partly provoked by zealous interest in the manner of Christ's real presence in the eucharistic rite.

Despite their impressive range and cumulative weight, these arguments are far from decisive. On the contrary, eucharistic controversies – with so many conflicting positions claiming to base themselves on the Bible – combine with higher critical methods of biblical interpretation to yield the verdict that sacramental theology is *underdetermined* by Scripture. Deep disagreements among theological professionals have always undermined the notion that the Bible is self-interpreting. If I disagree with Aquinas and Luther that literal location is demanded by relevant biblical passages, I would contend against Zwingli that it is not excluded either. So far as I know, no one has claimed that any positive position about eucharistic presence can be proved by reason and/or experience in such a way as to convince all rational persons. But Zwingli's and Calvin's philosophical and scientific objections to literal location are shown up as philosophically narrow-minded and unduly polemical when they simply ignore the variety of alternative philosophies of body developed by school theology to show how it is far from unintelligible that one body could be in two places or two bodies in one place at the same time.

---

[20] Calvin, *The Institutes*, Book IV, ch. XIV, sec. 4, vol. II, 1279–80, sec. 14, vol. II, 1289; Calvin, *Short Treatise*, secs. 48–52, 534–536.

[21] Calvin, *The Institutes*, Book IV, ch. xiv, secs. 14–15, vol. II, 1289–1291, ch. XVII, secs. 36–37, vol. II, 1412–1413, sec. 39, vol. II, 1416–1417; Calvin, *Short Treatise*, sec. 43, 512–513. Calvin's point of view was endorsed and imposed by the Anglican Thirty-nine Articles of Religion, no. 28.

3.2. Dinner-table dynamics

Ironically, Calvin's favorite image for the second sacrament – "the Lord's Supper," "the Holy Banquet"[22] – positively suggests a strong doctrine of Christ's corporeal presence to us in the eucharist, conjuring as it does a scene in which we meet *embodied* person to *embodied* person, make shared food the material medium with which to eat and drink, bite and chew our way into social identities and shared lives. Angels do not gather around family dinner tables. Lacking bodies, they do not biologically reproduce or come in families; pure spirits that they are, they have no need to eat. By contrast, dinner tables figure deeply in the psycho-spiritual formation of human beings.

Table fellowship is a risky business, for eating betrays our vulnerability. By opening our mouths, taking something from outside in, we prove that we are *not self-contained*. To be sure, our human bodies have a natural shape, boundaries giving definition. Paradoxically, these cannot be sustained unless they are regularly compromised – food, water, oxygen, enter to become part of us; carbon dioxide, useless leftovers expelled, in and out according to natural rhythms, necessary for life. The body's doors couldn't serve if they didn't open on passages that reach deep within us. Yet, precisely because they do, they put us at risk, allow the wrong things to penetrate too deeply, lock them inside for too long. Little wonder if the distinction between clean and unclean foods becomes sacred. What happens around the table is literally a matter of life and death!

At dinner tables, families bond, weave lives together. Where food is scarce, sharing means our lives are so tied together that I do not stand to gain by refusing you, while you win no advantage by withholding from me. If you give me the food that would sustain your life, by eating it I ingest part of your life, take part of you into myself, and

[22] Calvin, *Short Treatise*, 507–541. Cf. B. A. Gerrish, *Grace and Gratitude: The Eucharistic Theology of John Calvin* (Minneapolis: Fortress Press, 1993), ch. 1, 13.

vice versa. By eating the food the other could have eaten, we have carnal knowledge of one another. In a suspicious world, reciprocity is important. If I receive food from your hand, I not only consume something that you could have eaten. I take into myself something you have touched, prepared. I trust you not to be offering me poison. If I give, I reassure you by sipping first. Willingness to offer and to receive food from one another is a sign of covenant, a decision not to regard each other as enemies or strangers.

Family tables are meant to nurture, from cradle to grave, from infancy to Alzheimer's, to be centers of feeding and being fed. Our presence is required not only in periods of eager anticipation, vigorous work, and joyful accomplishments, but also in the midst of angry quarrels and hard-won resolutions, through seasons of grief and depression, frustration and diminishment. They are meant to be places where we grow up, from milk to pablum to solid food that has to be bitten, chomped, and chewed. Daily bread, broken and shared, is a tie that binds – for better, for worse, for richer, for poorer, in sickness and in health, for all seasons. Daily bread, broken and shared, makes us members of one another.

Yet, all too often and notoriously, dinner tables are scenes of mutual abuse and trust betrayed . . . Places where boundaries are violated, where families "eat at each other," "bite each other's heads off," gnaw away at self-confidence, throw up bones of contention, devour one another's sense of self-worth. Dinner tables can be set with venom and poison, children force-fed, their manners ritually mocked and insulted, while providers are heartily hated and scorned. How easily dinner tables become altars on which we make holocaust of others lest in flames of fury we destroy ourselves.

Other family tables freeze solid, iced by etiquette that folds indigestible truths in starched napkins, silently passes them under the table and on to the dog . . . Tables where mile-thick defenses guarantee disconnection . . . where dead and estranged families abort further conversation by appeal to their one mediator – the common TV.

So, too, Christ invites us, each and all to His supper. The Lord's table is a groaning board, heavy-laden with Heavenly Father's provisions, where adoptive sons and daughters gather to eat, drink, and be satisfied, to commune with one another and with God.[23] But the carnal knowledge to which Christ invites us is more radically intimate: instead of eating the food He could have eaten or sharing a portion of the food He is eating, Christ sets the table with His flesh and blood, with the food that *is* Himself! Christ fixes the appointment to meet us, embodied person to embodied persons, appearing under forms of bread and wine. Because we are horror-participants, Christ sets a specific agenda: all conflicts out on the table, immediately! We come, first and foremost, to show forth the Lord's death: "This is My Body!" "This is My Blood!" "Do this for the remembrance of Me!" Christ crucified is "in our face," Christ crucified is "in *God's* face," re-presenting, reminding God how in establishing material creation God "set us up," how in creating human being God has put us in the position of being radically vulnerable to horrors.

God in Christ crucified insists on swapping lunches, demands we bring our cups of spiced and foaming wine, our liquefying rage, the wormwood of our bitterness, the festering inflammations of horror-torn creation. Just as God in Christ crucified stretches out loving arms, drains the dregs of our poisons, sucks dry the pus out of our wounded world. God in Christ crucified offers us His Flesh to chomp and bite and tear with our teeth, invites us to get even, horror for horror, urges us to fragment God's own Body in return for the way God has allowed horrors to shred the fabric of our lives. God in Christ crucified invites us to come with anger and tears, with shame and humiliation poured out to the point of exhaustion. "I hunger and thirst for it all. For heaven's sake, don't keep swallowing it or try to force it down someone else's throat!"

God in Christ crucified refuses to leave the table, Emmanuel still plights His troth – for better, for worse, for richer, for poorer, for

---

[23] Calvin, *Short Treatise*, sec. 3, 508–509.

horrors descending down into the grave. "For heaven's sake, don't hold back! I can take it all in, and still rise on the third day!" Not always but in some cases, not right away but eventually, not all at once but from time to time and fleetingly, catching our breaths between bouts of thrashing and sobbing, the Easter recognition begins to dawn. This family will not break. This quarrel is between lovers. Love bade us welcome. Willy-nilly, recognized or not, Love has held on to us, all the while comforting us with its touch. From time to time, eventually, the storm may break, the air clear, the bread and wine bear the passion of lovers' kiss, of pleasurable embrace, of taking in one another's life.

3.3. Consistency of purpose

God's unitive aims in creation lead not only to the evolution of the material into the personal, but also to Incarnation, to God's expressing Divine love for material creation by becoming a human being. But God loves material creation by loving us. The Inner Teacher is omnipresent and ever helpful but difficult for personal animals to recognize or pay attention to. As animals we focus easily on what is sense-perceptible, on what we can see and touch and handle, on what is concrete and locatable in space and time. To grow up and flourish as human beings, we need embodied persons to care for us, to be role models of how to be embodied persons, of how to personify matter in wholesome ways. In the Incarnation, God enters into personal intimacy with material creation, not just through His Divine nature and across the metaphysical size-gap, but through His human nature. Jesus relates to Peter, James, and John, to the women suffering from hemorrhage and spinal curvature, to blind men and lepers, embodied person to embodied person. While Christ's earthly career climaxing in His passion, death, and resurrection are sufficient to accomplish Stage-I and to signal Stage-III horror-defeat, it does not bring to an end our need or the benefit to us as human beings of contacting God, embodied person to embodied person – of seeing, touching, and handling God in a determinate place and time. Our need for concrete interaction is all the more urgent given that our being embodied persons in a material world such as this exposes us to horrors. To suppose that God – even God Incarnate – is aloof from horrors while we continue to be exposed to them is alienating. If we are vulnerable to God and to the world, but God is now impassible in all His natures, then God is no longer meeting us on our level as He once did.

Wouldn't, why wouldn't, a God Who loved material creation, and Who loves us as a way of loving material creation, want – in Luther's language – to continue the Incarnation by becoming really present for us in the very sacrament that rivets our attention on horrors by showing forth the Lord's death?

4. The metaphysics of presence

4.1. *"Ego Berengarius"*

So far, I have been insinuating that a strong doctrine of corporeal eucharistic presence is congruent both with God's aims and our predicament in this world. I want now to defend "impanation," a recurrent minority report in Christian history, as a decidedly better fit than its more accredited competitors. The theory of impanation holds that just as the Divine Word becomes in-carnate (en-fleshed) when it assumes a particular human nature into hypostatic union with itself, so the Divine Word becomes im-panate (em-breaded) when – at the moment of consecration – it hypostatically assumes the eucharistic bread nature on the altar. Not only is impanation theoretically economical – reusing the notion of hypostatic assumption already deployed in accounting for how the Word became flesh the first time. I count it an advantage that impanation underwrites (makes literally true) the formula that eleventh-century Church officials made Berengar of Tours swear:

I, Berengar, acknowledge . . . that the bread and wine which are placed on the altar are after consecration not only a Sacrament but also the real body and blood of our Lord Jesus Christ, and that with the senses [*sensualiter*], not only by way of Sacrament but in reality, these are held and broken by the hands of priests and are crushed by the teeth of the faithful.

Although the bread and wine remain, so that the faithful "may not shrink through perceiving what is raw and bloody," it is the same body that Mary bore that is bitten into, torn, and chewed.[24] In my judgment, "Ego Berengarius" is pragmatically fruitful in suggesting how human participants in the very worst evils might make *ante-mortem* progress towards being reconciled to the Goodness of God!

4.2. *Spiritual eating, flesh-and-blood food*

In *Grace and Gratitude*, Brian Gerrish argues that – despite Platoniz-ing philosophical tendencies – Calvin does not think Christ meets us in the supper merely Spirit-to-spirit, but rather *embodied* person to *embodied* person. While Calvin repeatedly affirms that Jesus Christ is the gift and *spiritual* food in the sacrament, he also speaks of Christ's feeding us in the supper with His *Body and Blood*.[25] The *food* is not merely spiritual. But because Christ's Body and Blood have ascended into heaven to the right hand of God, the *eating* must be spiritual: it is not possible literally to bite and chomp a body that is not located in the same place where the consumer's mouth and teeth are! For Gerrish's Calvin, the real presence of Christ's Body and Blood and so

---

[24] S. Gregorius VII 1073–1085, Proceedings of his Sixth Council at Rome in 1079, "De ss. Eucharistia: Ius iurandum a Berengario praestitum," in *Enchiridion Symbolorum: Definitionum et Declarationum de Rebus Fidei et Morum*, ed. Heinrich Denzinger (Freiburg in Breisgau: B. Herder, 1911). Berengar's position was condemned by Leo IX at Rome in 1050, Victor II at the synod of Florence in 1055, by Nicolas II at Rome in 1059, and by Gregory VII at Rome in 1078 and again in 1079.

[25] Calvin, *Short Treatise*, secs. 3–4, 509, sec. 5, 510, sec. 11, 512–513.

of the embodied Christ to the faithful participant is not *spatial*, but *mysterious* and *spiritual*, because effected in some mysterious way by the Holy Spirit of God.[26] Likewise, the nourishment effected by this spiritual eating of the flesh of Christ is *spiritual* – a quickening not just of the mind's cognitive faculties, but of the whole soul.[27]

This view has the merit of emphasizing how the holy banquet is an occasion of *personal* encounter between the faithful and Christ. The pragmatic thrust of Calvin's critique of scholastic views is to steer our attention away from the physical onto the personal dimensions of the rite (hence his antipathy to liturgical ornamentation).[28] Calvin's account makes the literal eating and drinking of the elements *a metaphor* or *analogy* for the soul's feeding on the flesh and blood of Christ.[29]

Nevertheless, however much this account may seem to anticipate Piaget, I think it misunderstands dinner-table dynamics. It is true that my grasping of the cup is a metaphor, and *only* a metaphor, of my grasping the idea of a cup. This is because my grasping of the cup in no way constitutes my grasping of the idea. They are two entirely distinct actions. But at the dinner table, opening my mouth in your presence is not just an outward and visible sign of inward and spiritual vulnerability. It *is* a personal risk of vulnerability in relation to you. Eating what you prepare *is* an act of trust, sharing food *is* an act of social bonding. When I as an embodied person do these things, the one act *constitutes* the other.

Put otherwise, willy-nilly, human family dinner tables make the material the medium of the psycho-spiritual in such a way that they are humanly impossible to disentangle. Attempts to deprive bodily

---

[26] Calvin, *The Institutes*, Book IV, ch. XVII, secs. 1–5, vol. II, 1359–1365, secs. 8–10, vol. II, 1368–1371, secs. 32–33, vol. II, 1403–1408. Cf. Gerrish, *Grace and Gratitude*, ch. 1, 7–9, ch. 5, 137–138.

[27] Calvin, *The Institutes*, Book IV, ch. XVII, sec. 5, vol. II, 1364–1365, secs. 8–9, vol. II, 1368–1369, sec. 11, vol. II, 1372.

[28] Calvin, *The Institutes*, Book IV, ch. XV, sec. 19, vol. II, 1319–1320.

[29] Calvin, *Short Treatise*, sec. 17, 516. Cf. Gerrish, *Grace and Gratitude*, ch. 1, 11–12.

feeding of personal significance, or to pursue social bonding and personal nurture *only* outside the context of eating, are themselves psycho-spiritual moves, normally fraught with momentous psycho-spiritual consequences. I have no wish to deny that God provides Divine-to-human personal nurture outside the context of physical eating (as when the Word is preached or Scripture is read), or that God sometimes meets human persons spirit-to-Spirit (as in mystical contemplation). What I don't see is why God would invite us to *dinner* and then try to split table *fellowship* from the act of eating itself.

Calvin's position is also philosophically underdeveloped by his own admission. We can see how God can be present to the faithful spirit-to-Spirit, because God is Spirit and God is omnipresent, literally and/or at least in Divine awareness and Divine power to produce effects. We know from experience how encounters embodied person to embodied person build up trust and confidence. From some philosophical points of view (e.g., Aquinas'), we can understand how God might use the locally present bread and wine as instrumental causes to produce spiritual benefits in the soul. But how does the Spirit make it possible for us to meet or be united *embodied* person to *embodied* person when Christ's body is not located within the range of any of our sensory faculties?[30]

4.3. *Location without extension*

In thirteenth- and fourteenth-century eucharistic theology, both *transubstantiation* – the view that the whole substance of the bread (wine) is converted into the substance of the Body (Blood) of Christ, the bread (wine) accidents remaining – and *consubstantiation* – the view that the bread and wine remain as before but the Body and Blood of Christ come to be present *with* them where they are – continued to command attention. These positions shared the philosophically innovative thesis that bodies (like angels and souls) can be

[30] See Gerrish, *Grace and Gratitude*, ch. 6, 177.

literally located in a place without being extended in it. For a thing to be extended in a place (in their terminology, to be in place *circum-scriptively*) is for the whole thing to exist in the whole of the place and part of the thing to exist in part of the place – different parts in different places, so that some parts of the thing are at a distance from others of its parts. Taking their cue from Augustine, scholastic philosophers reasoned that angels and intellectual souls cannot be extended in a place because they are simple and so lack parts that could be positioned at a distance from one another. But a human being's intellectual soul is located in his/her body throughout his/her *ante-mortem* career. Hence, the intellectual soul must be whole in the whole body, and whole in each part of the body (which Scotus and Ockham call being *definitively* in place). By contrast, material things do have parts, and their natural way of existing is to be extended in place, with some parts at a distance from others.

Confronted with the problem of eucharistic presence, however, Aquinas, Scotus, and Ockham all reasoned that just because material things have parts and so can be and normally are in a place by being extended in it, it doesn't follow that it is metaphysically impossible for material things to be located in a place without being extended in it. Why would it be impossible for Divine power to make a material thing to exist in place definitively, so that the whole thing was in the whole of the place, and the whole thing was in each part of the place as well? Instead of making each part of a thing exist in a different part of the place, God could make all the parts of the thing exist in each and all parts of the place at once. Normally, there is no reason for God to exercise this power, perhaps even considerable reason against it. But in the eucharist, this isn't so. God brings it about that the Body (Blood) of Christ, which is literally located and extended (exists cir-cumscriptively in place) in heaven, also exists definitively in the place where the bread and wine accidents are still extended. Theoretically, Aquinas and Scotus observe, this allows the Body (Blood) of Christ to be literally located in heaven and on multiple altars at once without violating the intuition that two things can't be *extended* in the same place at once, and a single thing can't be *extended* in two places at once.[31]

In my judgment, these scholastic positions win a pragmatic advantage over Gerrish's Calvin, insofar as they allow the Body and Blood of Christ concrete locations in our world. God is Spirit, but we are personalized material. God is everywhere, but we are somewhere in particular, and – as noted above – it is difficult for us to notice and pay attention to what is not anywhere in particular. Like the Incarnation, literal location where the bread and wine seem to be is a concession to our condition: in the eucharist, the Body and Blood of Christ come to meet us literally where we are. That is why eucharistic veneration is not idolatry. We do not bow ourselves to bread and wine or their accidents (any more than we curtsy to the king's clothes). Rather we bend the knee to the really present, because literally located, Body and Blood of Christ which are themselves hypostatically united to the Divine Word Who is worthy of all worship.

Adherents of literal-location-without-extension counted it a further advantage that the Body and Blood of Christ could be thus present without being causally interactive with that environment. What is not extended in a place cannot be literally chewed and torn there. Neither can it be seen with the bodily eye or touched with the bodily hand or mouth. There is no need to wonder about whether the Body and Blood of Christ are digested or excreted by the normal biological routes. These conclusions were all the more important to them, because they believed Christ's post-resurrection body to be impassible. Thus, their theologically buttressed philosophical

---

[31] In fact, neither Scotus nor Ockham holds these commonsense theses to be metaphysically necessary. For a thorough discussion of the metaphysical merits and demerits of these positions as well as a fuller exposition of them, see my article "Aristotle and the Sacrament of the Altar: A Crisis in Medieval Theology," *Canadian Journal of Philosophy*, Supplementary Volume 17 (1991), 195–249.

account allowed them to distance themselves from the more vivid language of the "Ego Berengarius" formula.[32]

4.4. Ubiquity

If Luther often disparaged, he also entered the speculative fray in his zeal to preserve the corporeal presence of the Body and Blood of Christ in the eucharist.[33] He was singularly unimpressed with Zwingli's (and then Calvin's) insistence that the Body and Blood of Christ could not be literally located on the altar because they had ascended to the right hand of God. First, Luther denies that "the right hand of God" refers to a place (as if Christ were imprisoned in heaven like a bird in its nest); on the contrary, Luther contends, it refers to the hypostatic union of Divine and human natures.[34] Second, Luther rejects their philosophical assumption that a single body cannot be in more than one place at a time. Reviewing scholastic options, Luther denies that the Body and Blood of Christ are extended (circumscriptively) in place the way the bread and wine are, or that they are whole in the whole and whole in the parts of that place (definitively in that place) the way angels are. Instead, he maintains that the Body and Blood of Christ are in place repletively (*repletive*) in such a way as to fill all things.[35]

Luther's explanation (already alluded to in chapter 4) applied the *communicatio idiomatum* to the two natures of Christ to infer that

---

[32] E.g., Aquinas, *Summa Theologica* III, q. 77, aa. 3–7, esp. a. 7, obj. 3 and ad 3um; q. 81, aa. 3–4.

[33] Marc Lienhard puts Luther's reflections on the eucharist in the context of his wider Christology, in *Luther: Witness to Jesus Christ*, trans. Edwin H. Robertson (Minneapolis: Augsburg, 1982), esp. chs. 4–5, 195–267.

[34] Martin Luther, *Against the Heavenly Prophets in the Matter of Images and Sacraments* (1525), in *Luther Works* (=LW) vol. XL, 216, 220–221; Luther, *That These Words of Christ, "This Is My Body," Stand Firm against the Fanatics* (1527), LW vol. XXXVII, 55–70.

[35] Luther, *Confession Concerning Christ's Supper* (1528), LW vol. XXXVII, 223; see also 215–335.

properties from one nature can be truly predicated of the other *nature*. Thus, Luther reasons that, because the Divine essence is everywhere, *the human nature* is also everywhere, with the result that Christ's Body and Blood are too. This implies that the embodied Christ is *physically* as near to us as He was to Mary, Simeon, and the shepherds,[36] and that Christ is not only eaten spiritually by faith in the heart but physically with the mouth.[37] Yet, even in the mouth, Christ's Body is spiritual food that changes us into itself rather than corporeal food that gets changed into the consumer's body.[38]

To the objection that "everywhere" is overkill, indeed that it defeats one pragmatic purpose that real corporeal presence was supposed to serve – viz., of providing a particular concrete focus – Luther replies that we are not to seek God everywhere because that might lead to idolatry, but rather where God invites us to seek Him – viz., where the Word is present and especially at the Lord's table.[39]

Already Zwingli charged that Luther's use of the *communicatio idiomatum* was both philosophically incoherent and un-Chalcedonian insofar as it confuses the Divine and human natures. Interestingly, Duns Scotus did allow that not only Divine persons, but also the Divine essence (as maximally independent), could be the term of an ontological dependence relation grounded in an individual human nature.[40] By the same token, Scotus supposed, both the Divine essence and the Divine persons are essentially so independent as to be essentially unassumable by anything really distinct from them. Even if alien assumption of the Divine essence were not metaphysically impossible, and Christ's human nature were supposed to assume His Divine nature, my analysis of the *communicatio idiomatum* (in chapter 5) would not support Luther's conclusion.

---

[36] Luther, *That These Words of Christ*, 95–96.

[37] Luther, *That These Words of Christ*, 87–88.

[38] Luther, *That These Words of Christ*, 94, 100.

[39] Luther, *That These Words of Christ*, 69; Luther *The Sacrament of the Body and Blood of Christ against the Fanatics*, LW vol. XXXVI, 342–345.

[40] Scotus, *Op.Ox.* III, d. 1, q. 2, n. 6; Wadding VII.1.37.

The human nature's assuming the Divine would not yield the simple predication "Christ's human nature is everywhere" but only the qualified predication "Christ's human nature is everywhere with respect to Its Divine nature." In advancing his distinctive view, Luther seems genuinely to have been puzzled how – if the Divine Word really is hypostatically united to the human nature – the Divine Word could be anywhere without that human nature. Philosophically, this is worth pondering, but the claim goes to the heart of the Chalcedonian definition: that the person x can be F according to its Divine nature and not-F according to its human nature. Although in many places Luther denies that he is thereby confusing the natures, he can also be found to assert that because of such mutual participation the two natures should be called *one nature!*[41]

4.5. *Impanation*

If corporeal eucharistic presence is desirable so that we can meet *Christ* embodied person to embodied person, then it seems better if it is *Christ's* Body – rather than mere bread or mere wine or their accidents – that we meet. Impanation gives us this pragmatic desideratum without turning eucharistic reception into the biting and tearing of raw meat. To explain this, I will need to mobilize the medieval metaphysical machinery already used in my favorite account of how Christ can be Divine and human at the same time (see chapter 5, section 4).

Recall Scotus' claim that in Incarnation an individual human nature is united to the Divine Word by a relation of ontological independence – a relation analogous to that which whiteness bears to Socrates when Socrates is white. In Aristotelian metaphysics, Socrates is metaphysically substantial enough to be the term of the ontological dependence relation (in this case, inherence) because he is a primary substance supposit. Similarly, Scotus reasons, the Divine Word is

---

[41] Luther, *Confession Concerning Christ's Supper*, 296.

metaphysically substantial enough to be the term of the ontological dependence relation that the individual human nature bears to It. Stepping back to take a more general view, Scotus explains that what it takes to be the term of an ontological dependence relation is *independence*. Any Divine person is capable of the job, because a Divine person is as metaphysically independent as anything can be. But – Scotus observes – the Divine essence also qualifies. It, too, could be the proximate assumer of an individual substance nature. If the Divine essence were the proximate assumer, all three Divine persons Who necessarily supposit the Divine nature would be the remote assumers. Ockham agrees but goes further: by Divine power, even a created substance such as a stone could be hypostatically united to another individual substance nature; by Divine power, even part of a created substance (the intellectual soul) could be the thing that assumes.

These medieval reflections invite us to work out the doctrine of impanation in either of two ways. (1) If one preferred to say that only Divine persons and the Divine essence, or only complete substance things, are metaphysically independent enough to be assumers, then one should say that the Divine Word assumes the eucharistic bread the way that He assumes the human nature. In consequence, Christ's Body will have two natures – human nature and bread nature.[42] If we like, we can take a page from the scholastics and hold that Christ's Body is present on the altar without being extended *according to its human nature*, but present and extended *according to its bread nature*. Alternatively, we could hold that Christ's Body is not present

---

[42] Note that, Luther's sometime endorsement of the ubiquity of the Body and Blood of Christ is *not* tantamount to an acceptance of impanation. Ubiquity implies that the Body and Blood of Christ are located in the same place as the bread and wine on the altar (just as Christ is located in the same place as everything else in the physical universe). By itself, ubiquity implies no metaphysical connection between Christ's Body and the bread other than co-location – which makes the position sound like what Scotus and Ockham meant by consubstantiation, or more recently preferred Lutheran language to the effect that Christ's Body is "in, with, and under" the eucharistic bread.

on the altar according to its human nature at all, but only according to its bread nature. Either way, Christ's post-resurrection Body could be impassible or at least no longer vulnerable to horrors *according to its human nature*. But Christ's post-resurrection Body would be causally interactive and so capable of being literally touched and handled, tasted and seen, *according to its bread nature*. It becomes metaphysically possible for us to interact with Christ as with other embodied persons: to reach out for comfort, to ingest for nurture, to strike out in anger and confusion, to grasp and hold with desire, to gaze and gasp with amazement and awe. Just as the Divine Word could (but – according to medieval doctrine – never in fact will) lay down the human nature It assumed, so the Divine Word could lay down assumed bread natures at any time – once the bread enters the mouth, once it starts to be digested, only after it has ceased to be bread anymore, etc. My own estimate of what it takes to defeat horrors drives me to reverse medieval reluctance: for the Body of Christ to pass through the digestive process *according to its bread nature* would represent a continuation of Divine solidarity that descends to the depths of human degradation to be God-with-us!

Making the Divine Word the proximate assumer might seem to make it more natural to say that the Divine Word has not one but *two* bodies – an organic human body and a bread body. And so it would not follow that the Body of Christ that is really present on the altar is numerically the same one that Mary bore. So almost "Ego Berengarius", but not quite!

(2) Like a human soul, the human body of Christ is not a complete individual substance, but only part of one. If one allows with Ockham that God could make an individual substance nature depend on a substance part, then one could say that the human body of Christ is the proximate assumer of the bread nature. This would make it more natural to say that numerically the same body has two natures, a human nature and a bread nature. This version underwrites not only "Ego Berengarius'" assertion that the Body of Christ is held and broken by the hands of priests and crushed by the teeth of the faithful,

but also its claim that the very Body that Mary bore is present on the altar: Mary bore it according to its human nature, while it is touched and seen, bitten and chomped, according to its bread nature. "Ego Berengarius", wholly revived!

5. Sacrifice and priesthood

5.1. Mutual denunciations

Reformers gave many reasons for wanting to distance themselves from the notion of eucharistic sacrifice. For Luther, "sacrifice" connotes something that we do, whereas we are on the receiving end of sacraments. We do not do anything for or give anything to God; we simply accept that God's promises are true![43] Taking a page from Zwingli, Calvin allows that sacraments involve a two-way attestation: God seals our conscience with the promise of Divine good will, and we bear witness to our reverence for God in the presence of humans and angels.[44] Calvin is especially exercised over the idea that the mass is some kind of expiation or propitiation that somehow repeats or augments the sacrifice of Christ on the cross.[45] Appealing to Hebrews, Calvin insists, Christ's sacrifice is "once and for all" efficacious and accomplishes everything necessary for our salvation.[46] Calvin is willing, however, to speak of our offering a sacrifice of praise and thanksgiving, of our whole selves and all of our acts.[47]

Corollary to this, Reformers deplored the "papist" notion that priests are ordained to sacrifice. Luther denounces as unbiblical the idea that Christ ordained the disciples priests at the last supper, and suggests that there would be more biblical warrant for the idea that He

---

[43] Luther, *The Pagan Servitude of the Church*, 287.
[44] Calvin, *The Institutes*, Book IV, ch. XIV, sec. 1, vol. II, 1277, sec. 13, vol. II, 1289.
[45] Calvin, *The Institutes*, Book IV, ch. XVIII, sec. 1, vol. II, 1429, sec. 13, vol. II, 1441.
[46] Calvin, *The Institutes*, Book IV, ch. XVIII, sec. 3, vol. II, 1431–2.
[47] Calvin, *The Institutes*, Book IV, ch. XVIII, sec. 13, vol. II, 1441.

commissioned them to preach and baptize (see Matthew 28:19–20). In fact, all baptized Christians are priests with some authority over Word and sacraments, although no one has the right to administer the sacraments without a call from the majority of the community.[48] Likewise, Calvin embraces a priesthood of all believers that offers ourselves, our souls and bodies, as well as sacrifices of praise and thanksgiving.[49] But he denounces the "wicked" idea that priests are ordained to perform the sacrifice of Christ's Body and Blood. Some persons are set aside for the special functions of pasturing the flock and preaching the Gospel, but not for sacrificing victims![50] Despite Anglican attempts to chart various *viae mediae* between Rome and continental reformers, Pope Leo XIII in *Apostolicae curae* pronounced Anglican orders null and void, on the grounds that its ordinals did not make sufficiently explicit any intention to ordain a sacrificing priesthood.[51]

5.2. Eucharistic sacrifice

Horrors cut through these debates to expose holy eucharist as a scene of sacrifice in which not only Christ but we are both priest and victim. Holy eucharist liturgically condenses the whole of cosmic sacrifice (see chapter 8), which makes it many sacrifices at once. First and foremost, in holy eucharist, God sacrifices Christ to us, again and again. Impanation is the key to how God can *commemorate by repeating* the sacrifice of Calvary, without running afoul of Hebrews' "once for all"

---

[48] Luther, *The Pagan Servitude of the Church*, 340–346, 349; cf. Luther, *An Appeal to the Ruling Class of German Nationality as to the Amelioration of the State of Christendom*, in *Martin Luther: Selections from His Writings*, 409.

[49] Calvin, *The Institutes*, Book IV, ch. XVIII, secs. 16–17, vol. II, 1443–1445; IV, ch. XIX, sec. 25, vol. II, 1473.

[50] Calvin, *The Institutes*, Book IV, ch. XIX, sec. 28, vol. II, 1475–1476.

[51] *Anglican Orders: Essays on the Centenary of Apostolicae Curae 1896–1996*, ed. and intro. R. William Franklin; forward Hugh Montefiore (Harrisburg, PA: Morehouse Publishing, 1996), 8–9.

(7:27, 9:12, 10:10). Re-incarnating – hypostatically uniting the bread and wine natures to the Divine Word – puts God in a position to offer Christ as a *first-fruits offering*, the One in Whose human nature horrors are definitively defeated, Stage-I, Stage-II, and Stage-III. The "breaded" Christ is a *communion sacrifice*, God-with-us, embodied person to embodied person, each and every time; likewise a *gift sacrifice* expressing Divine gratitude to us for leading human lives in a world such as this. In holy eucharist, God offers the "breaded" Christ as something like an *expiation* by which God acknowledges and accepts responsibility for our plight. Likewise, the "breaded" Christ is both an *aversion* and a *propitiation* sacrifice to absorb and serve as the target we bite and chomp and tear with the teeth, returning horrors for horrors to God. Thus, at every eucharist, the sacrifice of Calvary is repeated with respect to the "breaded" Christ, for the purpose of working towards Stage-II horror-defeat for the communicants involved. Every eucharist is thereby a commemoration of Christ's horror-participation in His human nature, which stands as sufficient for Stage-I horror-defeat!

5.3. *Interim priesthood*

Maccabean martyrs reconceptualize torture, death, and dismemberment at Gentile hands as their own voluntary sacrifice for sin. Martyr priests bear witness, acknowledge that systemic evil (national apostasy and perverse social structure) is God's reason for stirring up foreign powers to initiate a pogrom as Divine punishment for collective sin, but ask that their voluntary and unblemished self-offerings be accepted as an expiation to bring the punishing consequences of Divine wrath to an end. Martyr priests cannot control the material circumstances of the sacrifice the way Levitical priests were supposed to do. But martyr priests thought to get the personal rubrics right by loving God with all their hearts, souls, strength, and minds – something that is everywhere and always appropriate (see IV Maccabees 5:4–6:30, 8:3–18:24).

Analogously, I suggest, martyr priests after the order of Job offer up human horror-participation, bear witness to its rootage in systemic mismatches for which God is ultimately responsible, badger God to do something to defeat horrors, hound God with questions and objections about what human horror-participation really means. Martyr priesthood after the order of Job is liminal and risky because it draws near to God and "sins with the lips." It is a priesthood that can be exercised on any ash heap or street corner. It finds liturgical focus in the sacrament of the altar, where it is exercised preeminently by Christ.

In eucharistic sacrifice, Christ *qua* human is martyr priest as well as victim. Turning Godward, towards the altar, Christ bears witness to God concerning the human condition, testifies to the horrors here below. Christ's intercession is partially self-fulfilling, insofar as His own solidarity with us is sufficient for Stage I horror-defeat. Turning towards the people, Christ presents Himself to us, and thereby bears witness to horrors and to horror-defeat, past, present, and yet to come. On the one hand, Christ presents Himself as God-with-us and therefore God-for-us in the worst that we can suffer, be, or do (i.e., as definitive Stage-I horror-defeat). On the other hand, Christ presents Himself as the first-born of the new creation: a human being whose human center of consciousness has grasped and appropriated positive meaning sufficient for stage-II defeat of His own horror-participation; a human being whose wounded human body is glorified, its relation to material creation so altered that – according to His human nature – He is no longer radically vulnerable to horrors (= Stage-III horror-defeat).

Impanation adds a third dimension to Christ's eucharistic priesthood. By hypostatically uniting to bread and wine natures, Christ sets Himself up for a repetition and commemoration of His "once-for-all" sacrifice on the cross. On the one hand, Christ's self-presentation as food bears witness to God-with-us providing for us in the midst of our continuing vulnerabilities. On the other, Christ's donation of Himself to be bitten, chomped, and chewed exposes Himself to our anger and frustration – anger and frustration so great that we would kill and cannibalize, even destroy God. Calvary's ironic reversal repeats itself. Biting and chomping our salvation confers immeasurable dignity, insofar as impanation turns the hostile act of eating into an act of intimacy with God. Thus, holy communion "balances off" the indignities of horror-participation whether or not any progress on Stage-II horror-defeat is made. At the same time, this very conferral of dignity and the possibility of communicants' winning through to Stage-II horror-defeat defeat the *prima facie* personal ruin thereby inflicted on Christ by being eaten and drunk, consumed and destroyed.

Christ ordains all who are willing to confront human horrors and Divine ambivalence into the priesthood of bold believers, which imitates and coattails on His own. Facing the altar, we bring before God not only bread and wine; ourselves, our souls and bodies; and the material cosmos God has made. We offer Christ, with the petition, "Just as You made Christ like us in horror-participation, so make us and all we offer like Christ in horror-defeat." Turning our backs to the altar, we present Christ for the world, the One in Whom horror-defeat is accomplished: His Stage-I defeat of all human horrors on Calvary; the "already" of Stage-II and Stage-III defeat in His own human nature; His freshly assumed vulnerability in bread and wine natures, really present to midwife Stage-II horror-defeat in us.

Merely human martyr priests also confront the less bold, the timid, and/or the unbelieving with their own present possibility of priesthood. The exercise of martyr priesthood is itself a great blessing, because it makes the priest an active participant in Stage-I horror-defeat. Trafficking with God is intimate and risky. But the priest's question-and-disputing intercession itself brings human horror-participation right in the middle of her/his own relationship with God. Moreover, faithfully exercised martyr priesthood gains "great confidence in the faith that is in Christ Jesus" (see I Timothy 3:13), because over time daily trafficking with God opens them – like Job – to experience Divine Goodness. Morning and evening sacrifice and daily mass convince martyr priests that God is *for* us, that – whatever the Divine reasons for delay – God is willing and able thoroughly to defeat horrors within the context of each and every horror-participant's life.

Some martyr priests become so persuaded that horrors are only *prima facie* ruinous that they offer themselves to others in ways that risk further horror-participation. Remember, for example, the religious who took the place of Jews in Nazi crematorium lines; those who joined civil rights demonstrations in the early 1960s, placing themselves among the crowds attacked by vicious police dogs; or the Jesuits tortured to death for organizing and empowering poor communities in Central America. Such martyr priests offer themselves as bloody sacrifices to bear witness to the outrage of human horror and to the faithfulness and resourcefulness of God. Their own horror-participation in solidarity with others is Stage-I defeated by virtue of its being an *imitatio Christi*, Who took flesh in order to participate in horrors, to cast God's lot with ours. Their heroic testimony challenges others to scorn horror-producing powers of darkness, and to fill up the sufferings of Christ (Colossians 1:24)!

5.4. *Priests forever*

In Genesis 14, Melchizedek, king of Salem, priest of God Most High, comes out to meet Abram, who has just defeated Ched-or-laomer and the kings who were with him. The liturgy is simple. Melchizedek brings out bread and wine. Abram pays tithes on all of the spoils. Melchizedek blesses Abram, the bearer of the promise, and blesses the promise-giver, God Most High. Proof-texting Psalm 110:4, the epistle to the Hebrews proclaims Christ priest forever after the order of Melchizedek (Hebrews 5:6; 7 *passim*). The ascended Christ is envisioned as exercising a heavenly priesthood to keep His once-for-all sin offering, the blood of His "once-for-all" propitiatory sacrifice before God's eyes. Christ is the anti-type of Isaac, the pleading of whose sacrifice wins forgiveness for the people of God.

When soteriology is approached from the angle of horrors, Christ still exercises a heavenly priesthood according to His human nature. Christ's human center of thought and choice forever brings before the Godhead the bread and wine of His humanity, scarred by crucifixion, glorified by resurrection. Between Ascension and consummation, Christ blesses Abraham's seed, Adam's race with martyr-priesthood's intercession: "human horrors are not yet utterly defeated; make good on all of them, in each horror-participant's life!" Between the "already" and "not yet," Christ blesses God Most High, the One Who has raised Christ Jesus to God's right hand, the One Who will finish what God starts.

Consummate horror-defeat in all three stages will complete the consecration of the whole material creation and of its best fruit, humankind. Christ (in His human center of thought and choice) will forever present us to God whole and holy, the trophy of His horror-defeating work. Now priests forever after the order of Melchizedek and under the high priesthood of Christ, we will draw near, present ourselves to God, bearing witness to our struggle and God's victory, to our *prima facie* ruin and God's re-creative powers. Best of all, we will present Christ, our prototype, pioneer, and Savior. The missal page will turn from accusation and intercession. Our common sacrifice will be praise and thanksgiving, honor, glory, and blessing forever more!

Bibliography

Adams, Marilyn McCord, "Aristotle and the Sacrament of the Altar: A Crisis in Medieval Theology," *Canadian Journal of Philosophy*, Supplementary Volume 17 (1991), 195–249.

"Biting and Chomping Our Salvation! Eucharistic Presence, Radically Understood," in *Redemptive Transformation in Practical Theology*, ed. Dana Wright and John D. Kuentzel (Grand Rapids, MI: Eerdmans, 2004), 69–94.

"Chalcedonian Christology: A Christian Solution to the Problem of Evil," in *Philosophy and Theological Discourse*, ed. Stephen T. Davis (London: Macmillan Press, 1997), 173–198.

"The Coherence of Christology: God Enmattered and Enmattering," *Princeton Seminary Bulletin*, 26:2 new series (2005), 157–179.

"Courtesy, Divine and Human," in "Three Great Theological Ideas from the Middle Ages" (The Dubose Lectures), *Sewanee Theological Review* 47:2 (Easter 2004), 145–463.

"*Cur Deus Homo?* Priorities Among the Reasons," *Faith and Philosophy* 21:2 (April 2004), 1–18.

"Divine Justice, Divine Love, and the Life to Come," *Crux* 13 (1976–1977), 12–18.

"Evil and the God Who Does Nothing in Particular," in *Religion and Morality*, ed. D. Z. Phillips (London: Macmillan Press and New York: St. Martin's Press, 1996), 107–131.

"*Fides Quaerens Intellectum*: St. Anselm's Method in Philosophical Theology," *Faith and Philosophy* (October 1992), 409–435.

"Hell and the God of Justice," *Religious Studies* 11:4 (1973), 433–447.

"Horrendous Evils and the Goodness of God," *Proceedings of the Aristotelian Society*, Supplementary Volume 63 (1989), 299–310.

Horrendous Evils and the Goodness of God (Ithaca, NY, and London: Cornell University Press, 1999).

"In Praise of Blasphemy," *Philosophia: Philosophical Quarterly of Israel*, 36:1–2 (2003), 1–17.

"The Metaphysical Size Gap," in "Three Great Theological Ideas from the Middle Ages" (The Dubose Lectures), *Sewanee Theological Review* 47:2 (Easter 2004), 129–144.

"The Metaphysics of the Incarnation in Some Fourteenth Century Franciscans," in *Essays Honoring Allan B. Wolter* (Franciscan Institute Publications, 1985), 21–57.

"Neglected Values, Shrunken Agents, Happy Endings: A Reply to Rogers," *Faith and Philosophy* 19:2 (2002), 487–505.

"Praying the *Proslogion*," in *The Rationality of Belief and the Plurality of Faith*, ed. Thomas Senor (Ithaca, NY: Cornell University Press, 1995), 13–39.

"The Primacy of Christ," in "Three Great Theological Ideas from the Middle Ages" (The Dubose Lectures), *Sewanee Theological Review* 47:2 (Easter 2004), 164–180.

"The Problem of Hell: A Problem of Evil for Christians," in *Reasoned Faith: Essays in Philosophical Theology in Honor of Norman Kretzmann*, ed. Eleonore Stump (Ithaca, NY: Cornell University Press, 1993), 301–327.

"Theodicy without Blame," *Philosophical Topics* 16 (1988), 215–245.

"Trinitarian Friendship: Same Gender Models of Godly Love in Richard of St. Victor and Aelred of Rievaulx," in *Theology and Sexuality: Ancient and Contemporary Readings*, ed. Eugene F. Rogers, Jr. (Oxford: Blackwell, 2001), 322–339.

"Universal Salvation: A Reply to Mr. Bettis," *Religious Studies* 7 (1971), 245–49.

What Sort of Human Nature? The Metaphysics and Systematics of Christology: The Aquinas Lecture, 1999 (Milwaukee, WI: Marquette University Press, 1999).

"What's Metaphysically Special about Supposits?," *Proceedings of the Aristotelian Society*, Supplementary Volume 78 (2005), 15–52.

William Ockham (Notre Dame, IN: Notre Dame University Press, 1987).

Adams, Robert Merrihew, "Existence, Self-Interest, and the Problem of Evil," in Robert Merrihew Adams, *The Virtue of Faith and Other Essays in Philosophical Theology* (Oxford, New York, and Toronto: Oxford University Press, 1987), 65–76.

Aelred of Rievaulx, *Spiritual Friendship*, trans. Mary Eugenia Laker SSND, intro. Douglass Roby (Kalamazoo, MI: Cistercian Publications, 1977), CF5.

Ambrose, *De excessu Fratris Sui Satyri*, II (Platrologia Latina 16, cols. 1315–1354; Corpus Scriptorum Latinorum 73.251–325).

Anglican Orders: Essays on the Centenary of Apostolicae Curae 1896–1996, ed. and intro. R. William Franklin; forward Hugh Montefiore (Harrisburg, PA: Morehouse Publishing, 1996).

Anselm, *Cur Deus Homo*, in *Opera Omnia*, ed. F. S. Schmitt (Stuttgart–Bad Cannstatt: Friedrich Frommann Verlag [Günther Holzboog], 1968), vol. II, 38–133.

De Casu Diaboli, in *Opera Omnia*, ed. F. S. Schmitt (Stuttgart–Bad Cannstatt: Friedrich Frommann Verlag [Günther Holzboog], 1968), vol. I, 226–276.

De Concordia Praescientiae et Praedestinationis et Gratiae Dei cum Libero Arbitrio, in *Opera Omnia*, ed. F. S. Schmitt (Stuttgart–Bad Cannstatt: Friedrich Frommann Verlag [Günther Holzboog], 1968), vol. II, 243–288.

Monologion, in *Opera Omnia*, ed. F. S. Schmitt (Stuttgart–Bad Cannstatt: Friedrich Frommann Verlag [Günther Holzboog], 1968), vol. I, 1–87.

Proslogion, in *Opera Omnia*, ed. F. S. Schmitt (Stuttgart–Bad Cannstatt: Friedrich Frommann Verlag [Günther Holzboog], 1968), vol. I, 88–122.

Appelfeld, Aharon, *For Every Sin* (New York: Weidenfeld and Nicholson, 1989).

The Immortal Bartfuss (New York: Harper and Row, 1989).

Aquinas, *De Potentia* (Stuttgart–Bad Cannstatt: Friedrich Frommann Verlag [Günther Holzboog] KG, 1980), vol. III, 186–269.

Scriptum super Libros Sententiarum, in *Opera Omnia* (Parma: Peter Fiaacaddorus, 1852–1853), Tomus VII.

Summa Contra Gentiles (Rome: Riccardi Garroni, 1918–1930), vols. XIII–XV.

Summa Theologica (Rome: Typographia Polyglotta, 1889–1906), vols. V–XII.

Aristotle, *Aristotle: On the Soul, Parva Naturalia, On Breath*, trans. W. S. Hett (Cambridge, MA: Harvard University Press and London: William Heinemann, 1957).

Ashby, Godfrey, *Sacrifice: Its Nature and Purpose* (London: SCM Press, 1988).

Bäck, Allan, *On Reduplication: Logical Theories of Qualification* (Leiden, New York, and Cologne: E. J. Brill, 1996).

"Scotus on the Consistency of the Incarnation and the Trinity," *Vivarium* 36:1 (1998), 83–107.

Beattie, J. H. M., "On Understanding Sacrifice," in *Sacrifice*, ed. M. F. C. Bourdillon and Meyer Fortes (London: Academic Press, 1980), 29–44.

Bernard of Clairvaux, *Liber de diligendo Deo*, vol. III, 119–154, in *Sancti Bernardi Opera*, ed. J. Leclercq, C. H. Talbot, and H. M. Rochais (Rome: Cistercian Editions, 1957), 8 vols.

Boethius, *The Theological Tractates*, trans. H. F. Stewart, E. K. Rand, and S. J. Tester (London: William Heinemann and Cambridge, MA: Harvard University Press, 1973).

Bonaventure, *Breviloquium*, in *Opera Omnia*. (Quaracchi: College of St. Bonaventure, 1891), vol. V, 201–291.

Commentaria in Quatuor Libros Sententiarum Magistri Petri Lombardi (Quaracchi: College of St. Bonaventure, 1832–1839), vols. I–IV.

De mysterio Trinitatis, in *Opera Omnia* (Quaracchi: College of St. Bonaventure, 1891), vol. V, 45–115.

Itinerarium Mentis in Deum, in *Opera Omnia* (Quaracchi: College of St. Bonaventure, 1891), vol. V.295–316.

Legenda Sancti Francisci (Quaracchi: College of St. Bonaventure, 1898), vol. VIII, 504–564.

Opusculum XXII: Epistola de Imitatione Christi, in *Opera Omnia* (Quaracchi: College of St. Bonaventure, 1898), vol. VIII, 499–503.

Brown, Raymond, *The Birth of the Messiah: A Commentary on the Infancy Narratives in Matthew and Luke* (New York: Doubleday, 1977).

Bultmann, Rudolf, *Jesus Christ and Mythology* (New York: Charles Scribners' Sons, 1958).

Bynum, Caroline Walker, *The Resurrection of the Body in Western Christianity 200–1336* (New York: Columbia University Press, 1995).

Caird, Edward, *Hegel* (William Blackwood and Sons, 1883).

Calvin, John, *The Institutes of the Christian Religion*, Library of Christian Classics, vols. XX–XXI, trans. Ford Lewis Battles (Philadelphia: Westminster Press, 1960).

Three Forms of Exposition: Short Treatise on the Holy Supper of Our Lord Jesus Christ, in *John Calvin: Selections from His Writings*, ed. John Dillenberger (Atlanta: Scholars Press/AAR, 1975), 507–541.

Carnap, Rudolf, "Empiricism, Semantics, and Ontology," in *Philosophy of Mathematics: Selected Readings*, ed. Paul Benacerraf and Hilary Putnam (Englewood Cliffs, NJ: Prentice-Hall, 1964), 233–248.

Cicero, *De amicitia*, in *Opera Philosophica: English and Latin Selections* (London: William Heinemann and New York: G. P. Putnam's Sons, 1923).

Coakley, Sarah, "What Chalcedon Solved and Didn't Solve," in *The Incarnation*, ed. Stephen T. Davis, Daniel Kendall SJ, and Gerald O'Collins SJ (Oxford: Oxford University Press, 2002), ch. 7, 143–163.

Cross, Richard, *The Metaphysics of the Incarnation: Thomas Aquinas to Duns Scotus* (Oxford: Oxford University Press, 2002).

Cupitt, Don, "The Christ of Christendom," in *The Myth of God Incarnate*, ed. Hick, ch. 7, 133–147, 205.

Dale, R. W., *The Atonement: The Congregational Union Lecture (1875)* (London: Congregational Union of England and Wales, 1902).

Douglas, Mary, *Purity and Danger: An Analysis of the Concepts of Pollution and Taboo* (London: Routledge and Kegan Paul, 1966).

Dunnill, John, *Covenant and Sacrifice in the Letter to the Hebrews* (Cambridge: Cambridge University Press, 1992).

Duns Scotus, John, *Ordinatio* (Vatican: Typis Polyglottis Vaticanis, 1950–1973), vols. I–VII.

Quaestiones in Lib. Quotuor Sententiarum [Opus Oxoniensis]; reprint, originally published as *Quaestiones in Lib. IV. Sententiarum* (Lyons: Laurentius Durandus 1639), (Hildesheim: Georg Olms Verlagsbuchhandlung, 1968), vols. V–X.

Theologiae Marianae Elementa, ed. Carolus Balić, OFM (Kačić: Šibenik in Yugoslavia, 1933).

Fairbairn, A. M., *The Place of Christ in Modern Theology* (New York: Scribner, 1894).

Forsyth, P. T., *The Person and Place of Jesus Christ* (London: Independent Press, 1909).

Gerrish, B. A., *Grace and Gratitude: The Eucharistic Theology of John Calvin* (Minneapolis: Fortress Press, 1993).

Girard, René, *Violence and the Sacred* (Baltimore: Johns Hopkins University Press, 1977).

Gore, Charles, *Dissertations on Subjects connected with the Incarnation* (London: John Murray, Albemarle Street, 1895).

"The Holy Spirit and Inspiration," in *Lux Mundi: A Series of Studies in the Religion of the Incarnation*, ed. Gore (London: John Murray, Albemarle Street, 1890), ch. 8, 315–362.

The Incarnation of the Son of God: The Bampton Lectures (1891) (London: John Murray, Albemarle Street, 1893).

S. Gregorius VII 1073–1085, Proceedings of his Sixth Council at Rome in 1079, "De ss. Eucharistia: Ius iurandum a Berengario praestitum," in *Enchiridion Symbolorum: Definitionum et Declarationum de Rebus Fidei et Morum*, ed. Heinrich Denzinger (Freiburg in Breisgau: B. Herder, 1911), 163–164.

Grosseteste, Robert, *De cessatione legalium*, ed. Richard C. Dales and Edward B. King (London: Oxford University Press for the British Academy, 1986).

Hall, Francis J., *The Kenotic Theory* (New York and London: Longmans, Green, & Co, 1898).

Hayes, Zachary, OFM, *The Hidden Center: Spirituality and Speculative Christology in St. Bonaventure* (Ramsey, NJ: Paulist Press, 1981).

Hick, John, "An Inspiration Christology for a Religiously Plural World," in *Encountering Jesus: A Debate on Christology*, ed. Stephen T. Davis (Atlanta: John Knox Press, 1988), ch. 1, 5–22, 32–38.

An Interpretation of Religion (London: Macmillan Press, 1989).

The Metaphor of God Incarnate: Christology in a Pluralistic Age (Louisville, KY: Westminster/John Knox Press, 1993).

ed., *The Myth of God Incarnate* (Philadelphia: Westminster, 1977).

Hubert, Henri and Mauss, Marcel, *Sacrifice: Its Nature and Function*, trans. W. D. Halls; forward E. E. Evans-Pritchard (Chicago: University of Chicago Press 1898/1964).

Illingworth, J. R., "The Incarnation and Development," in *Lux Mundi: A Series of Studies in the Religion of the Incarnation* (London: John Murray, Albemarle Street, 1890), ch. 5, 181–214.

Julian of Norwich, *Revelations of Divine Love*, trans. Clifton Wolters (London: Penguin Books, 1966).

Kaufmann, Gordon, *In the Face of Mystery: Constructive Theology* (Cambridge, MA, and London: Harvard University Press, 1993).

Kelly, J. N. D., *Early Christian Doctrines* (London: Adam and Charles Black, 1958).

Lawton, John Stewart, *Conflict in Christology: A Study of British and American Christology from 1889–1914* (London: SPCK, 1947).

Levenson, Jon D., *The Death and Resurrection of the Beloved Son: The Transformation of Child Sacrifice in Judaism and Christianity* (New Haven: Yale University Press, 1993).

Lienhard, Marc, *Luther: Witness to Jesus Christ*, trans. Edwin H. Robertson (Minneapolis: Augsburg, 1982).

Lombard, Peter, *Sententiae in IV Libris Distinctae* (Grottaferrata: College of St. Bonaventure at Clear Waters, 1971).

Luther, Martin, *Against the Heavenly Prophets in the Matter of Images and Sacraments* (1525), in *Luther Works* (St. Louis: Concordia Publishing House), vol. XL.

An Appeal to the Ruling Class of German Nationality as to the Amelioration of the State of Christendom, in *Martin Luther: Selections from His Writings*, ed. and intro. John Dillenberger (Garden City, NY: Anchor-Doubleday, 1961), 403–485.

Confession Concerning Christ's Supper (1528), in *Luther Works* (St. Louis: Concordia Publishing House), vol. XXXVII.

The Pagan Servitude of the Church in *Martin Luther: Selections from His Writings*, ed. and intro. John Dillenberger (Garden City, NY: Anchor-Doubleday, 1961), 249–359.

The Sacrament of the Body and Blood of Christ against the Fanatics, in *Luther Works* (St. Louis: Concordia Publishing House), vol. XXXVI, 342–345.

That These Words of Christ, "This Is My Body," Stand Firm against the Fanatics (1527), *Luther Works* (St. Louis: Concordia Publishing House), vol. XXXVII.

Mascall, Eric, *Christ, the Christian, and the Church* (London: Longmans, Green & Co., 1946).

Mauss, Marcel, *The Gift: The Form and Reason for Exchange in Archaic Societies*, trans. W. D. Halls, forward Mary Douglas (London/New York: W. W. Norton, 1990).

McEvoy, James, "The Absolute Predestination of Christ in the Theology of Robert Grosseteste," in McEvoy, *Robert Grosseteste, Exegete and Philosopher* (Aldershot: Variorum, 1994), 212–230.

Milgrom, Jacob, *Leviticus 1–16: A New Translation with Introduction and Commentary* (New York: Anchor Bible, 1990), 2 vols.

Moberly, R. W., *Atonement and Personality* (London: John Murray, Albemarle Street, 1901).

Morris, Thomas V., *The Logic of God Incarnate* (Ithaca, NY, and London: Cornell University Press, 1986).

Ockham, William, *Quaestiones in Librum Quartum Sententiarum (Reportatio)*, in *Opera Philosophica et Theologica* (St. Bonaventure, NY: St. Bonaventure University Press, 1984), *Opera Theologica*, vol. VII.

Ogden, Shubert, *The Point of Christology* (Dallas: Southern Methodist University Press, 1992).

Phillips, D. Z., *The Concept of Prayer* (New York: Schocken Books, 1966).

Pike, Nelson, "Hume on Evil," *Philosophical Review* 72 (1963), 180–197.

Plantinga, Alvin, *The Nature of Necessity* (Oxford: Clarendon Press, 1974).

Ramsey, Arthur Michael, *An Era in Anglican Theology, from Gore to Temple: Anglican Theology between* Lux Mundi *and the Second World War 1889–1939* (New York: Scribner, 1960).

Richard of St. Victor, *La Trinité/De Trinitate*, Texte Latin, trans. and intro. Gaston Salet (Paris: Les Editions du Cerf, 1959).

Sell, Alan P. F., *Philosophical Idealism and Christian Belief* (Cardiff: University of Wales, 1995).

Spiegel, Shalom, *The Last Trial: On the Legends and Lore of the Command to Abraham to Offer Isaac as a Sacrifice; the Akedah* (Woodstock, VT: Jewish Lights Reprints, 1993).

Stone, Darwell, MA, *A History of the Doctrine of the Holy Eucharist* (London, New York, Bombay, and Calcutta: Longmans, Green, & Co, 1909), 2 vols.

Swinburne, Richard, *The Christian God* (Oxford: Oxford University Press, 1994).

Taylor, Jeremy, *The Rules and Exercises of Holy Living*, vol. III in *The Whole Works of the Right Rev. Jeremy Taylor, DD* (London: Longman, Brown, Green, and Longmans, 1856).

The Worthy Communicant, vol. VIII in *The Whole Works of the Right Rev. Jeremy Taylor, DD* (London: Longman, Brown, Green, and Longmans, 1854).

Temple, William, *Christus Veritas: An Essay* (London: Macmillan & Co., 1925).

"The Divinity of Christ," in B. H. Streeter, *et al.*, *Foundations: A Statement of Christian Belief in Terms of Modern Thought by Seven Oxford Men* (London: Macmillan & Co., 1913), 211–263.

Thomas of Celano, *St. Francis of Assisi: First and Second Life of St. Francis with Selections from the Treatise on the Miracles of the Blessed Francis*, trans. Placid Hermann (Chicago: Franciscan Herald Press, 1963).

Weston, Frank, *The One Christ: An Enquiry into the Manner of the Incarnation* (London, New York, Bombay, and Calcutta: Longmans, Green, 1907).

Wiles, Maurice, "Christianity without Incarnation," in *The Myth of God Incarnate*, ed. Hick, ch. 1, 1–9.

God's Action in the World: The Bampton Lectures for 1986 (London: SCM Press, 1986).

William of St. Thierry, *De Natura Corporis et Animae Libri Duo* (Patrologia Latina 180, cols. 695–720).

Young, Frances M., *Sacrifice and the Death of Christ* (London: SPCK, 1975).

The Use of Sacrificial Ideas in Greek Christian Writers from the New Testament to John Chrysostom (Philadelphia: Philadelphia Patristic Foundation, 1979).

Zwingli, Ulrich, "An Exposition of the Faith," in *Zwingli and Bullinger*, ed. G. W. Bromiley (Philadelphia: Westminster, 1953), 249–279.

"On the Lord's Supper," in *Zwingli and Bullinger*, ed. G. W. Bromiley (Philadelphia: Westminster, 1953), 185–238.

Index

77767272R00207

Made in the USA
Lexington, KY
03 January 2018